MUSIC
ON MY BEAT

An Intimate Volume
of Shop Talk

BY

HOWARD TAUBMAN

Member of the Music Staff of
The New York Times

SIMON AND SCHUSTER
NEW YORK
1943

ABOUT THE APPEARANCE OF BOOKS IN WARTIME

A recent ruling by the War Production Board has curtailed the use of paper by book publishers in 1943.

In line with this ruling and in order to conserve materials and manpower, we are co-operating by:

1. Using lighter-weight paper, which reduces the bulk of our books substantially.
2. Printing books with smaller margins and with more words to each page. Result: fewer pages per book.

Slimmer and smaller books will save paper and plate metal and labor. We are sure that readers will understand the publishers' desire to co-operate as fully as possible with the objectives of the War Production Board and our government.

MANUFACTURED IN THE UNITED STATES OF AMERICA
BY H. WOLFF BOOK MFG. CO., NEW YORK CITY

CONTENTS

1. OF MUSIC ITSELF   3
   "Classical" vs. "Popular"—A Musical Vocabulary—The Fetish of Masterpieces—Contemporary Music, Eighteenth- and Twentieth-Century Style

2. COMPOSERS ARE PEOPLE   14
   The Russian Way—Juke-Box Boys—Stravinsky and Strauss— Schwanda *and a Swindle—Rachmaninoff's Prelude—Motion-Picture Scores—The Monk's Tale—Conductor and Composer —Kreisler's Deception—"Commercial" Art—Trio for Clarinet, Violin, and Piano—Schuman Is Not Schumann*

3. THE DO-RE-MI   27
   Toscanini, Koussevitzky, and Stokowski—More Conductors, Less Money—Horowitz and Rachmaninoff—Play This on Your Fiddle—The Poor Cello—Men, Women, and Singers—In Union There Is—Laissez Faire in Music

4. MUSICIAN IN THE PUBLIC EYE   40
   Temperament Tells—Toscanini's Tantrums—Beecham Waves The Star-Spangled Banner—*Moore vs. Kiepura—Flagstad vs. Melchior—Bruno Walter's Downbeat—Baccaloni the Buffo— Casals and Cello—White of an Egg, Blowing Bubbles, and Standing on Your Head—Handshakers—Warming Up—Hot or Cold?—Barnstorming—The Press—Paderewski Was Not a Mormon*

5. MEET THE GLAMOUR BOYS   57
   Toscanini the Monarchist—Watch the Birdie—Stokowski's Hands—"Life Begins at Forte"—NBC Symphony—Mitropoulos and an Ambulance—Koussevitzky Talks Back—Guest Conductor

6. THE GLAMOUR BOYS AT WORK   69
   *Toscanini the Singer—From One Cellist to Another—The Secret
   of a Good Memory—Stokowski and a Lone Flower—On His
   Hobbyhorse—"Hokey Stokie"—The Koussevitzky Beat—A
   Volga Boatman—A Smile for Bruno Walter—Temper and
   Klemperer—Beecham at the Met—Barbirolli—Damrosch on
   American Music*

7. THE GLAMOUR BOYS AT HOME   82
   *Tea for Two—Koussevitzky and Stokowski, Writers—The Gout
   —Growing Old—Two Toscaninis—Granddaughter Knows Best
   —Horowitz's Father-in-law—Pinball Game*

8. REFLECTIONS ON VIRTUOSOS   92
   *From Mansion to Water Tank—"All" Heifetz Can Do—Horo-
   witz's Inferiority Complex—Practice Doesn't Necessarily Make
   Perfect—"Perfidious Passages"—Two on Elman—Horowitz
   and Conductors—Paderewski in Self-Communion*

9. VOICES AND ARTISTS   105
   *Donkeys and Philosophers—Musicianship—The Ad Libber—
   Broadway or the Met?—Martinelli "Won't Do"—Kiepura on
   the Taking End—Seduction Scene—Singing What They
   Shouldn't—Flagstad Falls Asleep*

10. THE BOYS IN THE ORCHESTRA   118
   *The New York Philharmonic plus Stokowski—Baiting the Con-
   ductor—Orchestra Rehearsal—Woes of the French-Horn Player
   —Pulling Strings—Cards—Women in the Orchestra—Personnel Manager—Librarian*

11. THE AMATEURS, BLESS THEM!   131
   *Letter from an Amateur—Amateur Cellist—The Oratorio
   Society—Grand Opera in Raleigh—Doctors—Chamber-Music
   Fans—Amateur Meets Professional—Try It on Your Recorder
   —Al Smith Wonders*

12. ANY HOPE FOR OPERA?   142
   *The Metropolitan—Radames the Hero—The Prompter—
   Maestro Salmaggi—The New Opera Company—Nine O'Clock
   Opera Company—American Operas—Opera in English*

13. ORCHESTRAS—AMERICAN SPECIALTY   155
*Two Orchestras in One—The New York Philharmonic—The
Mexican Way—Radio Orchestras—Upkeep of an Orchestra—
Endowments—Giving the Public a Voice*

14. CONCERT FOLKLORE   168
*Concert Manners—A Singing Painter—Song with a Goose—
Recorder Recital—Only Albanian Singer in America—Curzon
and Paderewski—Cocktail Party in the New York Public
Library—How to Make Chimes—Stage Fright—The Society of
Timid Souls—Even the Doorman Knows Better*

15. THE NEGRO IN MUSIC   180
*Segregation—Marian Anderson and the D.A.R.—The Key to a
City But Not to a Hotel Room—The Negro in Opera—Porgy's
Bess*

16. THE CHANGING SCENE   189
*Radio—Background Music—Film Music—Jazz, the People's
Music—Jazz in Carnegie Hall—Federal Music Project—The
Four Freedoms—Music in the Armed Forces*

17. ON BLACK DISKS   200
*Concerts of Recorded Music—Add-a-Part Records—Caruso
Made It Respectable—Two Highballs Make History—"Bugs"
—Recording Technique—The Big Three*

18. FOR THE CHILDREN'S HOUR   210
*Music in School—Playing an Instrument—Concerts for Chil-
dren—The Prodigy—Music Teachers*

19. PATRON AND PATRONESS   220
*A "People's Opera"—The Public Chips In—Constructive
Patronage*

20. HAIL, THE AUDIENCE!   226
*The Initiated and the Uninitiated—Big Names—Applause—
Program Notes—"The Five Wise Apples"—Nelson Eddy,
Ladies!*

21. MIDDLEMEN OF MUSIC   236
*Managers—"Twenty Per Cent Was Not Too Much"—First
Concert—Press Agents—Critics—Mary Garden on Criticism—
Asleep in Town Hall*

22. IN THE AFFAIRS OF MEN   248
*The Difference Between Busch and Furtwängler—The Adven-
tures of Vaughan Williams—Toscanini and Fascist Italy—
Casals and Fascist Spain—Enemy Art—Social Significance in
Music—The Musician in the Community*

INDEX   261

MUSIC
ON MY
BEAT

1

OF MUSIC ITSELF

*"Classical" vs. "Popular"—A Musical Vocabulary—The Fetish of Masterpieces—
Contemporary Music, Eighteenth- and Twentieth-Century Style.*

THE MOST important element in the world of music is the music.
We sometimes forget this simple truth when we hurry to *see* virtuosos and prima donnas rather than to *hear* them. The lesser ones
tend to forget too, and behave as if their personalities counted for
everything and the music were incidental. One can't be blind to
the personality of the performer, but it should speak to one, after
a while, through his treatment of the music, and even there he may
be exhibiting himself to the detriment of the music. When he stoops
to obvious tricks that draw attention to himself, he clearly tells us
that he wants us to relish his personality more than the music, and
we have no choice but to watch. No one can blame us for watching
rather than listening to a tenor who postures like a ham actor, a
husky soprano who flutters like a soubrette, a glamour-girl performer whose *décolletage* is so low and her dress so slinky that she
looks like Gypsy Rose Lee about to disrobe, a pianist who tosses
his long locks as in a caricature, or a jazz player who jigs and
smirks. These boys and girls, whether by intent or accident, are
amusing shows. If you can concentrate on their music, you're a better man than I am.

Granting every performer the right to a personality that makes
its impact across the footlights, I want to concentrate on the music.
I don't expect the musician to be as timid as Casper Milquetoast
or as invisible as a wraith, but I want to be able to absorb what he
plays or sings, rather than to be conscious of the mannerisms of his
face and figure. The best procedure if the musician has annoying

mannerisms is to close one's eyes, but there is the danger that one will fall asleep. Or isn't that a danger?

Once we concede that the music itself is the thing, we will begin to be annoyed by some of the patronizing classifications in vogue. For music is music, whether it be a symphony, an opera, a musical comedy, a string quartet, a folk song, or jazz. Each form ought to be classified on its merits in its own genre. I dislike the designations of "serious" and "light" music, or "classical" and "popular" music, though, unhappily, I use them myself for want of more exact, short descriptives. Some symphonies are delightfully and truly light and popular; others are light and popular in the derogatory sense these words suggest when applied to jazz. There is jazz that is serious, and certainly jazz has developed its classics. There are folk songs— truly songs of the people—that have more excitement and vitality than some of the so-called classics. Are we using the word "classical" in a stricter meaning as relating to an era, a style, and form? Then we had better trot out a lot of other stylistic designations such as romantic, baroque, neoromantic, neoclassic, polytonal, atonal, polyphonic; presently we shall find ourselves mouthing polysyllables and forgetting about music altogether.

Why not just music? Such an approach might even lead to a new open-mindedness. If we listened to music and weighed it for its own qualities in its own field, we would find a host of prejudices evaporating.

People get set in their ways when it comes to music just as they do about a political party or a ball team. Minds are closed and carefully sealed in with storm windows, like a New England house in winter. When such people meet an unfamiliar thing in music, they are apt to dispose of it with the comment, "I know what I like and I don't like that." That is their privilege, but how much better the tolerance of the sixteen-year-old lad who was invited to a performance of Bach's B minor Mass. He was warned that it lasted from 7:30 to 11 P.M., and might seem a long and difficult affair at first hearing. His answer was, "If Bach could write it, I don't see why I can't listen to it."

Intolerance is to be found among high-brows as well as among low-brows. There are a host of musicians whose attitude toward jazz is patronizing. An eminent trumpet player, soloist in a major symphony orchestra, listened to a record of one of the finest jazz trumpeters in America. He agreed that the jazz player was a virtuoso, but he had reservations. "What I want to know," challenged the symphony-orchestra man, "is how does he sound when he plays legitimate?"

People who love jazz and simple tunes like *Yankee Doodle* and old-fashioned waltzes can be condescending after their fashion. They sometimes dismiss the more elaborate field of music with a shrug: "High-brow stuff," or "A lot of noise."

This is stating the case at its extremes. Actually there are people of good will who have blind spots, not for want of intelligence or capacity to understand, but sheerly because of indolence. They do not hear because they listen only in fits and starts.

Take the oft-discussed music of Wagner, and I see no reason to quarrel with people who refuse to take Wagner on any terms. But when some people say glibly that because they cannot apprehend any melodies in Wagner then there are no melodies, they are presuming to take in too much territory. I can sympathize, in the same way, with the point of view of Aaron Copland, contemporary composer, who is indignant at the stale charge that modern composers deliberately eschew emotion in their music. Copland replies that the charge is sheer nonsense. No composer, unless he be interested only in mathematics, avoids emotion. He is perhaps expressing his emotions in a different way that is hard for the average listener to apprehend.

I do not mean to say that because a composer knows that he has felt a deep emotion in writing a piece of music it is necessarily there for the listener. Nor would I expect everyone to be receptive to the same emotional content or to the same musical patterns. The world of music, like the planet itself, is infinitely varied. There is room for many points of view and many tastes, and each may have its validity.

Let us explore a little further the question of the melody in Wagner, even though it is academic for many listeners. There are still people, within your acquaintance and mine, who find no recognizable tunes in Wagner; their reaction to Wagner is symptomatic of an unfortunate attitude. Wagner himself needs no defense. He fought his battles when he was alive, and won them, perhaps too well for the comfort of his successors.

How many of us try to speak a language without knowing its vocabulary? What would be the reaction of grammar-school children just learning their three R's to Chaucer, Shakespeare, and Milton? One need not be a poet to read them, but one must have a mature grasp of the English tongue. One need not be a trained musician to follow musical works, but one needs a backlog of listening. Most people who are not tone-deaf can readily perceive the lilt in a simple waltz and can respond to the momentum and snap of a good march. These offer no serious problems. In the average childhood, even where there has been no musical training or experience, simple tunes are encountered constantly. From these tunes it is not difficult to acquire a fondness for music abounding in simple melodies, such as the early operas of Verdi or the operas of Puccini. These works make things easy because they spot their best tunes. They provide long pauses of recitative where one can relax and prepare for the next tune. The tune itself is introduced in a carefully selected situation. Everything is done to make the process simple.

Another composer also deals in tunes but his method of organization is different. He chooses to sing without pause and to build his contrasts in the very process of presenting his best tunes. What he does is to stretch or contract these tunes, to assign them to the different instruments, to contrast them, to vary them, to throw as many different lights on them as does a cloud-swept sky upon a mountainside. To follow him one must keep one's ears open steadily, not only at capricious intervals. That is all there is to the so-called hazards of Wagner and many other symphonists. When one says that Wagner has no melody, one means simply that one has not followed him with sufficient attentiveness to discover the melody.

There are people who find Wagner's music trying. They resent its hyperemotional content; its continuous assault on their senses; its piling of climax upon climax. You cannot quarrel with them. That is how they are built, but at least they know why they dislike the music. Their reasons are founded on understanding, not on ignorance.

Any music like Wagner's, which has a host of adorers and which has been established in the best-informed circles as having the quality of immortality, is advantageously situated. The average listener who cannot relish the music is on the defensive. Though he may not admit it, he is troubled by the feeling that he may be at fault.

But when it comes to music of our own time and our own land, the belittlers can take the offensive. Time has not bestowed on this music the sanction of being a classic. One may safely accuse it of shortcomings that may be within the hearer rather than in the music. Possibly we would not like the music even if we understood it, but if it can be apprehended by the effort of listening, then we should give heed, in justice to the composers and ourselves.

By the same token, a composition is not inferior merely because it is simple and easy to grasp. When we hear one of the wonderful arias from Mozart's *Don Giovanni* or *The Marriage of Figaro* or one of his deceptively simple symphonies, or a lovely song by Schubert, we may like it on first encounter. But we may think, "Mozart, Schubert; famous composers; they must be good." Well, they are. But would we as readily concede that a song by Stephen Foster, Dan Emmett, George Gershwin, Cole Porter, Jerome Kern, or Duke Ellington is good? The tendency of some would be to patronize them, to say that their songs are all right for that kind of thing.

The average American has been buffaloed into accepting snobbish musical standards or he has been harried into rejecting some things that he might with time assimilate. The explanation, in part, is that the development of musical experience among our people has not moved along at an even rate. In the large cities there is a nucleus of people who have heard a great deal of music and have made some themselves. In the smaller communities the nucleus is much smaller. The great diffuser of music in America is the radio, and it has been functioning only a little more than twenty years. Our best symphony orchestras and operas have not been on the air much more than a dozen years. The smaller and remoter communities have only recently begun to build their own symphony orchestras; they have just begun to take hesitating steps in the direction of opera, chamber music, and other forms. A vast new world has been opened, and its richness and variety may be somewhat bewildering. It takes time to find one's way in this world. Some people make up their own minds and form their own tastes sooner than others.

Most people would eventually find their own way if they were not bedeviled by the abracadabra of chatter about art and music appreciation. Music is seldom served up on its own. Too often it is accompanied by a jumble of strictures and exhortations. There is an endless outpouring of talk and writing on how one should listen to music and why one should like certain things. Innocent people are taken in by this pother. They listen to lectures rather than to music; they read words about it rather than hear the music itself.

One of the curious phenomena of our age is the cult of masterpieces. By and large, the masterpieces are of the eighteenth and nineteenth centuries. We know and hear little of the music before Bach and Handel; we know and hear a little more, but not enough, of the music of our own time. But mention a phrase like "the three B's," and the innocents bare their heads. They are conditioned in the same way to the other time-honored and highly sanctioned composers whose music is as standard as the Bible and Shakespeare. Of course, their music is part of the heritage of Western man, but it is not the beginning and the end of art. Let us love it, but let us not deify it so that we dare contemplate nothing else.

There was a time when the three B's—Bach, Beethoven, and Brahms—were also new. They claimed their right to be heard, and they were heard and properly valued. The theory has been spread by the sentimentalists that the music of some of the great composers was neglected by their contemporaries. Ernest Newman, Britain's great critic, has been fighting against this romantic tradition for years. He has contended and proved that the outstanding composers were recognized by their contemporaries provided that their music was faithfully presented. Only a small circle knew of Johann Sebastian Bach's prodigious accomplishments, but that was because of poor communications and the paucity of public performances. Intelligent contemporaries who had a chance to hear decent performances of the last works of Beethoven were quick to recognize their greatness.

The fetish of masterpieces has caused some of us to forget that the men who produced them were not alone among composers. Other men were writing music and having it performed. I daresay it would surprise some of the masters to learn that now they, and chiefly they, are almost the sum and substance of the music being played decades and centuries later.

Look at some of the old programs. Here are five of contemporary music played at the concerts of the Akademie der Tonkünstler-Societät in Vienna:

In 1777: a grand symphony by Ordoñez, a choral work by Haydn, a cavatina by Traetta, a violin concerto by Paisible, a grand symphony and a grand concertino by Kohaut, and a new cantata by Wagenseil.

In 1783: a symphony by Koželuh, a symphony and choral work by Haydn, choral works by Starzer, Sacchini, Hasse, and Dittersdorf, a violin concerto by Schlesinger, and a clavier concerto by Mozart.

In 1786: symphonies by Haydn and Huber and the second part of Dittersdorf's oratorio, *Hiob*.

In 1791: excerpts from Paisiello's opera, *Fedra,* a symphony by Mozart, a cello concerto by Pleyel, and an *Alleluiah* by Albrechtsberger.

In 1795: an oratorio and symphony by Cartellieri and the Piano Concerto in C by Beethoven, with the composer at the piano.

Now glance at some samples from the famous Spirituel-Concerte in Vienna some decades later:

At the tenth concert of the 1819-20 season: Beethoven's Symphony in D, a cantata and a motet by Mozart, a choral work by Preindl, and a psalm by Stadler.

At the eleventh concert of that season: Beethoven's Third Symphony, a Mass by André, and a choral work by Preindl.

At the fifteenth concert: Beethoven's Fourth Symphony and a requiem by Drechsler.

At the eighteenth concert: Beethoven's Sixth Symphony and sacred choral works by Mozart, Salieri, Stadler, and Mosel.

In the 1820-21 season of the Spirituel-Concerte, at the third concert this was the program: Beethoven's Fifth Symphony and a Mass by Hasse. At the eighth concert: a Symphony in D major by Mozart and church pieces by Asioli, Sechter, Preindl, and Stadler. At the seventeenth concert: a new symphony by Krommer and *Christus am Ölberg* by Beethoven.

Now look at a program of the Gesellschafts-Concerte of Vienna in December, 1846: Mendelssohn's Third Symphony, an aria from Verdi's *Ernani,* a violin concerto by Spohr, and an overture by Netzer.

So much for Vienna, which was a cosmopolitan center. But it was not unique. In 1791 at Mergentheim the Elector's musicians played a program that included symphonies by Mozart, Pleyel, and Winneberger in addition to other works. At a London concert on March 24, 1795, the program contained among other things a Mozart symphony, a Haydn quartet, an aria by Andreozzi, a concerto for flute by Ashe, an aria by Nasolini, a new symphony by Clementi conducted from the piano by the composer, a violin concerto by Janiewicz, who was the leader or first violinist of the ensemble, an aria by Anfossi, and an orchestral finale by Haydn. At the first Salomon Concert in London on February 17, 1792, there were, besides a new symphony by Haydn, a symphony by Pleyel, a violin concerto by Janiewicz, a finale by Gyrowetz, and such oddments as vocal pieces, an oboe concerto, and a concerto for harp.

The fetish of masterpieces does not prevail in some of the arts, though its oppressive influence makes itself felt in painting and sculpture. We behave differently in literature and the drama. We do not expect every new novel to be a masterpiece. We do not read everything with criteria of perfection. If we did we would read precious few novels, and almost none would be published. We do not expect every play produced on Broadway to be designed for the ages. If we did, there would be scarcely any theater. We are quite willing to spend an evening at an unpretentious show and we do not begrudge long hours of wrestling with the brood of thousand-page historical novels. We regard the entertainment of the evening sufficient for the time spent getting it.

It is high time we approached music in the same fashion. It is time we stopped looking for masterpieces only. It should be fun to listen to something new merely for the pleasure of that moment's listening. The new piece may well prove to be a masterpiece, or it may turn out to be junk. But we have spent plenty of sour evenings with bad books and bumbling plays and vile movies. We shrug them off as the luck of the draw.

There are plenty of contemporaneous works that have modest attractions and that would give us a satisfying experience if we took them for what they are. Let us forget about whether they are masterpieces or not. Actually we do not know. Only time winnows the masterpieces from the average product. Time may even determine that what we regard as a masterpiece is something less. Are there such things as immortals? In two or three centuries Bach and Beethoven and Brahms may be as neglected as Palestrina, Lassus, and Monteverdi, except by scholars.

Once the fetish of masterpieces were rooted out, the problem of the contemporary, including the American, composer would fall into place without difficulty. His work would be played as a matter of course. The public would not cry out that it had been cheated if this work did not measure up to the three B's. We would learn to look for contemporary works. We would experience the excitement of exploring new territory. We would find that the masterpieces of the past and the output of our own composers could appear side by side without fatal aftereffects.

Who is responsible for the fetish of masterpieces? Blame the critics and other writers on music in part, for we are given to constant hair-splitting over details of performance of the classics and to repeated panegyrics to their glories. We must also blame the cult of the virtuoso that has dominated our musical life, a cult that forms the staff and support of the concert industry. It is a setup that has been cheerfully promoted by business managers and directors of symphony and opera associations. It has been absorbed by a musical public still growing and finding its way, and still painfully anxious to take its standards from on high. The result is that most of our attention is given to the men and women who play, sing, and conduct our music and only a small proportion to the music itself and to those who write it. If you find, incidentally, that precisely this procedure is followed in these pages, charge it to a conscious sinner.

It is worth glancing back to what was happening in the world of music a generation ago. In those days the fetish of masterpieces was already strongly entrenched. The pundits were saying that little music of consequence was being composed, and they looked back nostalgically on the miracle of the past. Yet that day produced figures of importance in composition, figures who today begin to bulk as writers of masterpieces. There were Debussy and Ravel in France; Elgar and Delius in England; Stravinsky in Russia; Strauss and Schönberg in Germany; Sibelius in Finland; Falla in Spain. There were also men of solid accomplishment like Mac-Dowell, Foote, Chadwick, and Gilbert in this country.

Once we drop the blinders that the fetish of masterpieces places on our eyes, we shall discover that we are not poverty-stricken today. We shall find that we are producing composers that a succeeding generation will be proud to look back upon. We have men like Shostakovich and Prokofieff in Russia; Bartók of Hungary; Bloch of Switzerland, France, and this country; Milhaud of France; Hindemith, Alban Berg, and Kurt Weill of Germany; Vaughan

Williams, William Walton, and a group of younger men in England. We have Copland, Harris, Schuman, Barber, Randall Thompson, Virgil Thomson, Gershwin, and other talented composers in this country. We have Chávez in Mexico and Villa-Lobos in Brazil.

I could easily list several hundred compositions, written since the First World War, that could hold their own on the programs of the symphony orchestras, operas, chamber-music concerts, and solo recitals, but they would read too much like a catalogue. It would be preferable, in any case, to play and sing them and to hear them rather than to read about them. I do not contend that they would replace Bach, Mozart, Beethoven, Schumann, Schubert, Chopin, Mussorgsky, Tchaikovsky, and Debussy, nor would I want them to. We have not forfeited our taste for Shakespeare, Fielding, Dickens, Balzac, Flaubert, Cervantes, Tolstoy, and Hawthorne merely because we draw nourishment from Thomas Mann, Steinbeck, Malraux, and Sholokhoff.

The world is abundant with promise, and America shares in it overflowingly. We are not doing as badly in music as the mourners would have us think. Of course, we can do better, and we shall. In the meantime let there be recognition of our own contribution, whether it be in the concert hall or opera house, the radio, the theater, the hills and prairies where folk songs are made and sung, the night clubs, and the ginmills. The time has come to stop prating about the future of American music. The present is of more importance to us, for that is all we know, and, with no respect whatever to the pundits who perpetually fret about posterity, all we need to know.

2

COMPOSERS ARE PEOPLE

The Russian Way—Juke-Box Boys—Stravinsky and Strauss—Schwanda and a Swindle—Rachmaninoff's Prelude—Motion-Picture Scores—The Monk's Tale—Conductor and Composer—Kreisler's Deception—"Commercial" Art—Trio for Clarinet, Violin, and Piano—Schuman Is Not Schumann.

LIVING COMPOSERS have a singular weakness: they want to stay alive. They have the naïve notion that they ought to make a living out of composing. They know it is naïve because so few can swing it. Occasionally they get mad and tell the world exactly how cockeyed it is. Since being cockeyed on a planetary scale is normal routine for the world, it blithely shakes off the living composers' accusations and goes about its business of rewarding and bedeviling the just and unjust alike.

There are places, however, where the living composer's lot is a relatively happy one. In a visit to Soviet Russia some years ago, I was given facts and figures to show that there the composer was a prophet with honor in his own land. There it was taken for granted that the composer's function was to write music; that his music was meant to be played and sung; that the essentials of life—like food, clothing, and shelter—were things to which a composer was entitled as a matter of course, in return for his creative effort. Each composer, even one with modest talents, was guaranteed the minimum living standard of all workers. Talented or successful men had tremendous earnings. In one year Glière had earned 80,000 rubles, and Shostakovich 100,000. Those are a heap of rubles, representing a lot of purchasing power, in any form of society.

It may be argued that these composers worked under restrictions and that even in composing they had to follow the "party line." It is true that the authorities cracked down on what were called "left-wing aberrations" and that a composer like Shostakovich was chastised publicly for "smart-alecky superficialities" and "distorted intellectualism." He was told, in effect, to compose so that the masses of the people would be able to follow him. The advice was not bad, even though the method of giving it was drastic. The music he composed after the spanking, such as the Fifth and Sixth Symphonies and the Piano Quintet, had dignity, humanity, and easy comprehensibility without forfeiting a distinctively individual and modern idiom. Would Shostakovich have arrived at the same destination without the public excoriation? It is possible, even likely. I, for one, feel that his opera, *Lady Macbeth of Mzensk*, for all its brash realism, which subjected it to violent censure here and in the Soviet Union, had an honest, underlying compassion and a rich, assertive vitality.

A neighbor of Russia's and a recurrent enemy, Finland, also had to its credit a lively respect for its obligation to a composer. The government gave Sibelius a life grant. Considering that Sibelius was the pride and adornment of his country and possibly of advertising value to it, the grant was no more than his deserts. But it was an unusual procedure, and it was marveled at in other lands where composers have the rugged individualist's right to live or starve on their own. Even in Finland, lesser composers were accorded that delectable right.

How many composers earn a living by composing? I am not privy to their income returns or to their budgets, but I know that only a few make enough money to live even according to lower-middle-class standards. To live well, they must take on other jobs. If they have aspirations to cut a figure in society, they must depend on private means.

The composers who make the most money are the boys who write successfully for theater, movie, radio, night-club, and juke-box consumption. Irving Berlin, George Gershwin, Cole Porter, Jerome Kern, Richard Rodgers, Vernon Duke, Hoagy Carmichael, Harold J. Rome, and the others who write the nation's hit tunes are the most consistent money-makers in music in the United States. For the most part their songs have a short and merry life; they are played and sung *ad nauseam,* but at least they are played and sung. Most of the stuff is ground out according to formula, but some of it has class. Success falls on routine and classy tunes alike; it depends apparently on who you are and whom your publisher's pluggers know.

The writers of the song hits are generally content to keep working in a highly remunerative field. Vernon Duke has an alter ego, and under his real name, Vladimir Dukelsky, writes for symphony orchestra and other "high-brow" forms which pay him peanuts. Gershwin aspired to the larger forms and did pretty well with them. His interest in writing for symphony orchestra was not to make money, obviously. He felt that here was a challenge to his talent, and he longed to crash the world of "art." Actually, some of his songs were delightful expressions of American art, but they did not generally win such an accolade. Stravinsky is supposed to have made the point without snobbery when Gershwin went to him for composition lessons. Stravinsky asked George how much he earned as a composer, and Gershwin named what was an astronomical figure to Stravinsky. "I had better take lessons from you," murmured Stravinsky.

Stravinsky has been one of the rare composers who could make a living by composing. Beginning with the commissions from Diaghilev, he has been paid well for his music. His early works, particularly *The Fire Bird* and *Petrushka* Suites, have been played by orchestras all over the world year after year. They have been staples of the repertory, and the royalties have been substantial. But even Stravinsky has found it helpful to accept teaching or conducting assignments; the extra income was not to be turned down by a composer.

Richard Strauss is another composer who has had decent financial returns from his music. His tone poems and operas have become fixtures all over the world, and the composer and his publisher have not been shy about asking for stiff royalties. At the Metropolitan Opera the Strauss works commanded the highest royalty fee of the entire repertory, and when the company proposed to do *Der Rosenkavalier* on a Saturday afternoon when it would be broadcast nationally and internationally, the publisher demanded a much higher figure. Unfortunately, the Metropolitan Opera decided not to broadcast the work, but it was good to hear of a composer who had the bargaining power to make a hard deal.

Jaromir Weinberger may not be one of the great composers of our era, but for a time he was one of the shining elect who could make a living out of music in the larger forms. In fact, his success was predicated on one opera—and what a success! *Schwanda, the Bagpipe Player* had its *première* in Prague in 1927, became the rage of Europe, and in time achieved perhaps more performances than any other opera written since the First World War. Within a decade it had been produced in 160 theaters; it had been sung in more than twenty languages, including the Scandinavian; it had amassed a total of more than 4000 performances. One of its sections, the Polka and Fugue, is still played by symphony orchestras and bands, and in the United States alone has achieved more than 500 performances. It has been transcribed for small orchestra, chorus, various choral and instrumental ensembles. It has been recorded and the disks have sold widely.

The figures compare with those of the good old days of Verdi and Puccini. Weinberger earned enough to live in comfort and to have the time for further composition. But his good fortune ended with Hitler's coming into power in 1933. His royalties had arrived regularly and properly before 1933. Thereafter he had difficulties. His works were barred in Germany, but that was not nearly so serious as the fact that his publisher was German. For *Schwanda* continued to be performed in the remainder of Europe, while there was a substantial remainder that was not under Nazi domination. But the accountings from the German publisher became spasmodic and grossly inaccurate. Later, of course, they ceased entirely. Weinberger could not persuade the theaters of Europe to pay him the royalties directly. That would have been extralegal, and such was the passion for the letter of the law in the days when the Nazis were theoretically at peace that no one would have dreamed of stretching a point, even for the sake of real justice.

Thus the composer of an enormously successful opera that was still earning considerable sums had to do hack work in Paris, where he made his home for a time, just to live. He took cheap arranging jobs. He needed help to get to this country, and then it required the assistance of generous Americans to give him the opportunity to resume composing here, while his royalties—and this did not add to his peace of mind—went to the Nazis.

A composer who did well in music was Sergei Rachmaninoff, but not from composing. His piano playing made his fortune, though his compositions have been performed with reasonable regularity. The piece that might have brought him big money was the C-sharp minor Prelude, one of the smash hits of the twentieth century. But Rachmaninoff sold all his rights for twenty dollars. Had he retained the rights and received royalties on the piece for the more than four decades since he tossed it off, his reward would have been, at a conservative guess, something like $100,000.

That in itself would be sufficient reason for souring him on the composition, though he actually disliked it on musical grounds. For years he was expected to play it at his piano recitals, at least as an encore. Occasionally he dodged it, but his audiences were insistent. Even when he avoided it himself, he heard it on the radio or from a neighbor's window as junior or daughter struggled with it, and recently in hopped-up jazz versions. In the days when it was inescapable at his recitals, he decided to vary the monotony by revising it. He played the rewritten version at a recital, whereupon the critics declared that he did not know his own piece. He decided that it would be futile to tell them about the revision. He would just have to go on being a slave to a youthful indiscretion which made money for every publisher who wished to print it but not a cent for him.

Hollywood is the place where composers can make a nice, round sum for a job of composing. An assignment to do a score for an A picture may be worth as much as $10,000. It means concentrated work for a fortnight or a month. It means, unless the producer or director is a man who appreciates the uses of music for a movie, doing the best you can when the picture has already been filmed. In composing the score for *Citizen Kane,* Bernard Herrmann was called in by Orson Welles at the start and his music was an integral phase of the finished product. Aaron Copland had similar luck when he wrote the score for *Our Town,* produced by Sol Lesser. Generally, however, the composer fits his music to the completed film, and then, when the picture is cut and edited, he has to carpenter his score anew. But the composer has the consolation that there is money in it for him.

Suppose he writes a symphony which takes him, not weeks, but months and years. If he is outstandingly lucky, it receives ten performances in a season. That may mean a grand total of $750 in royalties, minus the publisher's share and minus the costs of paper and copying. Now and then a composer writes a symphony which, for musical or extramusical reasons, has a bullish market, and then the compensation approximates the value of the work. Shostakovich's Seventh Symphony, completed at the height of the Soviet Union's magnificent stand against the Nazis, was a natural, and conductors and orchestras clamored for the right to perform it. In the first year after its completion it had at least 100 performances throughout the United States. The American distributor, Am-Rus Music Corporation, charged $500 for three performances, which meant receipts of $1,500. Sixty per cent, or $900, was turned over to Shostakovich.

But most composers have to look to other sources for their living. A few have the good luck to be born into money; others marry into it. Some find patrons who give or "lend" them sums periodically. Others win prizes that carry large stipends. Commissions from august, moneyed institutions provide a *modus vivendi* for a few. Most of them, however, take jobs of one kind or another. They teach, lecture, conduct, become virtuosos, if they can, hold jobs in

orchestras, direct small and large choruses, and, in the case of one
or two, get by on literary pursuits.

In his book, *The State of Music*, Virgil Thomson maintains,
wittily and ingeniously, that the style of a composer's music is conditioned by the source of his finances. The fact that he does not
name a specific composer and composition does not alter the essential truth that the composer, like any other animal, is the product of
his environment. The way he gets his money, if any, is a vital factor
in that environment.

But composers are people, and the money problems are not the
only ones that exercise and stimulate them. There is the major
struggle to get performed. If a composer writes symphonic music,
it is not always enough to write good works, although that is helpful. It may be just as useful to know how to please powerful conductors, some of whom are not above being fond of an approach with a
touch of obsequiousness.

It is sad and amusing to observe how the composer must cater to
the conductor, flatter his vanity, praise his musicianship, and listen
to his strictures on art. A female composer may have additional
problems. A young woman, who was not bad-looking, brought a new
score to one of the famous maestros who was in New York on a
visit. He glanced at it and her and said, "This is very interesting.
We must talk about it." He suggested that she come to his apartment in his home town. When she arrived at his diggings, she was
struck by the simplicity, almost austerity, in which the great man
lived. "Why, this is ascetic," she said, "just like a monk." He came
close and whispered, "Not quite like a monk." There was no meeting of the minds.

Once a conductor agrees to program a work, the composer may
have the task of persuading the maestro to do it the way he imagined
it, not as the conductor would like to interpret it. If the composer
is within traveling distance of the town where the performance will
take place, he sits in on rehearsals. Most conductors discuss a score
with the composer in advance and are delighted to have him on hand
during the rehearsals. Some conductors feel they have done their

duty to the composer if they have agreed to play his music; the rest is up to his majesty. Such men have a way of making a virtuoso's holiday out of a composer's work under the best of conditions; when they do not bother even to consult with the composer, they really let themselves go as they mutilate the poor composition.

Dimitri Mitropoulos, who recognizes his duty to the living composer and plays a higher percentage of contemporary works than most conductors, approaches the task in the best of faith. He spent some time with Chávez going over his Piano Concerto before a New York *première*. I am sure that Mitropoulos' intentions were honorable. But he conducted the score in his supercharged, feverish style. The composer, who was in Mexico during the performance, was amazed later when he heard a recording. The orchestral sound was swelled out until the piano squeaked like a weary and overwhelmed voice.

Mitropoulos is an honest musician who probably had to conduct this way because it was his nature. He was certainly not toying with the composer deliberately. I happen to know that he takes seriously his obligation to the composer. Some time ago he wished to honor the memory of Busoni, and conducted a whole program of his music with the New York Philharmonic-Symphony. When he could not find time to rehearse this program on the regular practice schedule of the orchestra, he called a special session and paid for it out of his own pocket.

Toscanini's reputation for respecting the intentions of a composer has been beyond cavil. The chief quarrel with him, as far as the living composer is concerned, has been that he has not played enough of his music. When the maestro has done a work by a living composer, he has consulted with the author and spent hours studying the score with him. If he has made an alteration, he has known that he has sinned. After a radio performance of Samuel Barber's *Essay for Orchestra*, No. 1, the seventy-five-year-old maestro asked the thirty-one-year-old composer to come to his NBC dressing room. The maestro was embarrassed. "Barber," he said, "all day yesterday I tried to reach you. I know I had no right, but since I could not reach you, I did it anyhow." Toscanini had added a second trumpet for one note. "I hope," said the maestro, "you will forgive me."

A trumpet doubling on a single note is a minor matter, unless, of course, the note comes at a crucial point where several trumpets might distort the composer's intention. But some scores are edited more extensively by conductors, and if the composer is alive and within earshot, you can imagine his feelings. That is why some composers turn to conducting. They know that they are not virtuosos of the baton, nor do they aspire to that eminence. Some feel that they can do a more honest job than the gilt-edged maestro, and they are certain that they know how their own works should go.

Stravinsky has told his friends that he took up conducting because he found that few conductors, even among the most glamorous and best-publicized names, knew how to conduct his music. He found that in works like *Le Sacre du Printemps* and *Les Noces* the intricate rhythms were not faithfully established even by virtuoso conductors.

I have heard other composers complain of the same thing. It may well be that some works fail for this reason, though it might be argued that their very intricacy is explanation enough for their failure. The important thing is how a score sounds. If a proper interpretation will simplify ideas that seem complicated on paper, then it is unfortunate that world-famous conductors do not have the sympathy and contemporaneousness to project these modern works.

The truth is that the new crop of composers needs its own generation of interpreters, including conductors. Ideally conductors and composers should grow up together, absorbing each other's point of view and learning to solve common problems. It does not work out that way. The eminent conductors are likely to be men who, in orientation, belong to a preceding generation, while the composers are probably young and vigorous.

Being people, composers have foibles and delusions, sweetness and integrity, like the rest of us. I rather think that they have more of the latter two qualities than most musicians who perform in the limelight. If they are men of vision, it may take the rest of us a long time to catch up with them. Waiting and working without fanfare bring out the moral stature of a man. Of course, he may also go sour. I know of one distinguished composer who complained querulously that the world had forgotten him, though his work was being performed recurrently. On the other hand, there is Béla Bartók, the Hungarian composer, one of our most original minds in music, who has refused to take advantage of his prestige. At a time when he was in need of employment he declined an offer from a Western university to teach composition. He also refused to accept advanced students of composition for private lessons. He said simply that he did not know how to teach composition, nor did anyone else. The only way to learn to compose, he asserted, was to compose, to make mistakes and to learn to do better.

I have known distinguished composers to be less scrupulous. In return for a fee of $1000 for lessons in instrumentation, they have orchestrated a work for the pupil.

Fritz Kreisler was assailed when he confessed that he was the sole author of a number of compositions which he had published as arrangements of treasures rescued from ancient archives. It was a mild deception, and some musicians, including critics, were miffed that they had spoken and written in praise of Pugnani, Porpora, Martini, and half a dozen others when the credit belonged to a contemporary. The music had not become any worse because it was all Kreisler's. As for the deceiver, he had good reasons. As a young man he had written these attractive additions to a limited repertory, especially useful as encores. He feared that his rivals would not touch his music with a ten-foot bow. As matters turned out, his royalties were much greater.

Sam Morgenstern, a young composer, set to music a poem, *Dive, Bomber, Dive,* written by an enlisted man of the United States Army during the defense of Bataan. The song was considered for a big radio show, and the producer suggested that the composer sign over his rights to the author of the poem. It would have been a handsome gesture, but the composer needed at that time whatever

money his music could bring in, and he said so. The producer threw
out the song, accusing the composer of being "too commercial."

I cannot agree. Nor can I blame another composer who, having
set a fine poem to music, agreed to let a famous bandmaster use his
tune with new and corny lyrics. The composer did not admire the
substituted verses, but a performance in hand was worth a dozen
speculations. Let the well fed make moral judgments.

Composers come modest and immodest, wildly in quest of publicity and not giving a damn. Most of them, of course, want to be
noticed. Those of sturdy fiber insist only on dignified announce-
ments; some are tickled by any blurb or flattery. Some hire press
agents, though not many have the funds for such a luxury, and
others are their own drum beaters. The living composer has every
right to fight for his place in the sun. Too often he is submerged in
the shadow cast by the performer. For this reason I like this calm
letter sent to *The New York Times* by a young composer of New
York's High School of Music and Art, who felt that he had been
overlooked:

"Through an oversight I was not called into the classroom where
you were getting the interviews, so instead I'll give you the information, hoping you can use it in your article. My name is Charles
Schiff, I am fifteen, in sixth term, taking eighth-term theory. My
piece is a trio for clarinet, violin, and piano. This is the second time
I have had a piece accepted in this kind of contest. The reason I
wrote the piece is this. I am a clarinetist, my two best friends are a
violinist and a pianist. We often wanted to play together but there
was no available music for that combination, so I did the next best
thing, I wrote some.

"I don't know whether or not you need the following information
but if you can use it, O.K. I have written five pieces all together. In
order of composing, here they are. A clarinet duet (accepted in a
previous contest), a fantasy for orchestra, the trio, a sonata for unaccompanied violin, and a sonata for horn and piano.

"I guess I've covered everything. I sure hope you can use some
of this stuff. If you can, thanks."

Don't mention it, Charles.

Composers, like their critics, are capable of misjudging their own talents. Long before he composed *The Cradle Will Rock* and *No for an Answer,* Marc Blitzstein was advised by Douglas Moore, a colleague, to try writing for the theater. Blitzstein said, according to Moore, that he was anything but a theater composer. It turned out, in good time, that he was a composer *in excelsis* for the theater.

There are, on the other hand, men who try writing for the stage even though they possess no sense of the theater. Some write for orchestra when their milieu is the song; others write grand opera when musical comedy would seem to be their strong point. Some composers write too much and too fast. Shostakovich, it seems to me, has been too glib for his own good. In our country, Roy Harris and William Schuman, both greatly talented, have taken a long time to master self-criticism.

The tribulations of the composer are many, but William Schuman has a few extra to suffer because of his name. When Koussevitzky performed his Third Symphony in Pittsburgh, an enterprising merchant advertised that all his works were available on records, thus: "Buy the Third Symphony (the Rhenish) by William Schuman." Another time Robert Schumann's A major Quartet was credited in a program of New York's Town Hall to twentieth-century William. As Schuman (William, not Robert) said, "It seems I'm getting a lot of works free—so far my favorite is *The Happy Farmer.*"

Another thing composers get free, besides advice, is abuse. The living composer, because he usually writes in an idiom strange to ears accustomed to eighteenth- and nineteenth-century music, seems to receive more censure than other musicians. But let him cheer up. Let him recall Giuseppe Verdi, who, you would think, could not fail to please his public. Yet his letters, in *Verdi, The Man and His Life in His Letters,* show that a young Italian complained bitterly to Verdi about the expense to which he had gone to hear a production of the "disappointing" *Aïda.* Verdi's outraged correspondent wrote that after making a trip to another town to hear it again, he was sure he had been defrauded. He demanded that

Verdi refund the price of the tickets and traveling expenses. And Verdi did. The only item he refused to pay was the angry young man's food bills because, he argued, the chap "could perfectly well have eaten at home." Verdi made one further condition before authorizing the refund. He insisted that the young man sign a written declaration that he would never again hear another of his new operas.

3

THE DO-RE-MI

IN MUSIC, as in most businesses and professions today, a few people make a heap of money, and a heap of people just get by, or worse. Those who are struggling to make a living have fantastic notions of the riches that pour into the bank accounts of the top artists, and those who are living in luxury may forget the fret, the fever, and the misery of the musicians who have to manage at or below a subsistence level.

No musician makes the kind of money that a munitions or oil king accumulates. If it's any consolation to the musicians, they don't have to worry about explaining themselves periodically to Congressional investigators. A musician's stock in trade is his voice, his hands, and his head; a heart is useful but not obligatory. The performer cannot, save through recordings, earn *in absentia*. The only musician who can is the composer whose bodily presence is not required for earnings to accrue. But the composer—foundation of the edifice—has an illusory advantage. He is rarely performed enough to make a living while he is alive, and what happens to his work when he is gone is of value only to his heirs.

To make money in music, as in industry, you must have talent— at least for making money. The largest earnings are not always in direct proportion to the quality of the talent. Many fine artists, for one reason or another, never break into the big money. Some, with little artistic quality, clean up. But even they have something. A good figure and a photogenic face have seldom stood in the way of a woman's career, and some men have capitalized handsomely on singing loudly, if not well.

In the long run, class should tell and, curiously enough, it does. If occasionally it deals in half-truths, call them the inevitable exceptions. In a time when the vast apparatus of propaganda makes a genius of a general in one campaign and a stumblebum in the next, a statesman of a politician in one election and a blundering fool in the next, it is surprising that form in music stands up as well as it does. I don't know why. Perhaps the buildup, once it starts propitiously, just grows and grows until the object is beyond criticism. Perhaps the men and women who reach music's major leagues have something on the ball.

It looks that way, when you examine the figures. Who are some of the big-money musicians of the last generation or two? Among the conductors: Toscanini, Stokowski, and Koussevitzky. Among the pianists: Paderewski, Rachmaninoff, Horowitz, and Hofmann. Among the violinists: Kreisler, Heifetz, Elman, and Menuhin. Among the singers: Caruso, Chaliapin, Garden, Farrar, McCormack, Galli-Curci, Flagstad, Tibbett, Eddy, Moore, Pons, Anderson, Crooks, and Robeson.

This list does not cover everybody, but it is representative. If our standards are uncompromising, we would omit several in a roll call of great musicians, and we would look in vain for names that represent the finest and noblest achievements in art.

How much does a big-money man make in music? In a long career, Paderewski earned close to $10,000,000. Caruso's life earnings totaled four or five millions. Most of the really prosperous musicians have passed their first million, and some have earned their second and are working on their third.

If he cared to take on endless engagements, Toscanini could probably lead all conductors in total annual earnings, but he chose to work sparingly even before he had passed his seventieth birthday. The largest regular fee he ever received was the $4000 net per concert from the NBC Symphony Orchestra, for his contract required that the National Broadcasting Company pay his income taxes and other expenses. From other orchestras he could command at least $2000 a concert.

That sounds like a lot of money for a concert that does not take more than two and a half hours, counting the intermission. But the concert itself does not represent the time and effort that Toscanini expends in earning his fee. Consider this rehearsal schedule for one performance of Beethoven's *Missa Solemnis* which Toscanini conducted during the New York Philharmonic-Symphony Orchestra's centennial season. Long before he began practice sessions with the orchestra, the maestro worked with the soloists, spending hour after hour and day after day with them. The Westminster Choir of Princeton, N. J., was the chorus in the performance, and it had been well trained by John Finley Williamson, its conductor. But Toscanini made two trips to Princeton, holding morning and afternoon rehearsals each day—a total of four long rehearsals. This computation does not allow for the hours of private re-examination of the score, for Toscanini, despite his phenomenal memory, conducted nothing without painstaking review. All in all, Toscanini worked for several weeks preparing for one concert.

Koussevitzky has been paid up to $75,000 a season by the Boston Symphony Orchestra, one of the highest salaries drawn by a conductor from any orchestra. But Koussevitzky rebuilt the Boston and turned it into the finest and most consistent in the land. He has been a sound investment.

Calculating his immense earnings from records, radio, and movies as well as his concert fees, Leopold Stokowski has probably earned more than any other conductor in history. He was paid about $150,000 for his share in Walt Disney's *Fantasia*. The first eminent conductor to take recording on a large scale seriously, he has more disks to his credit than any other leader, and his earnings in this field have been tremendous. For a six-month period, he once received a check of $35,000 from the RCA Victor Company. Radio has paid him well, and his fee for conducting the Philadelphia Orchestra and such other engagements as he accepted have been hardly negligible.

The work with the All-American Youth Orchestra which he organized and took across the continent and down through South
America was not a profit-making venture for Stokowski. He put up
$50,000 out of his own pocket to assure the tour to South America,
when other guarantees fell through. The tour repaid his advance,
but he earned little or nothing for his tremendous job of organizing,
training, and conducting the orchestra.

The average rate of pay for conductors in this country is $1000
for a week's engagement. Usually there are two concerts each week,
though the New York Philharmonic-Symphony has three and four
a week. The New York orchestra has had to go higher than the
$1000 per week for some conductors; the top men also receive more
in other cities.

Eugene Ormandy has earned about $50,000 a year from the
Philadelphia Orchestra. He has directed the formidable total of one
hundred concerts a year, which has made his average $500 a con-
cert. That has been a favorable business deal for the Philadelphia
Orchestra, and not a bad income for Ormandy, considering that he
has also earned something from his numerous recordings with the
orchestra. But remember that one hundred concerts are a terrific
undertaking, demanding virtually a conductor's every minute.

Bruno Walter has also fared well in recent years. He has directed
at the Metropolitan Opera, where he received $1000 a performance,
and with numerous orchestras where his fee has been $1000 a week
and more. Walter has preferred conducting at the opera. Once he
has prepared and rehearsed a work for the stage, he is able to conduct it five or six times a season; he has found the task of whipping
into shape a fresh program for each concert or two comparatively
burdensome.

Several conductors have managed handsomely on permanent
radio jobs: Frank Black with the National Broadcasting Company;
Howard Barlow with the Columbia Broadcasting System, and
Alfred Wallenstein with the Mutual Broadcasting System. Wallenstein left a secure job as first cellist of the New York Philharmonic-Symphony, which paid him about $10,000 a year, for the

post of music director of radio station WOR. Here he began at a salary of $15,000 a year, and when he was made conductor of the Firestone Hour he started at $300 a broadcast, but in time his two jobs netted him more than $50,000 a year. Add fees picked up from guest engagements with orchestras throughout the country, and he becomes one of the most prosperous men in conducting. Recently he achieved the goal of any conductor, American or otherwise—his own symphony, the leadership of the Los Angeles Philharmonic.

There are about a dozen conductors in the United States who earn $25,000 a year or more. Among the others who crashed the inner circle were Artur Rodzinski of the New York Philharmonic-Symphony, the late Frederick Stock of the Chicago Symphony, Dimitri Mitropoulos of the Minneapolis Symphony, Sir Thomas Beecham of the Metropolitan Opera and half a dozen orchestras from the East to West Coasts, and André Kostelanetz, who has a big radio following. There are a fair number who average over $10,000 a year. A few earn more than $5000 annually. A good many others are rattling around trying vainly to employ their knowledge, training, and talent, grateful for a chance to conduct without fee, and willing, if they have or can raise the money, to buy a crack at conducting.

The story repeats itself with the instrumentalists and singers. Several at the top make enormous sums; a dozen or so consider that they have had a good year if they make more than $25,000; the majority scrape by on anything from $5000 a year to nothing. How they manage on nothing I don't know. If they have no private means, they must turn to teaching or abandon music entirely.

Vladimir Horowitz has been the dominant box-office figure among pianists in recent years. In his first season in America, when he made a triumphant debut, he earned $500 a recital. The fee went up to $1000 a date for the second year and to $1500 in the third, when he had a tour of one hundred engagements. That represents a healthy income for a man of twenty-six, but Horowitz was paying twenty per cent to a manager with whom he had signed up in Europe and another twenty per cent to his American manager. In time he sloughed off the European manager, reduced the number of appearances, increased his fee, and emerged with a higher net income. He has deliberately confined his season to three or four months a year and will not accept engagements on consecutive days. Generally he has averaged about two recitals a week, for he has declined to be rushed. But his fee has gone up to $2000 for an appearance with orchestra and $3000 and more for a recital.

Actually his earning powers could be greater even than the minimum fees. At Carnegie Hall he has always had a sold-out house and a net profit of at least $5000. In New York a musician pays the costs of putting on his concert and takes all the profit, if any. Since Horowitz's appearances have brought a profit wherever he has played, he would prefer to defray the costs, take the risks, and garner the profit at every recital in New York or out. He does not like the system of booking by groups for concert courses through the country. This system has obliged him to take a minimum fee and occasionally a percentage of the gross. But, he contends, his name on a series helps to sell the other concerts. He complains that the setup of the concert industry in this country has militated against him.

Horowitz scored a smashing success almost at the outset wherever he played. In Soviet Russia, where he began his career as a public performer in 1922, he played his first concert to deadheads, the second to a few paying customers, and the third to a sold-out house. In Berlin and Paris he had similar luck. It was good to have the feel of cash for one's work, for, at the start, Horowitz was not paid in cash in Russia. The early 1920's were agonizing days in the Soviet Union, and musicians took their pay in kind—clothes, food, and fuel. Horowitz kept his family well provided, but his earnings, he recalls, were trifling compared to those of Chaliapin, Russia's most eminent musician. "We used to say," he observes, "that Chaliapin had to rent a couple of warehouses to store his earnings."

Rachmaninoff kept his hold on a huge following through the years and commanded the highest fees. But he, like Kreisler, preferred not to be bothered with details. His manager guaranteed him

a flat sum of $2500 for each appearance, and he filled about thirty
dates a year. If the manager made a big profit on the deal, that was
his good fortune. If he earned less, it would not have been fatal,
because he could demand engagements for lesser artists in return
for giving Kreisler and Rachmaninoff to a local impresario.

Heifetz and Menuhin, like Kreisler, are violinists who have averaged close to $2500 a date. Because he has chosen to fill more en-
gagements than the other two, Heifetz has earned a larger total each
year. In his heyday Elman, whose earning power is not as great as it
used to be, received $2000 and more a concert. Were violinists like
Zimbalist, Szigeti, Milstein, Spalding, and Adolf Busch lesser musicians because they did not draw so well year in and year out? Your
answer will depend on your preferences. I consider Szigeti, for
example, as exciting a violinist as any man in the field. He has his
following, yet his fees are geared lower than the top. Among the
pianists, there are excellent artists like Artur Rubinstein, Artur
Schnabel, Egon Petri, Robert Casadesus, Rudolf Serkin—to name
but a few—who are not in the same league with the champs,
Paderewski, Rachmaninoff, and Horowitz, but they have been well
repaid by music, on the whole. Wanda Landowska, the harpsi-
chordist, is one of the greatest of living musicians—her command
of the instrument and her exquisite taste and vivifying imagination
are among the rarest in music. She is highly esteemed by connoisseurs, but I doubt whether she will ever make any ranking income
list.

Three or four pianists, and an equal number of violinists, earn
$100,000 or more in a good year. A limited group averages $50,000.
Then there is a precipitous decline, and a fine, talented musician
considers himself lucky to earn $10,000. Though the United States
books more concerts than any other country in the world, everybody wants the most glamorous names. And the men and women
who have just missed catching on with the wide public have to take
such fees as are given them.

Conducting, fiddling, playing the piano have been glamorized
and publicized with consistency. But what about the poor fellow

who plays an instrument like the cello? Highly regarded though he may be, he cannot approach the earning powers of his colleagues in the other categories. An excellent cellist like Emanuel Feuermann accepted $400 for a date. Gregor Piatigorsky, who has private means, can afford to hold out for more. Pablo Casals, venerated as one of the greatest string players of all time, could not command much more. As for the others, they have joined orchestras or taught; the leavings have not amounted to much in the recital or radio fields.

The singers have wider opportunities. The opera, radio, and movies have given them vast popular followings. The result is that many of them have jumped into the higher brackets. Nelson Eddy, a Hollywood star, has been able to name his own price. For a radio date he has received up to $5000. For recital appearances he has a percentage agreement that nets him close to that. In recent years he has had the biggest income among musicians in America from music only.

The Metropolitan has paid its stars a maximum of $1000 a performance since the depression, though in the good old days Caruso earned $2500 an opera and Chaliapin received $3000 a performance during a limited engagement. Singers like Grace Moore, Lily Pons, Kirsten Flagstad, Gladys Swarthout, Lawrence Tibbett, John Charles Thomas, Richard Crooks, and Lauritz Melchior have cashed in when they took to the road for recital dates. Occasional movies have paid some of them fabulously, and the radio has not stinted them.

Stars not of the first magnitude as draws receive less than the top at the Metropolitan and earn correspondingly lower fees on the road. But if the leaders can make more than $100,000 a year, these second-line draws, who may be as good or better as artists, earn $25,000 or better. Since the country employs more singers than instrumentalists, there is a larger representation of men and women in the middle brackets. But because the supply is immensely greater than the demand, there are hundreds in the lowest brackets.

Without benefit of opera or movie, Marian Anderson and Dorothy Maynor have been among the biggest earners. Miss Anderson has done a tour of eighty recitals, earning up to $2500 for each. Miss Maynor, whose fee has not reached this pinnacle, has managed nicely nevertheless and has had all the work she could take on.

Pianists and violinists can crash the big time overnight. They can take the world by storm, as did Hofmann, Heifetz, and Menuhin, as prodigies. However, not all prodigies have an easy time of it. Joseph Szigeti was an extraordinarily gifted lad, yet he missed the upper ranks as a draw for a good many years. Singers and conductors do not, as a rule, arrive overnight. Whether they like it or not, they take longer to scale the top. It is in the nature of their crafts.

Flagstad became a sensation right after her American debut, but by then she had twenty years' work and development. Dorothy Maynor worked and studied for years before she was "discovered." Many musicians could match the early experience of Marian Anderson, who earned the munificent sum of $5 for each of her first professional engagements. She would sing two or three songs as "assisting artist" at a church social. Often there was no accompanist, and she would play the piano herself. Since she was not a pianist, she sang all her songs in the key of C major; that disposed of the hazard of the black keys.

A determination to step up her fee to $10 generated a crisis. A men's society which she knew had ample funds offered her a date at $5. She held out for $10. The committee suggested a compromise at $7.50, but the young girl, trembling at her audacity, insisted on her price. The committee gave in, and one of the members told her mother: "That girl of yours sure is going to make money. I wouldn't be surprised"—and the prophet weighed his words significantly—"if someday she got fifty dollars a concert." The girl and her mother laughed. "We thought," Miss Anderson recalls, "that he was crazy."

Artists and managers don't like to talk publicly about fees, and the interested bystander occasionally has to make a shrewd guess. An oracle of wisdom, a doorman at Carnegie Hall, has given me his sure-fire rule of thumb for measuring the drawing powers of an artist:

"If there ain't no chiselers trying to crash the gate, then the musician ain't no draw. If there's a bunch of wise guys trying to crash, even after the intermission, he's a wow!"

Performing musicians are not the only ones with fancy incomes. The President of the Musicians' Union, James Caesar Petrillo, has had a good thing in music; his salaries from the international union and Chicago local amounted to $48,000 a year at their peak. His view of music was inclined, naturally, to be materialistic. During the period when his organization and the American Guild of Musical Artists, headed by Tibbett, were in a jurisdictional row, he and Tibbett had several conferences. Once he asked Tibbett, "What're they paying you?"

"Who?" Tibbett asked in surprise.

"Your outfit."

"My union?" Tibbett laughed. "Nothing."

Petrillo was incredulous, and Tibbett insisted, "Nothing. Not a penny."

Petrillo reflected, and then he seemed to see light. "I guess, Tibbett, you're fixing yourself a nice berth for when you can't sing no more."

Fortunately, Tibbett did not have to rely on this source of income, for success in the so-called high-brow realms of music is reasonably lasting. It is much more capricious in the field of jazz. A few of the best jazz players belong with music's financial elite, and a lad like Bing Crosby rates among the highest income earners of America. A host of good musicians earn modest incomes. Some have ups and downs, hitting it big one season and starving the next. The majority of the tribe fare no better than the majority of high-brow musicians. Ask the crowd on Broadway; it's an unpredictable racket.

Music may also have a dollar-and-cents value to a community. Samuel Rosenbaum, vice-president of the Philadelphia Orchestra, once declared that Philadelphia was known over the world for two things: the Liberty Bell and the orchestra. "We get untold thousands of dollars of valuable and favorable publicity every day in the year from reading matter, broadcasting, records, etc."

Cities that have booked visits of the Metropolitan Opera in the course of its annual spring tour have found, similarly, that it has been good business. The town has received publicity. People have come from long distances to hear the opera and to spend money in hotels and shops; the opera has been as salubrious for the town's cash registers as a big football week end.

Nevertheless, as stated at the outset of this chapter, music may reward a few, but it is a devilishly hard occupation for more than a hundred thousand men and women who try to practice it professionally. The United States turns out thousands of musicians of one kind or another each year. They come from the conservatories, music schools at the universities, innumerable music departments in colleges, and even finishing schools throughout the land. Then there are the youngsters who receive comprehensive training under private teachers. Add to them the products of institutions like music settlement schools that are privately maintained but run on a public basis to aid the underprivileged of the community.

What disposition is made of these musicians of varying qualities? A number of them get jobs as orchestral players in symphonies, on the radio, and in movie houses. Others are diverted into jazz, where a few find it easier to make a living. A considerable group turns to teaching music in the high schools, colleges, conservatories, elementary schools, or in private studios. Some obtain minor paying jobs in opera, radio, the theater, night clubs, or the movies.

It is impossible to calculate just how many men and women trained to be musicians earn a consistent livelihood from their profession. One thing, however, is certain: for every musician who makes a living out of music, scores of others flounder, earn in fits and starts, or make a substandard living.

It is time we began to think about that huge group of professionally trained musicians for whom we have no openings. I have known some excellent musicians who have knocked around from

pillar to post, taking turns at teaching, conducting small choirs,
composing, playing accompaniments, and trying their hands at various musical chores, none of which provided a dependable living.
There is no harm—there may be, in fact, great good—in a period of
practical experience based on many musical jobs. But this kind of
internship can be only harmful if the musician is subjected to it during the best years of his life. It is time we recognized that the laissez-
faire method of handling our musical resources is no more prudent
than the outworn laissez-faire management of our economy.

We need to know what we need. We must have some general idea
as to what the community's requirements are in music; whether in
performers, teachers, or composers. Just as the United States
needed a census of the unemployed and the employable among
them, just as the new army had to canvass the skills of its recruits,
so must an intelligently geared musical economy be based on the
facts.

We must know how many orchestras we have and how many
more the nation needs and can maintain. We must know how many
choruses we have and how many more could be organized. We must
know how many music teachers our schools employ, and the kind of
training they must be equipped to give. A survey of our musical
resources and potentialities would give us other invaluable data,
and the facts would enable us to devise programs of guidance. It is
deplorable that youngsters enter music schools without any conception of where they will be able to take their skill when they have
acquired it. It is a devastating indictment of our society that they
emerge from the schools with no clear idea of who needs them or
where they are needed, if they are needed at all. I have heard of
soundly trained musicians who, after a decade of batting around in
a capricious profession, gave it up to become X-ray technicians,
dental-laboratory assistants, factory workers, and salesmen. Possibly they are better off now, but it would have been social conserva-
tion and individual fulfillment if they had known what to prepare
for at the start.

It is true that some of the large conservatories maintain placement bureaus that keep in touch with the market for musicians. They try to find out where there are openings and they work hard to place their graduates. But even these institutions, with all their resources and prestige, succeed in placing only some of the boys and girls they train. How much more difficult it is for smaller institutions that have limited resources and much less prestige!

It is an enormous task that could be done only by the Federal government or by a lavishly endowed private foundation. The former would be the preferable agent for the job. Probably we would need to establish a department of fine arts in our government. Such a department, if it were to serve any useful purpose, would have to be developed on a down-to-earth factual basis. A department organized for speech-making and for the other genial and useless activities dear to politicians would have no meaning or utility.

We have propaganda enough in this country for the art of music. What we need is practical direction of the nation's resources and capacities in the field. No man or woman of talent should have to pine for or to turn from music. There should be useful work in music for all. A nation's artistic riches are too precious to be squandered.

4

MUSICIAN IN THE PUBLIC EYE

Temperament Tells—Toscanini's Tantrums—Beecham Waves The Star-Spangled
Banner—*Moore vs. Kiepura—Flagstad vs. Melchior—Bruno Walter's Downbeat—
Baccaloni the Buffo—Casals and Cello—White of an Egg, Blowing Bubbles, and
Standing on Your Head—Handshakers—Warming Up—Hot or Cold?—Barnstorm-
ing—The Press—Paderewski Was Not a Mormon.*

FOR GENERATIONS America's musical life has been geared to the
concert industry, which could not exist in its present form without
the idolizing of outstanding performers. The performing musician
is discussed, interviewed, and written about so consistently that he
begins to think himself the whole works. No one denies that the performing musician plays a vital role in the nation's musical life, but
he is not and should not be its be-all and end-all.

Some performers, who have little sense of proportion about themselves and their world to begin with, become the victims of their
own reputations. They come to believe that the musical world re-
volves around them. A famous American soprano wrote a letter recently complaining that some of the leading music critics were not
taking her seriously enough as an artist. But she added reasons why
she deserved to be taken seriously; one was that she, virtually un-
aided, had kept several opera houses in the country going.

When a performer begins to think that he alone can make or
break a big theater, he has been puffed up out of all reason or he
ought to see a psychiatrist. There are no indispensable performers.
Caruso died and the Metropolitan Opera went on; Flagstad left,
and the opera did business at the old stand. Toscanini retired from
the New York Philharmonic-Symphony, and the orchestra was
around to welcome him back six years later; Stokowski left the
Philadelphia Orchestra, and the ensemble has carried on.

40

Are musicians more self-centered than other people? The incidence of egomania is probably the same as in other fields where men and women play to an audience. When musicians act up as if the world revolved around them, it is partly because of the nature of their craft. A veteran manager summed up more than twenty-five years of observation of all shapes and sizes of musicians' egos with this explanation:

"The great difficulty for the musician is that he constantly carries his business with him. A man who opens a store to sell merchandise may leave it for the week end and, unless he is unusual, can forget about it for a while. But a musician carries his skill in his brain, hands, and voice. He can never get away from his business because it is himself. Every business kicks up a little hell now and then, and naturally, if the business and the individual are inextricable, the individual gets to be a little hellish."

No doubt the musician would reply that this managerial analysis reveals the mote in the analyzer's eye. A man who can think coldly of music as business pure and simple is a materialistic buzzard, and if he refuses to make allowances for human foibles, he is a money-making machine himself, and why bother discussing art with him.

There is no getting away from the fact, however, that the general public has the notion that most musicians are long-haired, wild-eyed, and unpredictable. It probably thinks much the same of the boys who work in the field of jazz, except that it is willing to concede that they are not long-haired. The public attributes any extraordinary behavior, short of arson, burglary, and murder, to temperament and is willing to excuse it and be amused. But the public is too indulgent. "Temperament" is a fine dodge that musicians and others employ for reasons a psychologist could easily explain.

There is no question that some musicians have delicate nervous organizations and that under tension they may behave impetuously. But don't think that this is true of the musician alone. I have found, as a matter of cold fact, that in musical affairs the finest musicians are perfectly sane and controlled individuals. They have to be. Greatness as a musician is not achieved without the capacity to think clearly and to organize one's resources—at least musically. The lads and lassies who are capricious and nothing more are usually inferior musicians.

Toscanini, you will say, is supposed to be the most temperamental of conductors and yet he is one of the greatest of our time. My answer would be that there is precious little temperament in Toscanini when it comes to the bedrock of musical thinking. He works calmly and persistently on his musical tasks. But what about the stories of his outbursts? Do they not constitute temperament? Yes and no. I suspect that the maestro sometimes deliberately puts on a bit of a show to scare the hell out of a recalcitrant performer. On the other hand, when he is angry and disgusted, he cannot always restrain himself. Toscanini has had the adulation of the world for many years and he may be more than a mite spoiled. A great soprano who had worked with him in opera and concert once confided that she thought so. He is used to having his way. Whether you call it temperament or not, it does not diminish the delightful quality of the things that occur when Toscanini is annoyed.

Notice, however, the effort at self-restraint. At one rehearsal, failing time and again to get just the effect he wanted from a trumpet, Toscanini worked into one of his rages, in which he humiliated the luckless trumpeter. Afterward several temerarious players spoke to the maestro, reminding him gently that the trumpeter was competent, a veteran musician of proved capacities, integrity, and character.

Toscanini was remorseful. "You are right," he said. "I am much to blame and I am sorry."

At the next rehearsal he apologized to the trumpeter in the presence of the entire orchestra. But as he talked, the memory of the previous difficulties and the unsatisfied musical ideal came back to him and overwhelmed him. The apology became a little angry.

"The trouble is," Toscanini cried, "God tells me how He wants this music played, and you—you get in His way!"

Another time Toscanini was rehearsing the four vocal soloists for a performance of Beethoven's Ninth Symphony. He sat at the piano, and the singers stood near by. The contralto was nervous, for she had never sung with him, and made a wretched entrance. Toscanini stopped and said, "*Da capo.*" They went back to the beginning, and she came in badly once more. Toscanini growled, "*Da capo!*" This time the contralto did not enter at all; she began to sob. As she wept, Toscanini brushed his mustache nervously, and the other singers stood in terror, awaiting the explosion. The contralto's sniffles diminished; she blew her nose and dried her eyes. The maestro struck the keyboard, said "*Da capo!*" glared at her, and murmured, "And they say that I'm impatient!"

Toscanini can even be utterly poker-faced, if it amuses him. He was strolling along a main street of Lucerne, in Switzerland, one summer when an American lady rushed up to him, brandishing a pencil and album, and cried breathlessly, "May I have your autograph?" Toscanini looked blank. The woman stammered, "Aren't you . . . aren't you . . . ?" With a bland expression, he shook his head. The poor woman began to fidget. "Good Lord, I've made a terrible mistake," she cried, as she got ready to run. "I thought you were Arturo Toscanini."

Given sufficient cause, even as self-contained and even-tempered a musician as Rachmaninoff had fits of irritation. He was disembarking from a train once in a Midwestern city. A young reporter grabbed his arm and gave it a painful tug. The pianist turned furiously. "Gangster!" he shouted and strode away. Another time an unruly audience got under his skin. He raced through the program, taking faster tempos than usual, cutting pauses between compositions to the bone, and, when it was over, vanished from the stage and left the hall, without playing a single encore.

Sir Thomas Beecham is an excellent conductor and a shrewd and witty citizen of the world. He can be as smooth as any person in the business, but he can also raise the roof. I suspect that occasionally he plays to the gallery. At a Philadelphia Orchestra rehearsal attended by some visitors, he spent a long time working on *The Star-Spangled Banner*. He carried on as if a great new symphony were being prepared. He shouted, grunted, yipped, hoorayed, tossed his arms and body about, and at the climaxes his voice soared over the orchestra like Flagstad's in the *Liebestod*.

Sir Thomas arrived for a Philadelphia Orchestra concert one afternoon to find that the program was under way and the assistant conductor was leading. Apparently the clock in his hotel room was wrong and he had started late for the hall. Since the concert was being broadcast, it had to start on the second. Beecham knew that he had only himself to blame, but he let go with a bit of "temperament" while sitting in the wings, fuming and sputtering. It was not serious, however, for when the first movement was over he dashed out to the podium and, like a runner in a relay race, grabbed the baton.

Artur Bodanzky was another conductor who could have seizures of "temperament." I never met a saner and more thoughtful man. And this was true of his musical work. He was easy to rile, and once riled he would swear, slap his baton viciously against the lectern, plunge out of the pit, mount the stairs to the stage, and, brandishing a long finger under a bewildered singer's nose, launch into a vicious tirade. People who experienced Bodanzky's wrath were sure that he was one of the prize temperamental babies, but after a while they learned that his temperament was his technique for enforcing discipline and strict attention.

The best indication of the fact that most temperament can be turned on and off like a spigot is what happened at the Metropolitan when the Second World War broke out. Conductors of Italian or German extraction who could be violent and unrestrained discovered that they owned the tongues of angels. For a time an ineffable and unprecedented glow of sweetness and light prevailed at the Opera House. Alien musicians realized that this was a time to be cautious rather than cantankerous, and they seemed to be able to control their passions quite nicely.

The prima donnas and tenors, arch-temperamentalists, if they are important enough, have method in their madness. If they want to make sure that no one will steal the show, they carry on to hog the limelight. Grace Moore is supposed to have the liveliest temperament currently at the Metropolitan Opera House, but I have always felt that it was well within her power to control it. She does, too, if everything goes according to her desires. But put a tenor like Jan Kiepura, who is no mean scene-stealer and with "temperament" in his own right, into a cast with her, and you get a fine stew. When they sang in *La Bohème* together, he strode up and down in the forefront of the stage while she tried to sing her aria, and then she suddenly pushed a chair into his knees when he was giving out with his solo.

Another prima donna, after appearing in *Carmen* with Kiepura, said flatly that she would never work in the same cast with him again. Grace Moore has also demanded that certain singers be eliminated from her operas. After a performance of *Tosca* in Chicago, she descended on the managerial offices to inveigh against John Charles Thomas, who had played Scarpia. The manager was not there, but his secretary was. Miss Moore cried, "I never want to sing in the same opera with Thomas!" The secretary, who had seen these bursts of fury before, said sweetly, "Pretty soon, Miss Moore, you'll be singing all the roles yourself."

For a time there was hostility between Flagstad and Melchior, when the latter jealously watched all the curtain calls the soprano received and demanded a like number. He once insisted that he appear in all the productions in which she was cast, probably so that she would reap no glory in which he could not share. And yet Melchior could be sweet and considerate to a newcomer. When Astrid Varnay, young Swedish-American soprano, made a hurried appearance as Brünnhilde, singing the role for the first time in her life, Melchior stood in the wings and encouraged her.

Jealousy is not the prerogative of the opera stage alone. A violinist ordered his manager to throw out a carefully planned advertising schedule and prepare a new one because a rival was using more advertising. When the American Guild of Musical Artists, of which Jascha Heifetz was a vice-president, was rowing with James Caesar Petrillo, president of the American Federation of Musicians,

Heifetz was scheduled to fill a date as soloist with the New York Philharmonic-Symphony at the Lewisohn Stadium. Another fiddler wrote a note to Petrillo reminding him that Heifetz was not a member of his union and that he should not be permitted to appear with a union orchestra.

There are, of course, numerous musicians who live and act like mature, intelligent citizens. Even if things do not go to their liking, they remember that there is no infallibility in this best of all possible worlds. Bruno Walter was listening to a playback of one of his recordings with orchestra. In one place an instrumentalist playing a solo passage faltered almost imperceptibly for a brief moment, but that was the only blemish. Walter's comment, at the end of the record, was, "Not perfect, but very good. Perfection is not for this world."

With maturity go consideration and a touch of humility. When Walter directed a revival of *The Bartered Bride* at the Metropolitan Opera, he worked with each singer individually and then with the group in ensemble rehearsals. He took special pains with the difficult quintet. On the night of the performance, he arrived early at the Opera House, assembled the five singers, and rehearsed the concerted passage once more. Throughout the rehearsals the singers had been worried about a delicately shaded diminuendo. Walter's beat became constricted as the diminuendo developed, for he was living through it in his gestures, and they could not make out clearly a strategic downbeat. They discussed the matter among themselves, and Ezio Pinza, as the veteran of the five, was deputized to speak to Walter. The basso began with some hesitation, "The downbeat at this point, maestro. Could it be more decisive? I am ashamed to say we can't see it." Walter smiled, abashed, and said quietly, "I shall try to improve."

Salvatore Baccaloni, the great comic basso, could be big enough to help out a younger singer without thought of self-aggrandizement. A young American baritone, Arthur Kent, was assigned for the first time to the role of Masetto in *Don Giovanni* one season.

One of the most ticklish places for him was the ballroom scene at the end of the first act. Here the orchestra in the pit is complemented by small ensembles on stage; in addition, the chorus is singing full blast and the ballet is bouncing around. Through most of this scene, Baccaloni as Leporello has to keep dancing and singing with Masetto, and on this occasion the basso deliberately kept his back to the audience through most of the scene to make sure that young Kent would have his eye constantly on the conductor. Moreover, Baccaloni seemed to be playing Kent's role too. His face showed suspense as the younger man waited for his cues and he glowed when Kent came in at the right place.

Szigeti had to fill a concert date in Canada and discovered that his accompanist, who was not yet an American citizen, would not be able to make the trip. He borrowed Emanuel Feuermann's accompanist, giving him a complete list of his repertory and telling him to choose the program. The pianist was astonished; virtuosos are not in the habit of letting the accompanist make up a program to please himself. But as Szigeti explained, "We have not played together before, and I want you to choose the compositions with which you will feel most comfortable."

Adolf Busch and a colleague paid a visit to the High School of Music and Art in New York City and were invited to listen to a rehearsal of the senior orchestra. The conductor offered the baton to Mr. Busch, but he declined it. His only wish was to sit among the sixteen-year-old New Yorkers and make music as one of them. The visitors borrowed violins and joined with the student orchestra in the Polonaise from Rimsky-Korsakov's *Christmas Night* and in passages from Mozart's Piano Concerto in A, with a youngster as soloist.

Casals was regarded by his manager, who had dealt with hundreds of musicians, as one of the calmest. One evening, during an American tour, his train was delayed by a snowstorm and he arrived in town fifteen minutes after his concert was to begin. When he reached the hall, the audience was restless and the local impresario was beside himself. "Do something!" he screamed, "do something, somebody!" Casals took out his pipe, lit it, puffed contentedly, and slowly prepared the cello for action.

Another time Casals put up for the night at a swank town house, and let the butler carry off his cello. He did not learn until concert time that the well-meaning flunky had deposited the priceless instrument on top of a hot radiator. When Casals began to play he found that the varnish was sticky instead of glossy and the tone was raspy instead of mellow. Here was ample provocation, but there was never a peep out of Casals, though he probably thought his thoughts about butlers.

Talk about the grace and tact of a gentleman—Casals was working on a Beethoven adagio, and he felt that his pianist was missing the heart of it. He proposed a rest, then asked a pupil, another cellist, to play the adagio while he sat down at the piano. His treatment of the piano part was a revelation to the accompanist, who whispered that he understood.

Since it is true that musicians carry their business on their persons at every sleeping and waking moment, they think about their health more than most people. Illness may raise hob with a tour, causing cancellations, postponements, shifts of schedule, and losses of large sums of money. An illness in midseason once cost Tibbett more than $50,000. When Kreisler was hit by a truck in New York City and was laid up for months, a season's tour and $75,000 were forfeited.

The most persistent fretters about health are the singers. They feel colds coming on every time the breeze changes, and their precautions against wind, weather, and smoke would make a hypochondriac seem like a daredevil. Some of their notions about diet and health are extraordinary. There are singers who take the white of an egg and try to keep it sitting in their throats for minutes on end before swallowing it. Gladys Swarthout says she blows bubbles as a daily dozen for her breath support. Tibbett says he can hasten the departure of a cold by standing on his head; at least he has some medical doctrine in his support.

I once visited Mitropoulos during the peak of a New York heat wave. The conductor had a bad cold and a touch of fever. He occupied a small hotel room, and every window was tightly closed. He wore a tweed suit, with a heavy cashmere sweater underneath his coat. A woolen blanket was draped around his shoulders and another covered his legs. It was more efficacious than a Turkish bath. I don't know whether this treatment cured Mitropoulos' cold but it came close to giving me claustrophobia.

The pianists, violinists, and cellists are as careful about their hands as a woman about her complexion. Kreisler has his insured with Lloyd's for $1,000,000. Heifetz has refused to insure his hands, for fear that he would become too self-conscious about them.

Calisthenics for the hands, arms, and shoulders are routine for some musicians, but most of them feel that their regular practice sessions and concerts are exercise enough. They are cautious about hard labor, but even here there are exceptions. When Kreisler arrived from Europe, he liked to toss his baggage around as if he were a porter. Heifetz, in the off season, has worked on his farm with handsaws, rakes, and shovels. He handles the wheel of his yacht and plays a slashing game of tennis and ping-pong. A fortnight before his season begins, however, he stops all strenuous activity, to soften his hands.

Musicians are especially wary of handshakers. At receptions where they must greet many people, many of them wear gloves and use each hand alternately. With an elephant's memory for athletic handshakers who affect a viselike grip, they will spot and avoid the brutes years after. A hearty greeter once clutched Paderewski's hand so violently that a muscle in the pianist's hand was strained and he had to postpone several recitals.

Musicians have their several recipes for warming up the hands before a concert. The majority bathe them in warm water. Paderewski's hands and arms were massaged by his valet for fifteen minutes, while Rachmaninoff used an electric muff before and between numbers. Some musicians use lotions, and Josef Lhevinne, who grew up in Russia, has been fond of rubbing his hands in snow, of which, as the Nazis discovered, there is an

abundance in that country. The most unorthodox is Horowitz, who
says, "I warm up my hands on music."

Diet is a problem principally for the singers. Most instrumental
musicians eat what they like, and they have as many vagaries as
the rest of us. Singers affect all manner of concoctions for their
voices before and after singing. Caruso sipped hot water before
and between numbers. Some singers like mouth washes. A few
take hot tea. A snifter of wine or something stronger encourages a
good many before a recital or opera. After the show Flagstad liked
to have champagne, and she could hold a good deal.

Stokowski is one of the careful diet boys, but he shifts from
diet to diet. For one period he ate only meats; then for a time
he became a strict vegetarian. He does not take coffee, and he now
sticks to green vegetables and fruits with simple dishes of meat
and fish. He avoids rich desserts, and the boyish figure stays
boyish. For breakfast he takes orange juice and a raw apple. Before concerts he has had a masseur rub him down as if he were
going out for a heavyweight-championship fight.

If a musician worries about his health, he begins to be sensitive
to temperatures of theaters. Paderewski had to have a concert
hall airtight, so that he would feel not the slightest draft on stage;
if a breath of air so much as stirred, he would refuse to go on. A solo
recitalist can command, and his wish is obeyed. But in an opera
house there may be singers who have different tastes in temperature. Rosa Ponselle liked the theater cool, and Martinelli preferred it warm. Once when they sang in the same opera, it was too
cool for him and he caught cold. He lost several performances and
the next time they were cast together, he warned her before the
performance, "If I catch cold on account of you, I'll sue!"

Artur Schnabel was playing a recital in New York, and it seemed
to be going badly. He stopped in the middle of the work and said,
"It's awfully cold here." The hall superintendent looked into it
and apparently made some adjustments. A little later the pianist
told the audience, "It's warmer now." The story got about, and a
Los Angeles musical journal commented, "We might recommend

to the distinguished Schnabel that he concertize in southern California, where icy blasts come only from critics."

Don't blame the musicians for being sensitive to wind and weather; their livelihoods are at stake. When something goes wrong, they have to go through purgatory to correct it. Edward Johnson once lost his voice when he was at the peak of his career. Something happened to his throat, and he could not sing. A throat specialist advised him to develop certain muscles he had used slightly before. He gave the tenor a set of exercises, and Johnson went about gurgling like an infant. With patient courage he followed this routine for weeks. In time the muscles loosened, and the physician was able to reach and remove a tiny obstruction which had been unapproachable. There followed another long period of gradual and determined exercises to restore the power to all the throat muscles. In the end, Johnson could sing again.

And yet, in the tradition of the trouper that the show must go on, some musicians take chances. One night Tibbett sang at the Metropolitan despite laryngitis, because the opera could not find a substitute at short notice. Several days later he gave a recital at Hartford, Conn., though his throat was painfully sore. His manager begged him to cut out the big arias and to sing simple songs. Tibbett said, "Nuts," and sang the program as promised.

For most musicians barnstorming is the necessity of their trade, and they grouse about it as ballplayers do. And yet if they did not have extensive tours, they would complain even more, and with good reason. Traveling is a burden, but it means money, prestige, and admiration from a huge public. If the musician is famous and successful enough, he can barnstorm in style. Paderewski traveled in a private railroad car, with a retinue that included valet, secretary, cook, special porter, and road manager. When his wife was alive, she went along too. For relaxation he had a threesome of traveling companions for bridge, and if the stop in any community was long enough, he would hire a car and spend hours seeing the sights and the countryside. He was avid for information, and his road manager once told me that they had to carry reference books to answer his many questions.

Some musicians make their shorter trips by automobile, but tire and gasoline rationing have put a crimp in that. Most top-notchers can afford the speed of airplanes, or, at the least, drawing rooms on luxury trains, but there are some who travel on the ordinary sleepers. Feuermann always hired an upper and a lower berth; the latter for himself and the former for his cello. At home the cello slept in a bed of its own. Valuable cellos are a trial to their owners; Joseph Schuster's wife says that whenever she, her husband, and the cello go out together, they have to take a taxi, and the instrument is deposited first, while the human beings take care of themselves as best they can.

During the long hours on the road some musicians read anything from mysteries to philosophy; some sleep; some play rummy, hearts, or solitaire; some study scores, like Mitropoulos, who memorized a symphony on a trip from Minneapolis to New York. Chávez completed part of a big job of orchestrating a new work during the three-and-a-half-day journey from Mexico City to New York. Piatigorsky writes poetry in Russian. Hofmann once sat quietly during a train trip, looking straight ahead of him, his eyes apparently unseeing, until his companion asked what he was doing. "Practicing," he said.

Alexander Brailowsky had the shock of his life in a theater in Colombia. The packed house gave him a big hand when he appeared on the stage, and after bowing his acknowledgment he turned toward the center of the stage. Something was missing—the piano! Nor was there a piano anywhere in the house. The local management had overlooked that detail, and the recital had to be called off.

Habits in strange towns vary. Some musicians take long walks to see the sights. Others, like Horowitz, sleep late and lounge around their hotel rooms until it is time to go to the hall. There are nearly always first-class hotels in the towns that hire famous musicians, but Rachmaninoff was once ushered into a room with plaster falling from the walls. His only comment was, "The life of an artist."

Relations with press and public are a source of joy and trouble. Musicians may boast that they never read the newspapers and magazines. Unless they are illiterate, they are not telling the truth. Toscanini has no need to worry about criticism, and it is probable that when in the midst of hard work he does not read musical news and criticisms unremittingly, but he does follow them from time to time.

One day there appeared in two leading New York newspapers reviews of a Philharmonic concert, reporting exactly contradictory stories. It was not a concert Toscanini had conducted, but the maestro, in a towering rage, phoned a friend at the Philharmonic offices and shouted, "How in the world can our public have any standards if our critics are so far apart?"

There have been other occasions when Toscanini has reacted to stories in the newspapers. One season, when the Philharmonic was conducting a public campaign for funds, the Sunday-afternoon concerts were doing especially bad business. The maestro programmed several works by the most inconsequential of Italian composers, and one writer observed acidly that it seemed incredible for an orchestra that was pleading for funds not to do something with its programs that would attract the public more than this warmed-over Italian trash. Perhaps it was a coincidence, but the Sunday programs of the Philharmonic under Toscanini were radically changed for the rest of the season.

Then there is the story about Toscanini returning to the Philharmonic's offices after an absence of more than five years. He was introduced to the new employees of the staff and when he met a blonde, attractive girl, he said, "Aren't you the girl whose picture appeared in *PM* this summer?" She was.

A serious, dignified musician whose personal and artistic standards are of the highest had done without a press agent for years, but decided to hire one. He explained that usually he did not bother with publicity, but as he talked he kept referring to various pieces about himself that had appeared in print, and out of the pockets of his trousers, vest, coat, and overcoat he fished out clippings.

If the best of them are terribly anxious about their press, consider how the less publicized individuals pant after their place· in the spotlight. It is in this group that you find the publicity hounds, the boys and girls for whom no stunt is too shabby or demeaning, and who dream publicity in all their waking and sleeping hours.

One well-known basso seldom passes up the opportunity to parade in the corridors of the Metropolitan. If he is in an opera and his role ends at the close of the second act, he takes his curtain calls in costume, and before the intermission is over, you will meet him in civilian clothes, parading along the corridors. Even when he is in costume and grease paint and has a long pause between appearances on the stage, he will sometimes come down to the press room to while away the time and, of course, to be seen.

Then there is the tribe of glad-handers, who are constantly on the alert for important people and who, even before they have finished greeting you, have their eyes turned in search of the next victim to be hailed. Don't think that this is a foible common only to musicians. It is human. You will find it in the theater and in the business world and even among newspapermen who should know better. One musician protested that he hated the ostentation and hurly-burly of gatherings in the concert halls and opera houses. Yet by some strange circumstance, for which he always had an excuse, he was invariably present at the flossiest events and always planted where the crowd was thickest and the most prominent people were to be encountered. The poor fellow was constantly being imposed upon, he said. People invaded his time and privacy with invitations to chi-chi affairs. It was an annoyance, but after all one had to be polite. He never missed a party unless he was desperately ill.

Then there was the musician who behaved as if the members of the press were a magnet. He assured you that he did not seek out the critics. But somehow it always happened that he was one of the first to meet any newcomer to the craft. He was constantly finding excuses to trot about with them, to chat with them, and to be their buddy. This compulsion became especially acute every time he felt a concert coming on.

Musicians may lack subtlety in every other aspect of their careers, but when it comes to reading between the lines of newspaper reports, they are the most perceptive of creatures. They can sense innuendoes that were never intended. If their names are omitted for any one of a thousand good and sufficient reasons, they are sure that the omission is part of a plot. Leave out an orchestra from a list summing up any week's events, and the manager suspects that the critic or editor has been offended and that he had better do something to make amends. Not only the wicked, but the innocent and pure of heart flee when no man pursueth.

Those who have been roasted may have reasonable cause for anger. Most musicians curse quietly or confide their indignation to their families and friends. But a few carry on as if an unfavorable judgment were a criminal act. Publicly and noisily, they threaten to bring lawsuits or even to mete out corporal punishment. There is nothing, on the other hand, to match the complacency and good will of the musician who has been lauded. To him such a criticism is the essence of reason, intuition, and definitive judgment.

The mature musician does not fret too much about his press. He keeps a dignified sense of proportion, if he does not fight against the inroads on his privacy. Toscanini has granted no interviews, and Rachmaninoff, toward the end of his career, had cut his down to the bone. A reporter once asked him for a two-minute interview, and the pianist agreed. He took out his watch, and at the end of two minutes he terminated the meeting. A photographer for *Life* tried to persuade Rachmaninoff to pose for a series of pictures illustrating a day in the life of a great pianist, showing him rising from bed, shaving, breakfasting, practicing, dining, walking, talking, and so on. Rachmaninoff said no, curtly and flatly. But, argued the photographer, a distinguished United States Senator had recently posed for such a set of pictures. "The Senator," said Rachmaninoff, "is a more important man."

The mature musician also goes out of his way to avoid receptions and adoration. Egon Petri was scheduled to play the piano at a benefit concert in New York and was to appear as guest of honor at a preconcert banquet. At banquet time there was no Petri. Frantic telephone calls were made and someone suggested notifying the police. Before this was done, the pianist walked in, smiling and unaware of the commotion. He had slipped off to see Walt Disney's *Dumbo*.

There is no harm in relishing the excitement of a host of admirers. There was the time hundreds of women of all ages, shapes, and sizes waited for Paderewski at the stage door of the Tabernacle in Salt Lake City. When he emerged, the girls rushed him as if he were a movie idol, trying to get his autograph, shake his hand, touch his clothing, and stroke his flowing locks. His retinue sweated and strained and finally deposited him, all in one piece, in his limousine. With the valet poised on one running board and the road manager on the other, the car plowed through the mass of femininity. As the bodyguards pushed and fumed on the running boards, they heard Paderewski gayly chanting, "If I were only a Mormon, if I were only a Mormon."

5

MEET THE GLAMOUR BOYS

Toscanini the Monarchist—Watch the Birdie—Stokowski's Hands—"Life Begins at Forte"—NBC Symphony—Mitropoulos and an Ambulance—Koussevitzky Talks Back—Guest Conductor.

TODAY'S GLAMOUR BOYS of music are the conductors. For a long time they have been catching up on the singers, pianists, and violinists and now they seem to have taken the lead. As long ago as 1872 Verdi cried out against their tyranny, for even then, when the singer was king of all he surveyed in Italy, the conductor was beginning his ascendancy. In this country, where symphony orchestras extend from coast to coast, the conductor is the spoiled darling. Years ago when Toscanini bawled out Geraldine Farrar in a rehearsal at the Metropolitan, she protested that she was, after all, a star; and the maestro responded that he recognized only the stars in heaven. He may still hold this view, but the public hails the conductor as the bright, shining star and regards Toscanini as the brightest in the firmament.

Being stars, conductors are usually idolized, pampered, flattered, and fawned upon. The spoiling is done by the public, by the conductor's fellow performers who seek his good will, by composers who wish his patronage, and by his own family. There was once a guest conductor of the New York Philharmonic-Symphony whose wife treated him like a particularly sensitive plant. She used to cart a bundle of bedding from the hotel to the backstage entrance of Carnegie Hall. Then she would have it lugged up to the conductor's dressing room, where she arranged it on a sofa, and during the rest periods of rehearsals she insisted that he be tucked in for twenty minutes of complete relaxation. In those days the conduc-

57

tor's room was separated from the quarters of the players by a drawn curtain instead of a wall, and the boys congregated on their side to peek, grin, and make bawdy and irreverent comments.

The essence of the conductor's job is to lead, and if he does so with success, he tends to become dictatorial. Toscanini has recognized this, for he has said that in life he is a democrat but in music a monarchist—with himself, of course, as the monarch. Watch him at rehearsals and you soon find out that he means it. He was once rehearsing the first performance of a new symphony with the New York Philharmonic. In front of him was the manuscript of the score, fresh from the composer's hand, the pages unbound. When the men did not give him what he wished, Toscanini picked up the score and flung it at them. The pages scattered like leaves in the wind. Several of the musicians hastened to pick them up, and the concertmaster slowly assembled them and handed Toscanini the ordered pile. Still raging, Toscanini promptly flung the manuscript at the men again, and once again a shower of pages fluttered over the orchestra.

Toscanini's habit of hurling the score to the floor troubled the orderly instincts of Emil Greinert, the orchestra's librarian; it also injured the valuable scores, and this bothered the librarian's aesthetic sense. He observed that the maestro's first move, when he became furious during a rehearsal, was to grip his baton in both hands and to snap it violently. If he succeeded in breaking it, he usually cooled off and the rehearsal went on; if he didn't, there was score flinging. The librarian made it his business to have on hand a large supply of reasonably fragile batons. If a rehearsal went badly, Toscanini might break as many as half a dozen batons, and the librarian would dash off to the wings to get spares, shouting to his assistant: "Lumber, lumber!"

The conductor's dictatorial urge expresses itself in many ways: Toscanini is tempestuous; Stokowski is coldly ironical; Koussevitzky flushes and becomes stern; Mengelberg used to deliver long, didactic discourses. Sir Thomas Beecham's manner is distant though biting. During a rehearsal with New York City's WPA

Orchestra, he discovered that there was no organist for a work that demanded the organ. He insisted on having an organist and would not go on until one was obtained. The orchestra manager, in the meantime, asked the pianist of the ensemble whether she could play the organ. No, but she was willing to try. The rehearsal began and the young lady entered—badly, of course—with the first measures of the organ part. Sir Thomas sat back, his arms folded, and said, "Young woman, what *are* you doing at the monolith?" Without a word, she slipped back to the piano.

Sir Thomas did not find it so easy to dispose of a photographer over whom he had no authority. A man from *Life* had obtained his approval to take pictures of Sir Thomas in action and, before the rehearsal, had set up his apparatus. The picture taking went smoothly until the photographer made one shot with a flash bulb. Sir Thomas was annoyed and shouted at the photographer, "Get off the stage!" The photographer shrugged his shoulders and proceeded to dismantle his apparatus. But the conductor, evidently annoyed at the calm, measured pace of the photographer, shouted once more, "Get off, I tell you!" The photographer continued to work with his equipment and said coolly, "Humility is a sign of greatness." Sir Thomas flushed and thundered, "Get off at once!" But it was Sir Thomas who dashed off in a pet, for the photographer replied, "The hell I will! I don't have to take orders from you."

Photographers seem to bring out the most temperamental aspects of the great men of the podium. When a cameraman took a flash-bulb shot of Toscanini at the end of a concert, the maestro refused to return to the stage for curtain calls, as if the adoring audience had been guilty of the breach of etiquette.

Stokowski handled an encounter with a photographer more amiably. After he had made *Fantasia* with Walt Disney, the studio decided that it wanted a new set of pictures of Stokowski rehearsing his Philadelphia Orchestra. A cameraman went down to Philadelphia and planted himself unobtrusively among the bull fiddles. Stokowski hurried in for the rehearsal and gave the signal to start, as was his custom, almost as soon as his feet landed on the podium.

When he turned to cue in the bull fiddles, he saw the stranger with the camera. He objected to his presence, but when the photographer argued, Stokowski relented. "All right, sit among the violas." The photographer, who knew nothing about music, wandered along the stage, peering intently at the instruments and looking vainly for violas. The men laughed. Stokowski, with a straight face, clicked his heels, bent from the waist, gave his arm to the photographer, and led him ceremoniously to the violas. Months later the photographer ran into Stokowski and greeted him with the challenge, "You don't remember me?" Stokowski smiled, "Aren't you the viola player?"

Most conductors, of course, like to see their pictures in the papers and magazines and on the billboards, and they enjoy having their photographs taken. But, being generals rather than privates, they insist on commanding. Some of them supervise even the angles from which they shall be photographed and like to decide what pictures shall be used.

The good conductor, like the good general, knows what he wants. That is his prerogative when it comes to music. Stokowski supervises every last item of his affairs. When he became conductor of the NBC Symphony Orchestra, he gave clear evidence of how he works. Before the auditorium in which he was to play his concerts was chosen, he tested the acoustics from every part of the house. He supervised every detail of the preparation of the orchestra shell and arrived early for the first concert, to look after the placing of the lights.

His belittlers would say that he was careful about the lights because he wished to be sure that his trim figure would be properly silhouetted and his elegant hands and flowing hair would be dramatically highlighted. In later years he carried his own podium whenever he went on tour, because, it was said, this platform had its own spotlight, cannily set to outline the Stokowski profile, hands, and hair. The hair, by the way, was not always there. Recently I saw a picture of him with his head close-cropped à la Rachmaninoff. That photograph would be a collector's item today.

Stokowski was always receptive to an original idea in lighting. When he was preparing the American *première* of Alban Berg's *Wozzeck* in Philadelphia, a spotlight was accidentally turned on at an angle that caused Stokowski's eloquently waving hands to cast enormous shadows. The light man apologized, and quickly turned off the spot, but Stokowski said, "Very effective," and asked that the spot be turned on again at the curious angle. Stokowski was right. *Wozzeck* was a lurid story, and the eerie shadows helped to build the atmosphere of impending doom.

In his broadcasts, Stokowski supervises the manner in which the controls are worked. The legend has it that when he first went on the radio years ago, he took over the controls and tuned himself off the air several times. On the other hand, the engineers at the National Broadcasting Company said that he was the first musician they had met who could speak their language.

With the NBC Orchestra, Stokowski insisted on approving even the kind of paper on which the programs were printed. He had a notebook at hand, jotting down ideas that occurred to him and keeping track of everything. He left his notebook around one day, and one of the men glanced at it. Recalling that Stokowski's signature is sweeping and quite illegible, the man glanced at the meticulous, legible notes, and cried out, "Look, he can write!"

Stokowski would probably like to dictate the style and form of every interview he gives. I know. Several times I have interviewed him, and he has requested in advance the right to approve the finished story. You can't blame a man for wishing to be quoted accurately. But he sought to control even the wording. Once he objected to the word "get." He said, "Get? What does it mean?"

Stokowski's meticulous regard for detail gratifies some people. A clerk in a music publisher's rental library once said that he preferred to deal with Stokowski rather than with any other conductor. For Stokowski was dependable. He always notified the publisher of the arrival of the score, took scrupulous care of it, and returned it on the promised date.

Conductors like best of all to conduct. The men who have not

arrived ask for nothing more than a chance to work. Even some of
the leading lights are quite content to hold the same post year after
year. Look at the way in which Koussevitzky has devoted himself
almost exclusively to the Boston Symphony Orchestra. It was
through his work with the Boston Symphony that he joined the
Berkshire Festival and through the festival that he founded his
Berkshire Music Center; thus his extra-Boston Symphony under-
takings have grown naturally out of the main job.

Detractors of Stokowski deplore his tendency to pop off into
other fields. An eminent musician, who admired Stokowski's gifts
as a conductor, said once that it was criminal for such a talent to
be diverted into trifling matters like the movies. But actually
Stokowski was far from precipitate. He conducted the Philadelphia
Orchestra for more than twenty-five years. Admiring American
willingness to "explore without maps," he was equally daring himself and was willing to experiment with new works, new players,
new seating, new gadgets, new ideas. In Hollywood he developed
for *Fantasia* a system of recording the score on multiple sound
tracks and reproducing it in the theater through multiple loud-
speakers with overwhelming volume, causing one musician to remark: "Life begins at forte." He has been a force for adventure in
music. Since he left Philadelphia, he has been adventuring still.
Let us salute an audacious musician.

If any conductor has been restless, it is Toscanini. Possibly his
longest continuous employment was with the New York Philharmonic, where he remained for eleven years. He served at the
Metropolitan Opera for seven consecutive years; before that he
conducted for seven years, broken into periods of five and two
years, at La Scala in Milan.

Certainly Toscanini has never been fired. Possibly those who
have employed him have rigged a situation that left the maestro
no alternative but to depart. I incline to the theory that he has
been so impetuous, so jealous of his rights, so insistent that they be
observed to the last syllable and in the full spirit, because he would
not brook opposition.

When he left the Metropolitan in 1915 there was a sharp dis-
agreement between him and Giulio Gatti-Casazza, the general
manager. In later years Gatti declared that Toscanini left because
he was deeply patriotic and chose to be in Italy when his country
was at war. There was also the story that an affair of the heart had
something to do with making the maestro uncomfortable at the
Metropolitan. The compelling reason was that Toscanini was good
and sore at the Metropolitan, fed up because he was not getting
his way on artistic questions.

More than twenty-five years later he still harbored a deep resentment against the Metropolitan. Perhaps he did not admit it
openly. He received Edward Johnson, the present general manager,
cordially when the latter came to visit him, recommended a talented
conductor for the opera, and listened to Johnson's proposal that he
himself conduct a revival of Verdi's *Falstaff* at the Metropolitan.
But to his close friends he kept saying that he hated the theater;
evidently the memories of years gone by still rankled.

What of the break with the New York Philharmonic? It is more
than likely that some Philharmonic directors were seeking ways
and means to cut down on the conductors' budget, and Toscanini
represented by far the largest item. But as the years went by,
Toscanini became more and more displeased with the board. As I
understand it, the breaking point came when he was deliberating
in 1935-36 whether to accept a new contract. A delegation from
the board is supposed to have visited him and demanded his decision promptly. This irritated him, and he said no, violently. He was
so resentful that when the Philharmonic invited him to return as
one of the distinguished guest conductors for its gala centennial
program, he refused for a long time, and gave in, finally, for reasons
of sentiment.

The break with the Philharmonic sent him back to Italy, apparently for good. But within a year and a half he returned to
conduct the NBC Symphony Orchestra, which was organized for
him. I suspect that Toscanini accepted partly to get even with
the Philharmonic directors.

After five seasons with the NBC Symphony, there was another temporary break. The resentments were, of course, beneath the surface, but bitterness there was. Toscanini insisted on having the orchestra at his disposal when he wanted it. Once when he was rehearsing a big work, he wanted to go on beyond the regular rehearsal time. The orchestra had an engagement to play on a commercial program, but that made no difference to Toscanini, who went right on with the rehearsal.

During this break NBC representatives telephoned him, tried to call on him personally to persuade him to conduct at least a handful of concerts with the NBC Orchestra, which, after all, had been organized specially for him. But Toscanini was obdurate. He held himself incommunicado; he would not answer the telephone; he would not come out of his study to see visitors. He broke a luncheon engagement when he heard that NBC business was to be discussed.

By a curious twist of chance he accepted a series of guest engagements with the Philadelphia Orchestra in the very season that saw the final rupture between the Philadelphia Orchestra and Stokowski, the man who had made it great. Stokowski turned up as head man of the NBC Symphony—at Toscanini's recommendation.

No matter what gyrations take place in the shift of conductor to orchestra and orchestra to conductor, the shifts are not unrelated to business advantages. Toscanini, Stokowski, and Koussevitzky have been paid well for their ministrations, though they have been ready to make generous gestures, conducting for many good causes without fee. A manager once said that Stokowski understood every angle of a business deal and that if, in negotiations, he began to hint that he did not understand business matters, beware. Note how astutely he maneuvered his affairs in Hollywood. After making the successful *100 Men and a Girl*, with Deanna Durbin, for Universal, he declined a munificent offer from Samuel Goldwyn because he refused to repeat himself and because the producer would not give him a veto power over the story. Instead he agreed to work with Walt Disney on a Mickey Mouse short for a trifling amount. The short later grew into *Fantasia*, but it was not money alone that Stokowski sought in Hollywood; he wished to be sure that he would appear in something worth while.

Toscanini knows the angles, too. When the Treasury Department invited him to direct the NBC Symphony in a series of radio concerts, he readily agreed to do so without fee. NBC officials suggested Tuesday evenings, the fixed broadcasting time of the NBC Symphony concert series. But Toscanini refused to appear on the regular series time; that might make it look as if he were still the permanent leader of the NBC Symphony.

Despite the stories of Toscanini's impetuousness, he has been anything but unreliable. He has fulfilled promises without signed contracts. Once an understanding has been reached, Toscanini can be counted upon to live up to it, and to begin concentrating on it immediately. The day after he promised to take over the NBC Symphony—it was more than six months before the beginning of the season—he told his wife that he had spent a sleepless night. "Why?" she asked. "I was planning the program of the first NBC concert," he said.

Even when he has fought with boards of directors, he has not lost sight of the values of the institutions they represented. He once had a violent dispute with La Scala in Milan and quit. He told his family he would not conduct there again; if necessary, he said, he would make a living by playing the cello and he actually got out the instrument with which he had begun his career as a musician. For a long stretch he remained inactive, living on his savings. However, when he heard that La Scala was in grave danger, he made a large gift anonymously. There was a plaque on La Scala edifice, commemorating the nameless donor, and to this day the Italian public has not been told who the generous friend was.

Generosity just as unusual in its way was revealed by Mitropoulos, who, offered an increase in stipend by the Minneapolis Symphony Orchestra management, requested that the money be distributed as increases to the lowest-paid members of his orchestra.

The man seems to be indifferent to money. During the 1941-42 season, his guest leadership in New York for four weeks brought him about $4000. He paid fifteen per cent as commission to his manager; he had to pay Federal and State income taxes, and he had to meet living expenses in New York. Nevertheless, he offered to match any sum that the members of the New York Philharmonic-Symphony might raise toward a Red Cross ambulance, and his gift turned out to be $1950.

If conductors turn into dictators, they are frequently obliged to do so by force of circumstances. Differences of opinion with boards of directors occasionally drive a conductor with ideas and personality to fight, and when he wins, more than ever he is likely to feel that he is the supreme high command. If he does win, it is perhaps better for his orchestra.

In the long association of Koussevitzky with the Boston Symphony, you would think that sweetness and light have always prevailed. Actually there have been conflicts, some of them highly charged, between conductor and trustees. Shortly after his assumption of the leadership of the orchestra, Koussevitzky decided to overhaul it. The trustees protested that firings and hirings would upset the town. When Koussevitzky threatened to quit, he was allowed to rebuild the ensemble. Koussevitzky suggested on another occasion that women were progressing as orchestral players, but the trustees made it clear that the sixty-year tradition of men only was not to be lightly overthrown in Boston.

The orchestra was nonunion, and though a campaign by the musicians' union forced it off the radio and out of recordings, there was no surrender. Koussevitzky himself thought this stand was silly and costly. His comment was, "Henry Ford had to recognize a union." In December, 1942, so did the Boston Symphony trustees, and when the contract with the union was signed, the orchestra returned to the radio and recording studio.

A trustee who contributed heavily to the deficit once said to Koussevitzky that if the men did something of which he disapproved he would disband the orchestra. The conductor's reply was,

"What right have you to disband it? Has it ever occurred to you that the orchestra could disband you?"

The most intense feelings were aroused in the spring of 1942 when there was talk of abandoning the Berkshire Symphonic Festival. When Koussevitzky heard that the Boston Symphony Orchestra's trustees inclined toward abandonment, he called them together, told them that it would be an act of vandalism and threatened to resign instantly if they carried the proposal.

Mindful of the power and responsibility of his craft, Koussevitzky thought that conductors should fight against overweening trustees. He proposed the founding of a union of conductors, and discussed the idea with other conductors. But it got nowhere.

Conductors are as chary and intolerant of each other as prima donnas with the same repertory. Toscanini, who has had little use for Tchaikovsky's music, listened to a recording of the "Pathétique" Symphony by Koussevitzky and became so indignant at what he called a maudlin, sentimentalized performance that he scheduled the symphony on one of his programs to show how he thought the music should be played.

Toscanini once paid a visit to Tanglewood in the Berkshires, where Koussevitzky was the dominant figure. Toscanini called on a friend of the staff at Tanglewood, to be shown the grounds. He did not ask to see Koussevitzky, nor did Koussevitzky ask to see Toscanini.

Conductors who have permanent posts at the head of big orchestras are sometimes wary as to who shall be invited to appear as guest leaders. There have been cases of guest conductors who did so well that they were never invited back. There have also been conductors who labored mightily, during the period of their guest tenure, to steal their host's job.

When they discuss each other publicly, conductors are diplomatic. The veil is dropped when they hold forth in their own circles. Yet most conductors acknowledge the leadership of Toscanini. Stokowski has paid high tribute to the older maestro. Typical of the attitude of the younger men is the reaction of Erich

Kleiber to the news, kept from him for weeks, that Toscanini was coming to Buenos Aires to guest conduct his orchestra. "All I ask," he said, "is a pair of tickets for every concert."

Toscanini's attitude toward other conductors has varied. He has been friendly and helpful to younger men, if he has liked them. A young conductor of the Metropolitan Opera raised a question about a point in an opera, and Toscanini invited him to his home, where, with the maestro at the piano, they went through the score. The meeting was repeated at intervals. Each time Toscanini would hold forth on another opera. For the younger man it was like taking a private master course.

Out of a similarly generous impulse Toscanini would turn up at rehearsals of the NBC Symphony Orchestra when guest conductors were in command. Probably he was trying to help. Actually he was a hazard to the conductor, for the poor fellow would become self-conscious and nervous.

Toscanini can be bitterly critical of other conductors. He has no admiration for Sir Thomas Beecham, damning his politics and demanding to know why he did not stay in England and be bombed like other Englishmen. "Sir Henry Wood remains at home," Toscanini said, "and he's my age. Of course," added the maestro as an afterthought, "he does not have my figure."

Toscanini once went to a rehearsal directed by a young conductor who shifted the seating of the players in the manner of Stokowski. After the rehearsal, the conductor asked his visitor for comment. "I don't hear the violins properly," said Toscanini. "The trouble with you young fellows is that you conduct by eye instead of by ear."

6

THE GLAMOUR BOYS AT WORK

Toscanini the Singer—From One Cellist to Another—The Secret of a Good Memory —Stokowski and a Lone Flower—On His Hobbyhorse—"Hokey Stokie"—The Koussevitzky Beat—A Volga Boatman—A Smile for Bruno Walter—Temper and Klemperer—Beecham at the Met—Barbirolli—Damrosch on American Music.

IT IS AXIOMATIC that a conductor is as good as his rehearsals, for the performance is the measure of what has been accomplished in the practice sessions. There are several brilliantly gifted technicians of the baton who can galvanize an orchestra into an electrical performance in a familiar work with little or no preparation. But they are rare, and the result is flashy. Nor do they get by for long on stunts.

Each conductor has his own rehearsal technique, but whether a man is mercurial or phlegmatic, violent or restrained, inspirational or didactic, witty or solemn, the essential requirement is that the conductor shall make the orchestra work. When a conductor lets his men off too lightly, he is likely to be rewarded by slovenly performances, although there are exceptions even to this rule.

Toscanini's rehearsals are fiercely concentrated and intense. "Every rehearsal is like a concert to me," he says, "and every concert like a debut." Wearing his shiny black-alpaca jacket, cut like a cadet's coat, with a stand-up collar, Toscanini comes out on the stage quickly, picks up his baton, and gets down to business. His comments are strictly on the music—in a mixture of Italian and English phrases. He pleads with his men to sing. He asks them "to put something into it." Once he asked a vocal soloist to "make a face like an angel." He sings along with the orchestra in a strangely cracked voice, low and hoarse. Sometimes he adds words

69

of exhortation to the singing of a phrase. Working with the trombones on an excerpt from *Götterdämmerung* he chanted their theme to the words, "Roar, like a lion!"

He sometimes forgets about this habit. Once, in Salzburg, during a tense dress rehearsal, his voice howled out above the instruments. He halted the orchestra in amazement. "For the love of God," he cried, "who is singing here?"

Musicians who do not give every ounce of energy infuriate him. He stands through the full two and a half hours of a rehearsal session. Even when he was past seventy-five, he drove himself mercilessly. His gestures are decisive and spacious; his whole body is enlisted. The instrumentalist who plays hard warms his heart. He once paid a fiddler the highest compliment. "He's wonderful, you should see him at rehearsals, he sweats more than I do."

Toscanini's outbursts of fury get results—sometimes. At other times they just petrify the players. He once bawled out a pianist so violently that the poor fellow turned white and could not do anything accurately during the rest of the session. Another time he flung a beautiful gift watch to the floor, smashing it to bits. He was then given a bulky Ingersoll by the players, with an inscription, "For rehearsals." He once attacked a rare, expensive score and with deliberate fury ripped out page after page, then trampled on the ruin.

When he took over the NBC Symphony Orchestra, the officials of the company prepared themselves for the inevitable rages. They assigned a functionary to sit in at rehearsals and telephone bulletins to top executives. Occasionally the bulletins went like this: "Clear, calm"; "Breeze coming up"; "Calm again." At other times they went: "Rough wind"; "Gale blowing"; "Tornado"; "SOS." The last meant that Toscanini had rushed off the podium and had barricaded himself in his dressing room. It took a veteran of many years' experience to deal with him at this juncture.

Lotte Lehmann, who has worked with Toscanini in opera and concert, thinks that occasionally he pounded away at a company until everyone got tense and could not do his best work. And yet, when she once made a horrible mistake in *Fidelio* and expected to have her head blown off, he was as sweet as if she had sung perfectly. She recalled that at Salzburg once he was in a dark mood throughout the long rehearsals and everyone in the cast was becoming a bit hysterical. Finally the singers held a meeting and somebody suggested to Lehmann, "You know him best. Why don't you tell him to let up or we'll all go to pieces?" Reluctantly, she went to his dressing room and told him what the cast thought. Toscanini was astonished. "I thought," he said, "you were all as interested in the opera as I am."

Don't think that Toscanini is rough on musicians all the time. He knows how to smile and praise, and he does not force his ideas on artists he respects. He was preparing a new cello concerto by Mario Castelnuovo-Tedesco, to be played by Gregor Piatigorsky as soloist. When Piatigorsky came to the first rehearsal, Toscanini showed him the score in which he had marked all the fingerings for the soloist. Piatigorsky was dismayed; he had worked them out for himself and his differed radically from Toscanini's. He suggested cautiously that he would like to use his own fingerings. "Use any fingerings you like, my boy," Toscanini said. "I worked these out to amuse myself. You see, I used to be a cellist myself."

When a performer violates in performance the preparations made in rehearsal, Toscanini's patience has a low boiling point. Years ago he fought against singers who held on to high notes as long as their breath lasted, since this was a liberty they did not dare take in rehearsal. Caruso did it once, and when he finally let go of the note with an explosion of sound, the maestro said in a stage whisper, *"E finito, Caruso?"* When Toscanini did *Otello* at the Metropolitan with Leo Slezak in the title role, the big tenor kept omitting the same measures, inexplicably, during rehearsal. Toscanini made a point of visiting Slezak in his dressing room before the performance to remind him of the phrase and to play it on the piano for him. When Slezak forgot it once more, Toscanini paused in the middle of the aria and yelled, *"Porco Slezak, porco Slezak!"*

When he prepared an opera, especially in later years, Toscanini bossed not only the musical end of the show but also the acting, staging, lighting, and scenery. Experts were assigned to these jobs, but Toscanini's ideas prevailed. During a rehearsal of *Meistersinger* in Salzburg, Toscanini, who was a good distance away from the stage, shouted at Charles Kullman, the tenor singing Walther, "Stand up straight, you're playing a nobleman!" Kullman straightened up, muttering, "I thought he was nearsighted."

An NBC Orchestra official once found out that Toscanini's eyesight was not so bad as it was cracked up to be. The official stood at the back of the hall, waving to some of the men in the orchestra to indicate that it was time for another radio engagement. The maestro turned suddenly on the official and ordered him out, shouting that he alone would dismiss the men.

At rehearsals Toscanini generally has the score before him, and refers to it from time to time, even if it is music that he has conducted frequently. He does not bother with the score at concerts because he is so nearsighted that he would have to bury his head in it. But, then, his memory is one of the wonders of music, though he has a simple explanation. "I will tell you my secret," he confided to a young conductor. "All my life I have been studying scores."

Study does not completely explain his memory. He once sat down and played Mendelssohn's forty *Songs Without Words* by heart, though he had not looked at the score for fifty years. One night, at a dinner party, a musician asked Toscanini about a point in Debussy. Whereupon the maestro, ignoring the other guests, went to the piano and played through *La Mer* and *Ibéria*, singing and discussing both works at the same time. A friend once recalled the remark of Richard Strauss about Ambroise Thomas' opera, *Mignon*, that there are good operas, bad operas, and *Mignon*. Indignant, Toscanini tackled the piano, discanting on the construction and quality of the opera, observing that no work that had survived so long could be indifferent. He played through most of it from memory, though he had not examined it for years. Then he singled out some of Strauss' worst tunes, played them from memory, and said, "How does he dare to talk?" As a footnote to this outburst, a month later he conducted a performance of a Strauss tone poem and gave it a memorable reading.

Leopold Stokowski's rehearsals, like the man himself, are dynamic. Even his costume is colorful. He usually wears a blue polo shirt with long sleeves, with socks to match, and flannel slacks in a nicely contrasting shade. He uses a special high stool, painted blue. He talks a good deal during rehearsals, mostly about music.

Stokowski knows how to train an orchestra perhaps better than any other man in the business. He took a group of young American boys and girls, bulwarked them with first-desk men of the Philadelphia Orchestra in key posts, and whipped them in a fortnight into a crack ensemble that compared favorably with our finest orchestras. Experts were astonished at the brilliance of tone, the cohesion and snap of the All-American Youth Orchestra. It was the best endorsement of Stokowski's sharp ear and keen mind.

He has a flair for dramatizing his thesis as well as himself. During a rehearsal of Schubert's "Unfinished" Symphony with the Philadelphia Orchestra, he thought that the fiddles were taking a simple, lovely melody for granted. He had each violinist play the tune alone, and for each he had a criticism. At first the men were self-conscious, nervous, and resentful; this was a tune they could play in their sleep. Then they realized that Stokowski had forced them to rediscover the melody.

He ordered his players to avoid the uniform bowings common in symphony orchestras, pointing out that it was natural for some fiddlers to take a longer stroke than others. If everyone bowed the same way, there would be holes in the sound. A musician of another orchestra observed, "You know, the guy's right, his string tone is juicier than any other conductor's."

Stokowski is brisk and aloof at some rehearsals, friendly and elastic at others. One day he stopped a player and asked why he took a phrase in a particular fashion. "That's the way I felt it," said the shrewd instrumentalist. Stokowski was delighted: "A very good reason, then that's how you must play it."

When a rehearsal went sluggishly, Stokowski told his men a parable of a lone flower on a mountainside that bloomed in all its fragrance and beauty with no one to notice it. To a passer-by who asked why, the flower replied, "Because I have so little time." Stokowski has reminded his players that music is not a vacuum. It means, he said, the rush of the northwest wind, the ripple of a forest stream, a field of tall, waving corn, a snow-covered peak, and the embrace of a man and a maid. He advised his men not to practice during vacations but to travel, read, visit museums, work on a farm, climb mountains.

Stokowski has even lectured his players about their posture on the stage. When he noticed that they slouched or sprawled during a rehearsal, he reminded them that they would play better if they sat erect and kept nerves and muscles alert. Some of the musicians did not heed his injunction, whereupon he had a hobbyhorse brought out at the next rehearsal, mounted it, and conducted from it to give the men an object lesson in posture.

He once worked out a signal system to facilitate rehearsals with the Philadelphia Orchestra. Knowing the value of hearing the orchestra from the rear of the auditorium, where a conductor can get perspective on the sound the audience hears, he would seat himself in the back of the house and ask his assistant conductor to take over. To communicate with the assistant, he pressed a set of buttons, and lights flashed on the podium. Red meant stop, and Stokowski would call out instructions; green meant proceed; yellow indicated caution.

The man's remarkable blend of artistic and administrative talent, which makes for the most successful showmanship in music, may be gauged from the manner in which he built the Philadelphia Orchestra from a mediocre ensemble into one of the world's best. He had a sixth sense for new talent; he hired young Americans when it was fashionable to go to Europe for orchestral players; he was one of the first conductors to welcome women players. He played the social game to obtain influential support for his orchestra. He cultivated people who might become regular attendants at the concerts. He worked with amateur choruses, inviting them to join in large choral performances. For one performance he assembled a thousand amateur singers and took them to New York for a repeat performance. He launched children's concerts and put them on with his usual showmanship. When he played *The Carnival of the Animals,* he had as guest artists livestock from the zoo, including an elephant. Once he had a gifted cellist impersonate Charlie Chaplin and do a slapstick act with a battered cello. He let the youngsters sing, and he talked to them. He also lectured his audiences in protest against apathy. To cure persistent latecomers, he once had half the orchestra drift onto the stage haphazardly after the concert had begun.

Stokowski has been a subject of controversy among musicians and public for years. Because he has kept himself in the news people have suspected his musical capacities. *Variety,* the theatrical trade journal, once headlined a story about him, unfairly, I think, "Hokey Stokie." He has been in tune with the times, using its techniques to further the cause of music. Naturally, he has also advanced his own career.

The men who have played under him know the value of his leadership. He has helped many of them to advance, recommending some for jobs as conductors. He has also made life miserable for others. When a stranger turned up at a rehearsal and became involved in a dispute with Stokowski, a member of the orchestra whispered to the stranger, "Give him hell!"

There have been the sour comments that Stokowski dispensed with the baton the better to show off his beautiful hands. I am willing to accept his explanation that he could direct just as, if not more, effectively without a baton. If a conductor wishes to direct with his coattails, that is his affair, as long as the orchestra plays well.

Stokowski has been described as the virtuoso interpreter *in excelsis.* He has said that a score is a sheet of white paper with black marks that are approximate indications of what the composer had

in mind, and that it is for the musician to bring the thought to life.
That perhaps best explains his approach to music. For Stokowski's
urge has been to create in music. Probably his deepest wish would
have been to compose memorably. Since he could not, he has sought
to be a part of the creative effort by arranging and transcribing and
by directing highly personal versions of other music.

Judging by the vagueness of his beat, you would guess that Koussevitzky sets up a performance entirely during rehearsals. His opening beat seems especially difficult to grasp, and Bostonians insist
that his men begin to play when his baton reaches the bottom button
of his vest. Some of the men have confessed that at the start they
have been at sea about the Koussevitzky downbeat, but after working with him for a while, they have developed an instinct for it. The
conductor and the men know each other so well that Koussevitzky
does not need to worry about fastidious baton technique. There are
moments when he does not bother to give any cues and when he
merely stands and mops his brow.

Since he was once a double-bass player, Koussevitzky likes to
work from the kind of tall stool that bull fiddlers employ. He begins
a rehearsal occasionally by going over fragments of a score, reserv-
ing the full playing through until he has explained his wishes about
the knotty pages. He does not go in for tantrums, but he can get
angry or scorchingly sarcastic. Nor are the players the only ones
who know the sting of his tongue. Some of the instrumentalists were
once being lectured by an official of the orchestra, when Koussevitzky appeared. The conductor pitched into the official: "Don't
you speak to the men like that! Remember, you work for them, not
they for you!"

The indispensable item of clothing for Koussevitzky during a
rehearsal, save during a heat wave, is an opera cape. He flings it
over his shoulders when he goes on and off the stage. If the stage is
drafty, he wears the cape while working. He uses English in talking to the men, and he speaks it correctly, though with a heavy
Russian accent.

Koussevitzky is a progressive musician. He believes in helping young conductors and composers, and has given young musicians their first chance to appear as soloists. He has fought for the recognition of American music, and he has preached the need of encouraging the great masses of the public to come to music. And he is confident that they will if they have the chance to hear the finest music at movie prices.

Koussevitzky experimented with this idea in 1909 in Moscow, when he formed his own orchestra, thanks to the beneficence of his wealthy father-in-law. Besides a fashionable season, Koussevitzky gave concerts for workers and students at thirty kopecks, or fifteen cents, a ticket. "The hall was packed, and the response was electrical," he recalls.

In 1910 he hired a Volga River side-wheeler and took his orchestra barnstorming the length of Russia, from Tver to Astrakhan. In Tsaritsyn, now Stalingrad, after a concert for workers at reduced rates, the conductor was placed in a sedan chair by an admiring throng and carried through the town to his side-wheeler. When he returned to the city two years later, the newly formed Koussevitzky Band was at the pier to serenade him.

Bruno Walter is gentle and persuasive in his handling of an orchestra. He works extensively on the emotional and interpretive aspects of a score, paying a major orchestra the compliment of assuming that it knows the mechanics. Rehearsing Strauss' *Don Juan,* he said to the New York Philharmonic-Symphony, "If I were a woman, I would not believe in your seductiveness." If an orchestra has not the graceful touch he seeks, he suggests, "Now you must smile."

There is grave danger in this approach, for instrumentalists, as a rule, are literal-minded, and they want instructions in precise musical terms. Bruno Walter is experienced enough to get away with the poetic touch. Lesser men run into trouble. One conductor used highfalutin talk through a rehearsal, and at one point said to a horn player, "Now you must sound as if we were alone on a high mountain." The weary horn player wailed, "Tell me one thing, maestro: what do you want, piano or forte?"

Otto Klemperer, a brilliant musician, tends to be nervous. He
lectures the men in a high-pitched voice, and occasionally he begins
to bawl them out and forgets, on the way, what the bawling out is
for. His absent-mindedness and explosions have fed on each other
amusingly. In 1935 he came over to be guest leader of the New York
Philharmonic-Symphony. The pianist of the orchestra was Ignace
Strasfogel, who had joined the orchestra in 1933 and had previously
worked under Klemperer in Berlin. During an audition for singers,
Strasfogel played the piano. At the end of the audition, Klemperer
asked the accompanist his name. "Strasfogel," said the pianist.
Klemperer exploded, "But where were you? I have been looking
for you all this time."

Outbursts at rehearsals are not confined to the men who are
famous for them. Gustav Mahler, who left a host of admiring dis-
ciples and who was described as one of the most sensitive conductors, could be as savage and bitter as any maestro. Richard Strauss,
when he was young and conducted a great deal, could be a harsh
taskmaster. Artur Bodanzky once plunged into Gatti-Casazza's
office, seething about a singularly unfortunate cast in *Tristan und
Isolde*. He cried out, "If you ever put those dogs in my cast again,
I'll quit!"

Sir Thomas Beecham, through a career of more than forty years,
has become a law unto himself. The basic reasons are understandable. A rich man by inheritance, he has been able to accomplish
what he wanted, fighting against stuffy tradition and speaking his
mind bluntly. Now in his sixties, he is a wonderfully crotchety and
outspoken citizen. When an audience applauded a soloist before
the orchestra finished, he shouted at them, "Respect for the music!"
There are two schools of thought about his rank as a conductor. One
regards him as the greatest of our time; the other looks upon him as
a greatly talented man who can perform wonders or be erratic and
indifferent.

His entrance upon the scene as a guest conductor at the Metropolitan Opera was something new even for that home of eccen-
tricity and temperament. Sir Thomas began by breaking all the

rules. He walked into his first rehearsal with a big fat cigar stuck in his mouth and kept puffing away under a SMOKING PROHIBITED sign.

His method of rehearsing was different, too. He didn't seem to be troubled by details. He did not bother to go over a new score completely with all the elements—orchestra, singers, chorus. He was content to leave the work to assistant conductors and did not bother to confer with them. With his own company in London, he said, he would spend three months rehearsing an opera, and since the Metropolitan gave him only a couple of rehearsals, what was the use?

At a rehearsal of *Phoebus and Pan,* he stopped the tenor, Frederick Jagel, and said, "What's the idea! Why don't you make that cut?" Jagel said, "What cut?" Sir Thomas thought for a moment, then answered, "I suppose I told only the orchestra to make the cut."

Another time he sat with folded arms, puffing at a cigar, and listened to the chorus sing through a long scene. He did not interrupt to criticize or comment. When the passage was over he said, "It reminds me of the Salvation Army."

He was asked whether he would like to attend a stage rehearsal for one of the operas he was to conduct. Normally the conductor insists on being present at rehearsals run by the stage director, and more often than not the conductor and the stage director have at each other. Sir Thomas was told the time and place of rehearsal and finally said, when asked whether he would like to come, "It might be amusing."

A veteran of the conducting wars, Beecham has stayed calm through most emergencies. He did get furious when a critic wrote that the orchestra was out of tune with the piano soloist at one of his concerts. He wrote the critic an indignant note, challenging him to listen to records of the concert and inviting him to bring musical seconds and he would do likewise. The thing that probably burned him up most in New York was that he was not invited recently to conduct the New York Philharmonic-Symphony. He made no bones about his indignation. He accepted an invitation to conduct

the New York City WPA Orchestra; then he agreed to conduct the
newly organized Brooklyn Symphony Orchestra. He was said to be
irritated with John Barbirolli. Probably Beecham felt that it was
insulting that the younger man had been offered the post of permanent conductor of New York's biggest orchestra.

As for Barbirolli, he is one of the most untemperamental conductors. A man of simple tastes and adult manners, he has not raved,
made scenes at rehearsals, bawled out the audience, or issued statements. He has tried to do his job as best he could. His chief difficulty
with the Philharmonic-Symphony may have been that the job was
too big for him, as it is for most conductors of flesh and blood. He
was overworked and overmatched. He felt, I know, that the critics
disliked him personally. I am sure that they did not, but when you
are battered and bruised periodically, you have every reason to
think that there is a cabal functioning against you.

Walter Damrosch never had such worries, or never acted as if he
had. At eighty-one he is still sailing through life serenely, accepting
honors and staying in the limelight consistently and without apparent effort. He is not remote or standoffish. Did the press want a
statement? The good doctor was glad to oblige. A reporter once
asked him whether he was in favor of state aid for music. He spoke
vigorously of the need for such action. But his wife interposed cautiously, "What will that do to our taxes, Walter?" The subject was
closed.

Damrosch is the perfect diplomat. I once interviewed him and
asked him about America's younger composers. He answered in
general terms, saying they were serious, promising, and so on.
"What do you really think of them?" I asked. "Well," he paused,
"I hate them."

Damrosch is not the only conductor who feels that way. Some
do not express their thoughts privately. Their actions are cavalier
enough to speak for them publicly. A well-known American composer called up a newspaper one day to ask whether his work was
on a certain orchestra's forthcoming program. It was. The conductor had not bothered to notify the composer.

Being a young man himself, a chap like Erich Leinsdorf shows more regard for the feelings of the young composer. He was preparing a half-hour broadcast of a Mozart symphony and two short pieces by Paul Creston, an American. A couple of minutes had to be cut from the program. "Let's not leave out the living composer's music," he said. "Let's cut out the Mozart minuet. Who knows, maybe it was written by Süssmayer."

7

THE GLAMOUR BOYS AT HOME

Tea for Two—Koussevitzky and Stokowski, Writers—The Gout—Growing Old—Two Toscaninis—Granddaughter Knows Best—Horowitz's Father-in-law—Pinball Game.

WHAT SORT OF MEN are the Caesars of the podium when the white light of publicity does not beat upon them? How do they look and act in the privacy of their homes, in the bosom of their families, and in the circle of their intimate friends where they can let their hair down?

One or two seem never able to relax. The part they play has been grafted on their personalities; they are always acting the role of the maestro. Most of them, however, have private lives apart from the glare of the public gaze. They spend pleasant evenings with their families; they get into carpet slippers, light up a pipe, and read a book; they go out on benders; they play bridge; they lose on the horses; they make love; they listen to the news broadcasts; they talk politics; they are amateur strategists. They are, in short, like you and me—with some differences.

Not many of us achieve the splendor of absent-mindedness that Otto Klemperer reached one day when he went into a barbershop. The barber asked briskly, "Haircut or shave?" Klemperer said, "Just change the oil."

But a good many of us hate to miss our weekly bridge games. Artur Bodanzky loved to play cards. In New York he would frequently get together with Lauritz Melchior, the tenor, and Friedrich Schorr, the baritone, for a session; a fourth was easy to obtain in town. But when Bodanzky went to his summer home in Vermont he had difficulty in finding companions for his card games. If he could not get a fourth locally, he would import one from New York.

Our servants sometimes deflate us, and that happened to Stokowski one afternoon when he was entertaining a visitor from New York in his Philadelphia apartment. Stokowski suggested a cup of tea. He struck a Balinese drum which he had brought back from a trip to the south Pacific and which now served as a signal for his maid. The Negro girl entered, and Stokowski said impressively, "Some tea. Let's see, for today's mixture, let's have . . ." He named a string of exotic teas. The girl blinked, "Done made the tea, Mr. Stokowski, out of the one can we got!"

You would think that Stokowski would be the last man in the world to be ingenuous. Yet one day he approached a friend for advice. He was planning a trip to Europe with Greta Garbo, and he wanted to know how they could sail from New York and make the trip incognito. The friend said, "Try blackface."

When his second wife, the former Evangeline Johnson, sued him for divorce on the grounds of cruelty, Stokowski took occasion to answer the specific charge. "I could not," he said, "be cruel to the mother of my children."

Stokowski's home has been remarkably simple for a man of his position and income. When he appeared in *100 Men and a Girl* in the role of Stokowski, the studio rigged up an opulent set for his home. He protested that he did not live like that, but the studio people insisted it was necessary for photographic effect. Later the director of the movie visited Stokowski at his apartment in Philadelphia and discovered that the place was really simple. "A man like you," said the director, "ought to live better than this."

Koussevitzky lives elegantly but not ostentatiously. His summer home in the Berkshires, high on a hill overlooking the festival grounds as well as the hills and lakes, is a meticulously kept estate, and here there is always good food, wine, and talk. Koussevitzky has not traveled extensively in late years, and he likes to entertain; his friends are always welcome. Music is his vocation and avocation, but one of the things that he, like Stokowski, enjoys doing is writing.

He once showed me—with the hesitancy and pride of the amateur writer the world over—an essay he had composed on Debussy. He said he had done several others. Later they were published in *The Atlantic Monthly*. They were philosophical in cast, keenly considered, and well written.

People who know him say that Sir Thomas Beecham is one of the most erratic of the lot, privately as well as publicly. Being an English baronet, he, almost inevitably, is subject to gout. His tastes in food and drink are the gourmet's; unhappily, those tastes rise to plague him. He once waddled up to the podium with a swollen foot swathed in bandages and conducted a concert seated on a stool. During this period of physical tribulation, Sir Thomas had to go on tour with the orchestra, and he used to sit in a drawing room on a Pullman with his bandaged leg propped on the knee of his secretary, looking, with his goatee and ample figure, like a Hogarth character in a twentieth-century setting.

Sir Thomas' sense of humor, like that of other Englishmen, disported itself, at least before the war, at the expense of Americans. When he came here years ago to be guest conductor of a New York orchestra, an official of the ensemble met him at the pier and drove him uptown to a hotel. Looking out on Fifth Avenue, he observed, "I don't see any machine guns in the streets." The official was sweet about it. "No," he said, "we save them for the nice, quiet, respectable hotel you are going to stop at."

Women have made and marred the careers and private lives of many conductors, as they have of other men. And conductors have used the ancient stratagems to be near their friends. A visiting celebrity was taken by his New York manager to the Savoy-Plaza. The celebrated conductor inquired, casually, whether there was not a Plaza Hotel in New York. Apparently he had promised to look after a cousin—female—staying at the Plaza. The manager moved him over to the Plaza and made sure that his room adjoined that of the comely cousin.

Ettore Panizza relinquished his job as leading conductor at the Metropolitan Opera because his wife did not like traveling by air.

They went down to Buenos Aires, where he conducted opera at the
Teatro Colón in the summer of 1942. When the time came to return,
he decided that the voyage through the submarine-infested sea
would be too perilous. His wife decreed that the trip by airplane
would be just as bad, and the conductor sorrowfully notified the
Metropolitan Opera that it had better hire someone else.

Growing old worries conductors as much as other men. When
Toscanini reached seventy-five, his friends and colleagues thought
of observing the birthday with parties, but the maestro said, "When
you get to be seventy-five, it's a tragedy." When Stokowski reached
his late fifties, something happened to his birthday in the record
books. The old encyclopedias showed his birthday as 1882, but the
new Stokowski-approved publicity insisted it was 1887.

I liked the way Walter Damrosch achieved eighty. Here was no
display of false modesty. If the world wished to honor him, he was
available; if interviews were required, he was helpful. Many of
the details of the nation-wide observance of his birthday were
handled by his secretary, whose office was in the Damrosch home.
One of the surprise gifts Damrosch received was a beautifully made
book of tributes from fellow members of the National Institute of
Arts and Letters. About one hundred and fifty of America's most
famous writers, artists, and musicians each contributed a page of
poems, essays, drawings, or music. The volume was presented to
Damrosch at a dinner held by the Institute in his honor. It was just
a happy coincidence that the assistant secretary-treasurer of the
Institute, who arranged for these tributes and supervised the collecting, was Damrosch's private secretary.

Arturo Toscanini seems to have discovered the source of the fountain of youth. Save in rare moments of despair or fatigue, he does
not think of himself as a septuagenarian. He attended a party one
night with swarms of people milling around. At midnight a close
friend prepared to leave. Toscanini demanded, "Where are you
going?" The other said, "Home." Toscanini protested. "Wait a little
while," he said. "Soon the old people will go and we'll have fun."

The maestro once said, in explaining his wild outbursts, that there were two Toscaninis: the musician and the man off the concert platform. The first Toscanini may occasionally be uncontrollable, but the second is anything but forbidding. It was the second Toscanini who, on taking over a new orchestral assignment at the height of his powers, paused in the corridor before stepping out for the first rehearsal, placed his palms together and prayed, silently and humbly, for the success of the venture.

It is this Toscanini who loves a gay party or an evening of quiet conversation. His home is a vivacious place. For years he stayed in New York in a rambling suite at the Hotel Astor. In Italy he owned an island on Lago Maggiore, and the big house was always filled with friends and relatives. In recent years he has occupied a house in New York City's Riverdale section, where he has a commanding view of the majestic sweep of the Hudson River and the Palisades. His wife, Carla, and his granddaughter, Sonya, are almost always with him, and frequently so are his son-in-law and daughter, the Vladimir Horowitzes; his son, Walter, with his wife and their son, Walfredo.

Though her husband has earned tremendous sums, Carla has fretted about the terrific cost of maintaining the establishment. The Horowitzes have a house in Fieldston, a short distance away, and Mrs. Toscanini has complained about the cost of heating both homes. She found that food was more expensive in her neighborhood, and when the family car was on the way to town anyhow, she would go along to do some shopping in the Italian market, where she could get bargains. The maestro once invited a protégé, a South American conductor, to stay at his house during a long visit in New York. Mrs. Toscanini allowed the young conductor, who had a good job here, to be a paying guest.

Toscanini loves the throb of family life. He has worked, read his scores, and rehearsed in a vortex of noise. Occasionally he has risen in his wrath and protested. He has been heeded for several minutes and then the hubbub has built up again. A friend once visited him at his villa in Lucerne. On the lawn before the house a flock of children were playing ball shrilly. Inside, relatives and friends rattled around and chattered volubly. The visitor figured that the maestro must be in town somewhere, but Toscanini was in his study, rehearsing with a soloist. The door to his room was closed, but it was not a soundproof vault. He was so absorbed he did not seem to be aware of the tumult.

When he took over the NBC Symphony Orchestra, he was provided with a lavish suite—office, reception room, and dressing room —carefully located to shield him from the turmoil of Radio City. He used the place only to change his costume. He preferred to wander around the building and visit in the offices of other NBC officials. Nothing pleased him better than buzzing quarters. The more telephone calls, messengers, visitors, and noise, the better he liked it.

Toscanini is fond of practical jokes. A friend once showed him a set of collapsible knives. He borrowed one, planted it at his wife's place, and watched delightedly as the blade bent when she tried to cut the meat.

One day he was invited to a friend's house for a dinner party. A young woman, of the host's family, a Toscanini favorite, rigged herself out as a slatternly maid; bunched her hair in repellent fashion, blackened her teeth, and lined her face. When Toscanini was told that the young lady was out of town, he was disappointed. During the meal, the pseudo-maid gave him the works. She nudged him, swung her hips sensuously, stuck the meat under his nose, and brushed his chin with the ice cream. With the last course served, the girl plopped into the maestro's lap, and he sputtered as if he were about to explode. The girl disclosed her identity, and his mood changed from fury to hilarity. He roared with laughter, and months later he related the story with enormous gusto, giving a detailed and flavorsome account of the young minx's behavior.

Toscanini went to a New Year's Eve party and, with the joy of a small boy, tried on tin hats and false noses and went about blowing a tin horn. He piled up a stack of favors and took them home for Sonya. In the morning, when she joined him at breakfast, he was wearing a pair of Falstaffian cheeks.

Toscanini could also let his hair down and have fun with music.

A group of artists arranged a benefit show for the Chatham Square
Music School. Tickets were sold to a select group at fancy prices,
and illustrious names took part in foolish and delightful shenani-
gans. Vladimir Horowitz, in huge sweater, check trousers, and
gloves, played children's pieces at the piano. Heifetz wore a ditch-
digger's overalls, and a corncob pipe hung from a mouth that had
been made up to look gap-toothed; he played a battered fiddle like
a hillbilly. Lawrence Tibbett, in overcoat and muffler, coughed and
wheezed through *Drink to Me Only with Thine Eyes* with peculiar
modulations. The *pièce de résistance* was the appearance of Toscanini, who had agreed to conduct Mozart's *Musical Jest* with a small
orchestra made up of players like Heifetz, Adolf Busch, Nathan
Milstein, Mischa Mischakoff, William Primrose, Emanuel Feuermann, Alfred Wallenstein, and others of similar standing, all
dressed up in knee pants, middies, and short socks. The maestro
had made one proviso—that he be permitted to provide his own
costume. He turned up in a long frock coat, pants tight at the knees,
and flowing string tie, looking like all the seedy maestros of Italy's
provincial theaters of his youth. He walked with a mincing step. He
held his hands cupped to his ear. He grimaced. His gestures were
hammy, and he took his bows with beaming and pompous unction.
He lamented one forgotten detail. He had planned to bring a huge
red handkerchief and let it dangle from a hip pocket below the flaps
of the frock coat.

He went out to Hollywood for a holiday, and when he returned
to New York, he talked excitedly about a wonderful dancer. His
friends thought he was referring to a queen of the classic ballet, but
he meant Eleanor Powell. Someone asked him what she looked like,
and Toscanini replied, "I don't remember. All I know is that she
danced wonderfully and then she kissed me and I kissed her."

Toscanini likes our movies, especially Mickey Mouse and the
other Disney products. He was enchanted with *Snow White and
the Seven Dwarfs*. Sonya and he shared an admiration for the music
from *Snow White*. One day the two were discovered in his study,
Toscanini playing "Heigh-ho, heigh-ho, it's off to work we go,"

while little Sonya stood on a chair beside him, beating time with a baton as long as she was tall. Later he assured his friends, "Her beat was correct."

Sonya occasionally has played four hands with her father and even oftener with her grandfather. At one period the piece for her and Toscanini was Schubert's *Marche militaire*. After a session, she once told him that he was "not so hot as a pianist." Another time she said, "I don't know why you can't keep up with me." Sonya is a gifted little pianist, and Grandpa has boasted about her prowess. But she has no illusions about the piano as a career. Her grandfather once asked her which she would rather be, a conductor or pianist, and she replied, "A conductor—it's easier."

Toscanini was also proud of his grandson, Walfredo, who, at the age of nine, was a redoubtable bridge player. The lad would play with adults and hold his own. Toscanini would sit beside him, another kibitzer. One day the boy lost a trick unnecessarily. He flung down his cards, smote himself on the breast with clenched fist, and shouted, *"Io stupido!"*—the very *mea culpa* phrase and gesture of Toscanini annoyed with himself.

Toscanini likes to relax by toying with the radio dials and listening to the flow of programs. He has taken in stride opera, symphonies, jazz, balladry, news, and commentators. Whether he likes or detests what he hears, he keeps on listening to and talking back at the machine. He bawls out a bad performer, reviles a conductor, and sputters at a tenor. Once he tuned in on the middle of a symphony. "Not bad," he observed to the people in the room. "That fellow has a feeling for tempo, and the phrasing is good." When it ended, the announcer said, "You have been listening to a recording of Beethoven's Sixth Symphony, conducted by Arturo Toscanini." The maestro snapped off the radio ferociously and stormed out of the room, chagrined not to have recognized his own reading.

Toscanini has avoided interviews and publicity. Yet when his daughter Wanda and Vladimir Horowitz were engaged secretly, Toscanini was responsible for letting the news out to the American press. He wrote a letter to American friends, and they did the rest.

It was Toscanini too who, after Horowitz wrote an old-style formal note asking for his daughter's hand, suggested a quick marriage.

Toscanini and his famous son-in-law get on amicably privately as well as when they make music. True, they are a little wary of each other. Horowitz is sensitive about being patronized as the maestro's son-in-law. He is also cautious about displaying signs of temperament in the maestro's presence.

When Toscanini paid a visit at the offices of the New York Philharmonic-Symphony after an absence of five years, he made a tour of every room, shaking hands with each occupant, familiar or not. He passed through the room which has a counter for the transaction of business with subscribers and shook hands with a couple of bewildered customers. Finally he said good-by and started down the hall, followed by a delegation of well-wishers. He entered the elevator, shook hands with the operator, and the latter closed the door and said, "We'll make it an express this trip."

Another elevator boy, at Radio City, is one of his pals. One day Toscanini suddenly deserted a party of bigwigs, to comfort this lad who, he knew, was having trouble with his eyes.

During an ocean trip, Toscanini listened to a ship's concert, played by the usual makeshift band, with more attention than most of his fellow passengers. The players struck up a rarely performed Johann Strauss waltz. Toscanini had heard it as a youngster and retained a fondness for it. He went up to the leader of the ship's band and, with the respect due another conductor, said, "Tell me, maestro, where did you get that waltz? It was delightful."

He once went to a café, and the wine that he ordered was not to his taste. The waiter, who recognized him, served him with the panache of a man who reveres his customer. Toscanini sipped the wine and, with the waiter out of earshot, pronounced it vile. His friend suggested that he order another wine, but Toscanini declined; he didn't want to hurt the waiter's feelings.

Toscanini's simplicity has sometimes been almost naïveté. He was taken once to New York City's widely ballyhooed night club, the International Casino. The place was jammed. Toscanini's table was on the edge of the dance floor. He sat there enraptured, watching the entertainers through opera glasses and drinking in the excitement like good wine. "Marvelous, marvelous," the maestro said to his host, and then in a confidential whisper, "How did you find this place?"

When the NBC Symphony Orchestra traveled to South America, the road manager was Lawrence Fitzgerald, who had once served Paderewski in the same capacity. On board the ship, Fitzgerald became attached to a pinball game that cost fifty cents a round, and his friends among the musicians could not drag him away. Finally they appealed to Toscanini to do something with Fitzgerald. The maestro went off to try. A little later Fitzgerald's friends discovered that Toscanini, with a batch of half dollars in his hand, was feeding the machine, as Fitzgerald looked on.

8

REFLECTIONS ON VIRTUOSOS

From Mansion to Water Tank—"All" Heifetz Can Do—Horowitz's Inferiority Com-plex—Practice Doesn't Necessarily Make Perfect—"Perfidious Passages"—Two on Elman—Horowitz and Conductors—Paderewski in Self-Communion.

CONDUCTORS MAY have challenged and outstripped the virtuoso's dominance, but his day is not over. He still bestrides the world of music out of all proportion to his importance in a soundly geared musical economy. He is still dear to the hearts of the public, his manager, and himself. And what he does with a piece of music is still, unhappily, more interesting to many customers than the music itself.

Recognizing that the virtuoso exists and flourishes, one must add that changes are taking place. Possibly the last of the grand line disappeared when Paderewski died. For none of his successors and survivors have chosen to live in the grand manner which was so natural to him. You do not hear today of pianists who are followed by a procession of admirers from the concert hall to their hotel, as was Paderewski in Manchester, England, not long ago. You do not read of virtuosos who attract a throng of adoring men and women to a railroad station in a Texas town, as did Paderewski. That sort of acclaim is reserved for the moving-picture stars, and for them too the bliss of having people descend on them, tearing bits of their clothing as souvenirs, as worshipers of Paderewski once snipped off the tails of his dress suit.

The modern crop of virtuosos lives differently. The most dazzling violinists and pianists still pack them in, but they try—most of them honestly—to keep their private lives private. However, they still value themselves inordinately. Recently two famous virtuosos made a joint appearance for a war-relief society, earning a huge sum, but when they were asked to permit radioing of the program, they said that they would agree only if a speaker like President Roosevelt or Prime Minister Churchill joined in the broadcast.

Families have a way of deflating the great men. Horowitz gave a slashing performance of Tchaikovsky's Piano Concerto one day, and at the end his keen-eared seven-year-old daughter, Sonya, told him she heard some wrong notes in the crashing chords of the finale. Joseph Szigeti sold an article to a publication for thirty-five dollars and proudly sent the check to his wife. Later, when he asked her why she had not acknowledged his triumph, she said that she had not noticed the origin of the check but had simply turned it over to her seamstress.

If they are in the chips, virtuosos still know how to live stylishly, but their fine homes are usually in the country. Gone is the day when a Josef Lhevinne, at the height of his success in Berlin, bought a mansion that had been occupied by the Chinese ambassador. He made his purchase in the spring of 1914; the ambassador knew, and Lhevinne did not, that war was imminent. Through the First World War, he and his family, being Russian subjects, were kept in Berlin, and they rattled around in the forty-room mansion, consuming their savings but living in grand style. In recent years Lhevinne's notion of a way of life was to buy an old water tank in Portage, Wisconsin, where he would go off alone in the summer to rest, practice, and follow his hobby as an amateur astronomer. The old tank was divided into three stories of one room each. The first served as a living room, bedroom, and repository of fishing gear; the second was a studio, housing piano and music; the third, which had the telescope in a place of honor, functioned as an observatory.

It is no longer seemly for virtuosos to strut and preen themselves in public; if they must make a show of themselves, they have learned that the best way is through the music. The general public does not always recognize self-display, and the composer is usually beyond protesting. But even this form of exhibitionism is on the wane. Honest workmen are appreciated increasingly. People are

learning the difference between personal display and sincere, dignified musicianship. It is more fashionable to practice the latter, if
possible.

You will find, in fact, an inclination on the part of virtuosos to
shun an excess of public adoration. Jascha Heifetz took his fiddle
to Camp Roberts, in California, in the spring of 1942 to entertain
the boys. Having no illusions about the universality of art, he naturally had some reservations when he saw the hall packed with
soldiers. Perhaps an officer had passed the word down the line that
the visiting artist must have the courtesy of a full house. Heifetz
spoke briefly before starting to play.

"This is all I can do," he said, holding up the violin modestly. "If
you like it, fine. If you don't, that's all right, too. You won't hurt my
feelings if you walk out on me."

The crowd cheered. Heifetz began to play, and presently four or
five soldiers took him at his word. They got up and strolled out. The
empty seats were quickly filled, and those who remained to hear for
themselves gave Heifetz a rousing vote of confidence.

Fritz Kreisler refused to let his friends make a celebration of the
fiftieth anniversary of his first appearance in America. He did not
want the inevitable profusion of guff; nor did he want himself
treated as a museum piece. Let the public judge him on his merits on
the day of his performance, not on his accomplishments of years
gone by. When the thirtieth anniversary of Rachmaninoff's first
appearance in America came along, he too stood out against dinners,
speechmaking, and ceremonial. The Philadelphia Orchestra offered
to produce a special cycle of concerts of his music; that and nothing
else was acceptable.

Look at the way Rachmaninoff entered on the stage and seated
himself for a recital. The poise and dignity of the man were as
palpable as the fact that his hair was cut severely in the Russian
style. Look at the calm, benevolent demeanor of Kreisler; the cool,
businesslike appearance of Heifetz. Go down the roll call of virtuosos. There is restraint in the bearing of each. If anything, one or

two are so shy and deferential in their manner that you would think
they were neophytes.

Horowitz, in fact, gets the jitters before every appearance, even
after a career of twenty years in public. His manager observes a
special procedure for him, calling for him in his dressing room three
minutes before concert time and escorting him slowly to the stage
entrance. On the way, the pianist fidgets and wrings his hands and
his pallor seems to deepen. Once when he was to be soloist with the
New York Philharmonic-Symphony Orchestra, he announced that
he simply could not play. The manager, who had been to the wars
with him, said, "All right, Volodya, if you can't, you can't. But you
must do one thing. Go out on the stage and tell the audience that you
do not feel like playing and ask to be forgiven." Horowitz nodded
his head and said, "That's fair enough, I'll do it." He charged out on
the stage, sat down at the piano, and plunged into the concerto.

Horowitz admits frankly that the sight of an audience does things
to him. He confesses, "I have an inferiority complex." To put it
more accurately, he has a deep sense of responsibility to the thousands who pay to hear him play. He fears that he will not give them
value. It happens, of course, that he is the pianist above all others
whom the public throngs to hear these days, but that does not make
him any easier in his mind.

"I don't mind playing for a lot of people," Horowitz once explained. "If I had several hundred in my home, or your home, I
could sit and play for them all night. It is the concert hall that
terrifies me."

Nor can it be the fear that one's command of the music or the
instrument will be deficient. Musicians who achieve the standing of
Horowitz have poured a lifetime of study into their work. Horowitz laughs when the uninitiated ask him how many hours a day he
practices. "I don't practice at all," he says. "I study scores from
time to time." But his friends tell of a pleasant ruse he affects. In
conversation he swings the talk to music. A point needs illustration.
He walks to the piano. There he will sit for minutes—and hours, if

you let him—illustrating. As another musician summed it up, "That's the smartest way of getting in your practice."

On the other hand, Rachmaninoff would not practice while other people were in the room, even close friends or family. His practice sessions were strictly private, like a woman making her toilette. A photographer, making some pictures of him, suggested that he sit at the piano. Rachmaninoff agreed. Please play a few chords, the photographer said. The pianist put his hands on the keyboard, but he would not strike a note.

Rachmaninoff tried to practice a couple of hours each day. He once said that he had to be faithful to make up for the sins of his boyhood. Then he would go fishing, swimming, or ice skating when he should have practiced, and later he had to pay dearly for the youthful neglect. His experience is the clue to the needs of other virtuosos for practice. If they were kept sedulously at their work as youngsters, their technique became so sure that they could afford to spend less time when they were mature. Heifetz appeared to need less practice than most violinists. Paderewski, on the other hand, who used to tell that his first lessons had been maladroit, slaved at the piano, practicing eight, ten, and twelve hours a day before a tour and several hours each day even when on tour.

Joseph Szigeti devised a system out of the strains of his own life. When he was twenty-one and reaching the peak of his fame as a virtuoso in Europe, he became dangerously ill. For months he was flat on his back in a Swiss sanitarium. Somehow he prevailed on his doctor to let him practice for twenty minutes each day after lunch. To get the most out of these sessions, he would think about the problems of a composition and during the blessed twenty-minute session, he would work with relentless concentration on the difficulties that seemed most acute. Out of this grew his habit of concentrating on "perfidious passages," the intricate, virtuoso pages that require flawless co-ordination of fingers, arms, wrists, head, and heart. He plays these passages out of their context, without piano or orchestra, and they sound like the wailing of a battalion of cats. One morning, while practicing in a New York hotel room, there was a knock on the door and a young woman, trembling with anger, confronted him. She demanded that he stop the confounded noise or she would smash the fiddle over his head. The violinist thought of the price of his Strad, tried to placate the angry girl, closed the door, and sadly put the fiddle in its case. Now when he rents a room, he warns the hotel he is a noisy neighbor and they put him next to businessmen who have to be up and out early. He does not blame people who object to "perfidious passages." Once when he was practicing such excerpts from the Alban Berg concerto, his wife turned on him in irritation. Resignedly he repaired to the bathroom, where he worked for the next hour.

The hazards of practicing take strange forms. Iturbi once stayed at a small New York hotel, and when he sat down at the piano for a workout, his neighbor in the next room seemed always to be busy at his piano. The neighbor turned out to be Arpad Sandor, a pianist of parts himself and a well-known accompanist. The practicing of the two did not jell, and they had to have their rooms changed.

The layman does not always mind the practice sessions of a famous musician. In the days when the Menuhin family made the Ansonia Hotel its New York headquarters, Yehudi would practice in one room, and his younger sisters would play the piano in other rooms of the suite. A neighbor who lived above them used to lie on the floor to listen to the gifted youngsters. Paderewski practiced in his private car during his tours through the United States as the car rested at a siding, and workers would assemble to eavesdrop on his music-making.

Solving an elusive problem in music is one of its joys for the virtuoso. Pablo Casals, the greatest cellist of our time, would devote a year or more to a new composition before exposing it to an audience. One summer in Paris he spent days driving himself relentlessly to find the choice way of playing a simple melody that another cellist might toss off at a glance. He worked himself into such a nervous state that his friend, disciple, and fellow cellist, Maurice Eisenberg, persuaded him to forget the cello and come to the Stade Roland Garros to watch a tennis match. Usually Casals applauded, shouted

"Bravo!" and hopped out of his seat with delight at a well-placed passing shot. On this occasion, however, through the first two sets of a tingling game, he did not seem to notice what was happening. Suddenly he slapped his knee and shouted, "I have it!"

Eisenberg was puzzled. "Have what?"

"The passage worked out! Look!" He grabbed his friend's arm, ran his left hand over it as if it were the fingerboard of a cello, and sang the tune loudly, blissfully ignoring his gaping neighbors.

After years of seasoning in the public glare, some virtuosos slough off the timidity and self-consciousness that condition the actions of more constrained mortals. They don't mind being different, if the divergence suits their purpose and convenience. Szigeti, who was unaccustomed to playing chamber music in public, agreed to do a program with Gregor Piatigorsky, the cellist. The final work of the concert was a composition that moved, from beginning to end, at a vertiginous pace. The violinist had no time to memorize this composition, and he worried that he would have trouble turning the pages of the printed music. He adopted an ingenious though unconventional plan. He purchased a number of copies of the score, had a long line of music stands set out on the stage, and placed a page on every music stand. He played, reading from left to right, not only with skillful musicianship, but sashaying with brilliant footwork.

One of the conventional notions about virtuosos is that they are impractical—geniuses in music but without sense or prudence in business affairs. The truth is that they are as alert to their interests as the average merchant or banker. They keep in close touch with prevailing fees. They know about box-office returns. Paderewski made bets with his road manager on the size of the take from a glance at the audience. Though he was shrewd, he could be generous. When some unforeseen factor like bad weather injured the attendance, he would order that part of the guarantee be turned back to the local manager so that he would not sustain a loss. There have been other artists who agreed, at the last moment, to a smaller fee from a local manager when the latter showed that the sale had been below expectations and that he simply could not pay what he had promised. On the other hand, some have canceled a concert rather than take a cent less than a contract called for.

No manager puts anything over on some of these virtuosos. When Horowitz discusses a season's terms with his manager, he demands that every point be put into writing, and he drives a hard bargain. Heifetz has precise ideas about his affairs. He likes to decide about the extent and design of his advertising; he determines how many press tickets shall be sent out; he peruses box-office statements. One world-famous virtuoso made an incredible fuss over the expenditure of twenty dollars for throwaways announcing a New York concert; he thought the price too steep. If the virtuoso is himself indifferent, he usually has a wife, father, mother, or other relative who wants to handle business affairs.

Why shouldn't virtuosos be alive to practical matters? They earn large sums. Frequently they are investors. A good many of them lost fortunes in the stock-market crash of 1929. Fritz Kreisler has been an inveterate Wall Street follower. His wife once said, "It's a remarkable thing about Fritz, whenever he opens a newspaper, he always seems to happen on the financial pages." Paderewski once met an oil man at a party and talked about wells, borings, distribution, and income as if he had been in the business himself. Well, he had; oil investments had stung him for plenty.

The virtuoso usually has shrewd ideas as to the drawing power of various towns, and he insists on having a voice in the making of his itinerary. The more famous he is, the greater is his power to influence decisions. He knows generally which town likes him best, and he wants to be booked there often. He knows about hotels, food, and traveling conditions. Alexander Brailowsky became an expert on railroad timetables; he collected them as others collect stamps, and he could work out a better itinerary than anyone in his manager's office.

It isn't only their own affairs that concern the virtuosos. They keep themselves informed on their rivals, and that either pays off or makes them profoundly unhappy. Mischa Elman, who has had as many anecdotes pinned on him as any musician in recent years, has always been alive to business trends. He once encountered the late Mischa Levitzki, the pianist, when they were both stopping in Philadelphia. It was Elman's birthday and he invited Levitzki to celebrate it with him. They went to dinner, and then to *The Ziegfeld Follies,* which happened to be in town. The only seats available were in a box near the stage. In one of the extravagant scenes, when a group of gorgeous Ziegfeld girls were making generous display of their charms, Mischa Elman tapped Mischa Levitzki on the shoulder and said, "Tell me, Mischa, what has happened to John McCormack's drawing power?"

Your true virtuoso begins to act more like the figure of tradition when he deals with other virtuosos. As a rule, he does not run down his colleagues; in fact, he speaks so flatteringly of them that it is obvious he means his comments to be discounted heavily. If he criticizes a rival, he does so with exquisite tact. He will place his judgment on the highest plane of art. He will talk about the intentions of Beethoven or Schumann or Chopin. Whatever he says, it is for private consumption.

Which brings to mind the legend of the debut of Heifetz in America. Sitting with Leopold Godowsky, the witty and brilliant old pianist, was Mischa Elman. As the program pursued its course, Elman mopped his brow and muttered, "It's very warm tonight." Godowsky replied, "Not for pianists."

If you want the measure of the close watch they keep on each other, observe what happened in the basement showroom of Steinway Hall where the eminent virtuosos come to try out and select their pianos for their recitals. The man who presides over this department decided that the bare walls needed decoration. He clipped a photograph of Hofmann from a magazine and hung it on the wall. Then he mounted and displayed pictures of Horowitz and Rubinstein. One day Brailowsky looked in, and a little later he went upstairs to the head of the Steinway concert department to inquire why his picture was not on the wall downstairs. A photograph was duly hung. A little later Alexander Borovsky turned up and made the same complaint, and he too had to be pacified.

Recently a new pianist, Witold Malcuzynski, was scheduled to make his first American appearance. According to grapevine, he was a thundering virtuoso. Every pianist of consequence was in Carnegie Hall that night, or had an emissary there. It turned out that the pianist did not live up to the puffs, and at intermission time, you could observe the smiling, pleased faces of several eminent virtuosos.

The virtuosos are not all jealous of their rivals. Occasionally you meet one who can be generous. Perhaps he has achieved a position which puts him beyond fear or envy. Thus it was Kreisler who, in an effort to give a younger colleague a lift, told Americans twenty years ago that the most talented violinist in Europe was Joseph Szigeti. It was Kreisler too who said of Casals, "He is the greatest musician to draw a bow." When Kreisler was recovering from an accident recently, he made a practice of going to New York's concert halls, listening to artists. One had the feeling that he was delighted to be catching up with what younger musicians were doing, after years of preoccupation with his own work.

When virtuoso brushes with conductor, explosions may take place. Where the conductor is a man as respected as Toscanini, there is no difficulty, although you may have noticed that the maestro does not engage many soloists, and when he does, they are generally young people. There is seldom any difficulty with men like Stokowski, Koussevitzky, and Walter. If the soloist is pre-eminent and the conductor is younger, the position is reversed, and the conductor is happy to pay homage to the virtuoso. When Rachmaninoff was soloist with the Philharmonic-Symphony under Mitropoulos, the conductor gave up his dressing room to the pianist. When Schnabel appeared as soloist with a young conductor, he determined the outlines of the entire interpretation, establishing his ideas of tempo and other musical factors.

It is when the virtuoso and conductor have an equal stake that the waters are muddied. Vladimir Horowitz made his first appearance in this country as soloist with the New York Philharmonic, with Sir Thomas Beecham, making his American debut at the same time, as the conductor. It was apparently each man for himself. The rehearsals did not go well, and the performance was worse. As Horowitz tells it, he felt from the opening bars of the Tchaikovsky concerto that it would be a disaster and that the only hope of redeeming it would be to strike out on his own. He played like the mythical wild Russian, with the abandon and passion of youth; he confesses he played louder, faster, and more notes than Tchaikovsky intended. The performance became more disorganized as it progressed, and Horowitz arrived at the end long before the orchestra. Years later the recollection of the bad taste of it made him shudder. But it worked. He scored a tremendous success.

Horowitz was rewarded with an abundance of curtain calls, but Beecham, who was overshadowed, evened matters the next day at the repeat performance. At the end of the concerto, conductor and pianist joined in two curtain calls. When they emerged for a third, Beecham made a little speech to the audience and Horowitz stood by awkwardly, like a stage hand caught in front of the footlights after the curtain had gone up. Horowitz has no use for conductors who talk to the audience.

Years later Beecham invited Horowitz to be soloist with his orchestra in London. "This time," says Horowitz, "he conducted with a score and we gave a fine performance." And Beecham might add, "This time he played like a musician, not a frantic virtuoso, and we gave a fine performance."

Horowitz was once engaged to be the soloist in the Brahms Second Concerto under Wilhelm Furtwängler in Berlin. The two met in advance of rehearsals, and Furtwängler, who could behave with the arrogance of the Prussian, told Horowitz, "I will show you how we play Brahms in Germany," and he began to illustrate his ideas at the piano. "Here we don't articulate every note clearly but give a general, solid impression," he said. "This, you know, is not America." Matters did not improve during the rehearsals, and the performance was miserable. When it was over, pianist and con-

ductor took a bow jointly, and then Furtwängler left Horowitz in
the wings while he acknowledged the remainder of the curtain calls
himself. Horowitz plunged out of the hall in a fury. Years later
Horowitz, now Toscanini's son-in-law, strolled into the maestro's
dressing room in Salzburg to find that Furtwängler was paying a
call. Furtwängler extended his hand in greeting, but Horowitz
wheeled and, without a word, walked out.

The life of a virtuoso is not all success, fat checks, and adoring
audiences. Heifetz broke his career down into statistics once, and
the figures were formidable, as statistics always are. He estimated
that up to 1942 he had played the fiddle more than 70,000 hours.
In the twenty-five years since his American debut in the fall of
1917, he had traveled 1,500,000 miles, more than 300,000 by air.

To endure such a regimen, the virtuoso must love money and
fame dearly, or he must derive abiding satisfaction from his work.
The nonmaterial rewards are the sense of having done a job well,
the feeling that an audience has responded to what you have been
playing, the knowledge that you have the power to affect the lives
of your fellow men. Artur Rubinstein told of the thrill of having
a woman say to him that she felt he had played a program especially
for her. Paderewski's audiences had regulars who attended his
recitals annually for a generation and more. After a concert, once,
he was out of sorts because of the absence of a woman whose kindly
face had become familiar to him. Whenever he played in this town,
he discovered her down front, and when she was missing he worried
lest something had happened to her.

The best of artists have often known how to relax and play.
Paderewski liked to sit alone in his dressing room before beginning
a recital. He felt that he needed the ten minutes of self-communion
to bring himself to the right mood. If this interval was disturbed,
he would get angry. Once he delayed a program because his period
of privacy was invaded. He returned to his dressing room and sat
for many minutes to achieve the mood he sought. And yet he could
wear the mood lightly, even to the point of ribbing his retinue. One
evening he emerged from the dressing room and, as he walked down

the corridor, encountered his manager. Paderewski suddenly stopped; his shoulders drooped; he sighed and leaned against the wall. The manager turned livid, and his heart thumped. Paderewski sighed again, braced himself, and walked onto the stage with a slow step. The manager ran to the other members of the retinue. "Good Lord!" he gasped, "the Boss is sick!" The others grinned. They reported that the Boss had left his dressing room in the gayest of spirits, singing and doing a little dance step.

There may even be hazards in getting to the audience. Szigeti recalls that as a youngster he toured the cities of England as assisting artist to various famous musicians. Whenever they gave a concert on a Sunday they ran into trouble. For the Salvation Army was virulent in those days, and it resented Sunday concerts. Its followers would assemble in front of the concert hall, beat the drums, and harangue the customers, warning them that they were breaking the Sabbath when they entered to hear music.

Virtuosos are not bothered much by blue laws or people with blue-law ideas today. Their chief problem now is to obtain an audience. After that, to hold it. If they can do both, brothers, life is good.

VOICES AND ARTISTS

*Donkeys and Philosophers—Musicianship—The Ad Libber—Broadway or the Met?
—Martinelli "Won't Do"—Kiepura on the Taking End—Seduction Scene—Singing
What They Shouldn't—Flagstad Falls Asleep.*

ALFRED HERTZ, who conducted at the Metropolitan Opera thirty
years ago, drove his charges hard, according to the recollections of
Frederick Jacobi, American composer, who was his musical assistant. During the rehearsals of a new work once, a young soprano
fainted, and Giulio Gatti-Casazza, the general manager, later suggested that Hertz let up on her. "Let the poor creature alone," said
Gatti. "We Italians have a saying that a living donkey is better than
a dead philosopher."

Though I would not, even roughly, classify singers as donkeys
or philosophers, they may be grouped as those who are musicians
and those who are not. Naturally, there are border-line cases, like
the soprano of whom it was said, "She is an excellent musician, she
always makes the same mistakes."

It is the theory of those who are fond of paradoxes that the
singers with extraordinary voices are poor musicians and those
with mediocre voices are fine musicians. There is some truth in the
theory, and a great deal of falsehood. I can name many singers
with fine voices whose musicianship is first-rate: Flagstad, Lotte
Lehmann, Marian Anderson, Kerstin Thorborg, Friedrich Schorr,
Alexander Kipnis, Ezio Pinza, Salvatore Baccaloni. I pick them
at random, omitting many deserving artists. We have the testimony
of experts that in preceding generations a host of richly endowed
men and women knew their way around a musical problem. As for
the owners of poor voices who are also vile musicians, name your
own list.

To be sure, there is basis for the tradition that a beautiful voice often resides in a bosom without a heart and issues from a skull without a brain. Nor is this phenomenon confined to tenors in whom it seems to appear most frequently. I have seen and heard empty-headed baritones, and I have known bassos who loved themselves not wisely but too well. Among the sopranos and the mezzo-sopranos and the contraltos there is also a prevalence of the addlepated and the utterly insensitive.

It is also true that there are a handful of singers who triumph over limitations of voice to establish themselves as artists. To them a song or a role in an opera is something to be studied in the round. A song has words and a piano part as well as a vocal line; the singer must seek to integrate all its factors. Povla Frijsh, a soprano who ranks among the artists, once said, "I never sing a song unless I am interested in the words. I am a singer of songs, not a diva. And I never sing in a language I don't speak fluently."

These principles should apply to an opera singer approaching a role. But here the duty is greater, for the singer should know not only his part but have a thorough knowledge of words and music of the opera as a whole. You can get a fair notion of the quality of an opera singer from the manner in which he tackles a new role. When Gian-Carlo Menotti was preparing for the *première* of his opera *The Island God,* he had interviews with several singers interested in the leading roles. A famous soprano looked over the part for soprano. An illustrious baritone glanced at the part for baritone. It remained for a young artist of conscience like Astrid Varnay to suggest that she wished the composer to go over the whole opera with her, not merely the soprano part.

When a singer is too successful, he tends to take much for granted, for he prefers filling all his engagements to giving up a few for such things as rehearsals. I do not presume to pass moral judgments on this attitude. After all, a singer's musical life may be short, compared with that of other workers in music, and he had best gather dollar bills while he may.

John Charles Thomas belongs to the happy-go-lucky persuasion.

It is obvious, when you watch him perform, that he likes his work and the feel of a crowd liking him. He has moments of conscientiousness; but he also has a reputation for relying on his quick mind to keep out of trouble. On the opera stage he is one of the best ad libbers. After a half dozen appearances as Figaro in *The Barber of Seville,* a friend exclaimed, "That's the first time I ever heard John Charles sing every word in the *'Largo al factotum.'*" Thomas is supposed to have told a conductor once, "I enjoyed that show tonight; the next time I sing it I'm really going to know it." For his appearance in the title role of *Falstaff* in Chicago, it was arranged to hold one full rehearsal with orchestra, but Thomas had other engagements and could not appear. He was willing to chance the tough role without one orchestral rehearsal. I salute his nerve and his courage, and I hope that young singers will not imitate him.

Astrid Varnay promises to be one youthful singer who will pursue the slow, thorough path—if her managers, friends, and family help her. As a youngster of twenty-three, she made her debut at the Metropolitan during the 1941-42 season, in the exacting role of Sieglinde in *Die Walküre,* at short notice, replacing Lotte Lehmann, who was ill. And for her next role, she took on, again at short notice, the even more exacting Brünnhilde in the same work, in place of the indisposed Helen Traubel. She followed these parts with Elsa in *Lohengrin,* Elisabeth in *Tannhäuser,* and with the lead in the new Menotti opera—quite an assignment for a girl in her first season on any opera stage. But she assured friends that she would not be stampeded into too many engagements. She recognized that it would require years to master the operatic roles.

I hope her manager encourages her to follow the path of wisdom. The chance for quick gains has broken down the resistance of more experienced artists. The problem of the young singer who makes a splash overnight has troubled many experienced teachers, conductors, and other thoughtful musicians. They say that our singers want success too rapidly, that if they win public approval suddenly, they may never become artists. They have no time to ripen; some, in fact, have no time to finish learning the fundamentals of their business.

Marion Talley was rocketed into the limelight when not ready for it. Possibly she could not have made the grade in any case, but the girl never had a real chance. Her debut at the Metropolitan Opera was turned into a front-page affair which did not help her growth as an artist, though she prospered famously for several seasons. In a few years she dropped out of the picture and could not carry off a comeback.

Dorothy Maynor was also skyrocketed into fame overnight. She owned a magnificent natural voice, but she was far from being a well-rounded artist. There were flaws in production and she was unfamiliar with foreign languages. Fortunately, she has humility and artistic conscience. Neither money nor adulation has turned her head. She told her manager at the outset that she hoped there would not be too many concerts, because she had extensive projects for studying. And she kept on working, with commendable results. She has even been surprised by the tide of success. When she was advised, after her successful debut, to go to a Fifth Avenue shop for some fashionable clothes, she said, "I can't afford it." She planned to forgo giving Christmas presents, as she had in the lean years, until she was told that she had a drawing account.

The apparatus of our concert world is responsible, in large part, for driving too many of our young singers ahead too rapidly. Managers, press, and publicity feed the public curiosity. The managers try to cash in; the others try to supply colorful reading matter. In the face of this buildup, which we have all had a share in perpetrating, it is almost inevitable that the young singer's head should be turned.

But let us not absolve the singer. We have in America an abundance of wonderful young voices, possibly more than at any other time in our history. But too many of these talented singers cannot bide their time. They are not willing to begin modestly and to learn slowly and painstakingly. We are a nation that has suffered from an excess of ballyhoo in almost every field, not least in music. Perhaps habits and attitudes will change. It is to be noted that young American conductors are eager to take on obscure and onerous posts so that they may burnish their skills in a hard school. Possibly the singers will follow suit.

Edward Johnson, general manager of the Metropolitan Opera, is one of those who cry out against the haste of the young singer. His experience on both sides of the footlights entitles him to an opinion. When he was a young tenor, fresh from Canada, he landed in New York, right side up. He found a good church job and presently was cast in the lead in a new operetta, *The Waltz Dream*, on Broadway. He was featured, and his salary was $600 a week. He was twenty-eight, and in several years, he was assured, he would be the dominant singing star on Broadway. The Shuberts, producers of the operetta, offered him a long-term contract, starting at $800 a week. They wanted him to tour with the show, and they had grandiose plans for him. But he turned them down and went to Europe to work at becoming an opera singer. It took years of labor to learn his art, but he knew what he wanted and was willing to give himself time.

Broadway is not less desirable as a career than the Metropolitan Opera or the concert circuit, if that is where the singer's taste and talent lie. But there are practical reasons for preferring the latter two. On Broadway you do eight shows a week, and you have to pray for a part. On the concert stage, you are on your own, and in the opera house you sing twice a week. And nowadays you can move into radio or the movies just as easily from opera and concert as from the Broadway theater.

The conscientious singer takes as much pains with his work as any other musician of quality. Consider the scrupulous preparations that Lotte Lehmann makes for her appearances. She spends a considerable period planning her selections so that they will have contrast, curve, climax, and a binding over-all unity. There are no casual singing tasks for her. She once agreed to do four songs at a private gathering, and she rehearsed each song as carefully as if she had never seen it before, though each had been in her repertory a score of years. She knew that her voice needed absolute repose before singing, and before an appearance she would avoid even small talk.

Sometimes, of course, it pays dividends to be less than intense and earnest. At any rate, resilience may be useful, as Giovanni Martinelli will bear witness. At twenty-four, with six months' experience as a professional singer, he was engaged to appear in *The Girl of the Golden West* in Rome, after an audition before Puccini, Toscanini, and the publisher Ricordi. The style of the music was different from the three operas in which he had sung, and it puzzled him. At the first rehearsal with Toscanini, he fumbled the lines, mangled the music, and stumbled like an ignoramus. Toscanini glared at him, and banged the score shut. "Impossible," he cried, "you won't do!"

As Martinelli tells the story, "At twenty-four I should have been crushed! But what the hell! I was a boy from the provinces, and this was my first visit to Rome. I told the maestro, quite cheerfully, that at least I could go home and say that I had seen Rome and had rehearsed with Toscanini."

Probably this was Toscanini's first encounter with such a sanguine reaction. It seemed to change his mind. He smiled and said, "Let's try again, perhaps we can do something."

They did. Martinelli learned the part thoroughly, scored in Rome, and was engaged to appear in the opera in many cities throughout Europe.

It had also required resilience to survive the embarrassments of his debut in opera some months before, in the Teatro dal Verme in Milan. Singing in *Ernani*, he forgot the words of one of his big arias and had to ad lib. In a dramatic scene, he dropped his sword with a crash, and the audience roared with laughter.

These things happen to all singers, whether they work in opera, radio, or concert hall. The good trouper prepares himself so well that he encounters a minimum of difficulties, but he is also ready for the unforeseen and unpredictable. An experienced opera singer is always prepared to cope with a scene stealer and perhaps to do a bit of filching himself. Each congenital scene stealer develops a technique of his own. One acts all over the lot, another muggs excessively, a third does his most ornate acting while a colleague has a solo to sing. If you cultivate a reputation for "temperament," a mild bit of scene stealing will be passed over by your fellow artists with gratitude that it is not worse.

Jan Kiepura, who has committed some of the prize larcenies on the operatic stage, is a tenor from whom other singers don't like to take it. His encounters with Grace Moore have been classic; they almost came to blows. He tried stealing a scene from Lily Djanel, the Metropolitan Opera's new Carmen, recently, and he met his match. For Miss Djanel was a product of the Paris Opéra, where they know a trick or two. Kiepura embraced Djanel in one of the passionate scenes, and found later that his wig had been loosened. During his singing of the Flower Song, he rested his head on her lap as he started to sing, but she moved suddenly and his head took a severe bump.

Singers even try to steal the limelight from each other on the concert stage. Kiepura was booked for a joint recital with Anne Brown. Since he was the more experienced singer, he assured everyone backstage, "I will keell her." She heard about this prediction and sang with irresistible intensity. The audience not only saved Miss Brown from being "keelled," but it did a little slaying on its own.

Salvatore Baccaloni, if he chooses, can steal a scene in diverse ways. I have seen him overwhelm an expert singing actor like Ezio Pinza in *Don Giovanni* with details of business carefully injected where they would do the most harm. I have seen Pinza try the same technique on him. One of Baccaloni's neatest jobs was dominating a scene in *The Barber of Seville*, when Pinza and Thomas stood on either side of him, singing and acting, while he remained, almost immovable, on one spot. On another occasion Norman Cordon was the Basilio when Baccaloni was in *The Barber*, and Cordon played with sweeping gestures. As Cordon's acting became more extravagant, Baccaloni's took on delicacy and restraint; he seemed

to be making a deliberate point of poking refined fun at Cordon's
broad style, and in the end the audience got the idea.

Competition brings out the worst in some singers. Grace Moore
and John Charles Thomas had an encounter in a performance of
Tosca in Chicago recently. The soprano, irritated with Thomas,
tried the alluring technique. In the seduction scene of the second
act, Tosca put herself out to get the Scarpia wrought up beyond
the needs of the theater, which might give Tosca the advantage.
But Scarpia was indifferent. During the scene, the two had an
acid exchange, and people down front were astounded to hear the
kind of talk that took place during a passionate scene.

Lily Pons' favorite conductor at the Metropolitan Opera for
many years was Gennaro Papi, who was a model of tact and sympathy in handling her orchestral support. If she wished to hold a
high note a mite longer, he let her do so; if she wanted a fraction
of a second more before attacking another phrase, he waited. Papi
died early in the 1941-42 season, and Ettore Panizza took over
one of Miss Pons' performances. He was more rigid than Papi and
would not hold back or speed up even for a star coloratura soprano.
The result was a sour performance, and Miss Pons protested. The
management had to assign her operas to other conductors.

Because singers in the opera house are in constant rivalry, or
so it seems to them, they are always on the alert. Some do not talk
to each other, but keep a close watch on each other. Elisabeth Rethberg resigned from the Metropolitan Opera after nineteen years
as a leading soprano because she resented the management's assign-
ing some of her roles to Zinka Milanov. Melchior has fought hard
for his rights. It is said in the trade that he would battle all comers
—conductors, managers, and singers—if he thought that his position at the top was threatened. He has insisted on top pay, top
billing, and top consideration. As long as he has had them, he has
been as sweet as a soubrette, but when he has thought that somebody has been getting the better of him, he has turned difficult and
stubborn. He built up a record of never missing a performance in
fifteen years at the Metropolitan Opera. In the longest and most

exacting roles of the repertory, his energy and power have seemed inexhaustible. He has sung several nights in a row, and has even sat up most of the night at a party and then sung the next day with amazing freshness.

If there has been a more difficult singer at large than Grace Moore, the trade has not heard of him or her. She has been a handful for people who had business dealings with her, especially managers. It was a normal thing for her to bombard her New York managers with complaints when she went touring; she would blame them for a draft in a hotel room, a bad train ride, an uncomfortable bed. A lad in her manager's office, who had been on tour with her, was inducted into the army, and after his first day in camp, he sent a wire to his old office, "My tent is drafty and my bed is as hard as nails. What are you going to do about it?"

Miss Moore, however, has given value when she has sung. Audiences have been fond of her, and she has studied sedulously, trying hard to make herself an artist. When she has undertaken a new role, she has not spared herself. She has worked with experts; she has tried to improve her interpretation with each repetition of role. But her handsome face and figure, as much as her singing, have helped win her audience.

Like most human beings, singers long to be what they are not. It was said that Galli-Curci hated coloratura singing, and that, of course, was the style which made her famous and earned her more than a million dollars. Emma Calvé wanted to sing Wagner, but admitted that it was not her milieu. She felt, in a day when most prima donnas sang Wagner, that she needed this repertory to be the complete artist. She once went through an act of *Tristan und Isolde* in a rehearsal with Anton Seidl. The conductor suggested that she go on to the second act, but she realized that she would ruin her voice if she sang Wagner, and abandoned the idea.

Rosa Ponselle, in her last years at the Metropolitan, was constantly seeking to sing roles for which her voice was unsuited. First, it was the high tessitura of *Traviata,* then the low of *Carmen.* The dramatic soprano roles which she did magnificently she seemed to

resent. Finally, she quit singing in opera. Her friends reported that
a set of savage reviews had caused her to retire. Nevertheless, she
longed to sing. At a party recently she went to the piano and sang
scenes from *Norma* and *Tristan und Isolde*. The voice, I am told,
was darker and richer than it had ever been. The years of rest had
helped rather than impaired it. She even hinted that she would consider returning to the Metropolitan. But she talked of coming back
in an out-of-the-way opera that was not for her, instead of in a role
for which she was admirably equipped.

Even a shrewd chap like Bing Crosby was talked into trying
opera, but not for long. Someone prevailed on him to study Rigoletto, with a performance at the San Francisco Opera as bait. He
worked on it for a week and decided that this was not his dish. Wise
Bing!

Have you ever heard a singer hold forth on the blindness of an
operatic management in giving a role to a rival? But the part was
written for me, he will cry, even though the part was composed 150
years ago. I have heard bassos hold forth like that, and you would
think that they would be above such envious chatter. When Pinza
was detained by the F. B. I. after the United States went to war
with Italy, the malicious gossips in the theater insisted that other
bassos had reported him to the authorities. I happen to know that
a young woman, harboring private resentments, made the complaint.

But observe how the singers rally round when there is an emergency. During a recent tour, the Metropolitan Opera did *Lohengrin*
in Boston. The heat was miserably regulated backstage, and the
temperature soared so high that Thorborg developed a nosebleed.
Then someone opened windows and doors, and the drop of the
temperature was so sudden that Astrid Varnay's sore throat became
aggravated and she could not continue with the last act. Maxine
Stellman, who had never sung Elsa before, was called from the
hotel and hurried into a costume while the curtain was held. Miss
Varnay helped her with costume, wig, and make-up. Women in the

chorus kept singing the words into her ears and giving her instructions for her stage business. Melchior aided her by beating time with his fingers on her shoulders.

Singers can be a gay, fun-loving crew. I have run into fewer brooders among them than among other musicians. It must be that wearing grease paint helps them to get outside themselves. Tibbett is one of the jolliest. When Gatti-Casazza was general manager and his wife, Frances Alda, was a leading light of the Metropolitan, Tibbett, singing opposite her in *La Cena delle Beffe*, swung her around in a violent scene as if she were a partner in an Apache dance. After the scene, friends passed by his dressing room whistling a funeral march. He once went to a party honoring a Russian princess—at least she claimed to be a Russian princess—and he sang what purported to be a Russian song, using a wild gibberish of his own. The princess complimented him on his Russian.

Among the women, the best natural comedienne at the Metropolitan has been young Irra Petina, who has a sense of humor off stage as well as on. Before singing at a luncheon, she was served a heaping plate of roast beef. She said, "If I eat that, I'll be able to sing Brünnhilde."

Some singers play a role out of the theater as well as in. Chaliapin was constantly acting, and doing a good job, too. Mary Garden could be either the *grande dame* or as chummy as your Aunt Sue, and could carry off each role with style. Calvé was another who always played a part. She once asked an interviewer who was the greatest singer he had ever heard. The honest fellow said, "Lilli Lehmann." Said Calvé sweetly, "I agree with you."

Flagstad has been one of the most unaffected of human beings off stage. After an appearance in Detroit, she was rushed with a motorcycle escort to the railroad station, where the train was being held for her. She did not believe that the train would be there, until she found it waiting, and she complained that the escort was not strictly in Hollywood style, for the motorcycle cops were not blowing their sirens.

She was delightfully simple in her struggle to master the American idiom. When she started on her first tour, her road manager said, as they got into the Pullman, "I'll take care of you." She looked at him suspiciously. "You will not!" she said.

Kirsten Flagstad, who was meticulous about her artistic duties, once had a terrific scare on the stage of the Metropolitan Opera House. She was singing Kundry in *Parsifal,* and in the first act had to lie onstage for about fifteen minutes, her head in her arms. Like some of the helpless sinners in the audience who are dragged to the opera to hear Wagner, Flagstad fell asleep. Somehow she awoke, with a fearful start, just before her cue. She did not consider that moment fun.

Flagstad's departure in the spring of 1941 caused sorrow at the Metropolitan, for it was feared that she would not be back. She reached Norway safely, but the management's fears were confirmed. She did not return for the following season. In her absence, the rumors spread that she was sympathetic to the Nazis. Otherwise, why should she have willingly gone back to a Norway that was under the domination of the Nazis and the Quislings?

I investigated the charges, and I could find no confirmation that she favored the Nazis or the Quislings. Nor could I find proof that she had sung in Nazi Germany at the invitation of Goebbels, though she did travel through Germany to sing in neutral Switzerland. But this I did discover: her husband, Henry Johansen, was not out of favor with the Quisling "government." When he visited this country, he told friends that he feared Communism more than any other force in Europe. A wealthy lumberman, he had been one of the richest men in Norway. After the Nazis invaded Norway and handed the government over to Quisling, Johansen seemed to be able to obtain and accept favors from the men who had betrayed his people. Once every week he would telephone his wife in America from Norway, and certainly he could not make such calls without the sanction of the Nazis. Flagstad went home, promising to return. She may have been warned that her family would suffer if she did not go home or perhaps she could not resist the temptation to see her mother, sister, brother, and husband again. Possibly she is an unpolitical person who did not reflect that her return to Norway would undermine her standing wherever the fight for freedom was valued. At best you may say for her that she was an unreflecting and unwilling prisoner of her environment.

10

THE BOYS IN THE ORCHESTRA

The New York Philharmonic plus Stokowski—Baiting the Conductor—Orchestra Rehearsal—Woes of the French-Horn Player—Pulling Strings—Cards—Women in the Orchestra—Personnel Manager—Librarian.

THE FIRST MEETING of the one hundred members of an orchestra with a new conductor is like an encounter of diplomats. The rigidities of protocol are scrupulously observed, while each measures the other. Will they take to each other, or will they pursue the amenities as they quietly distrust and detest one another? Will there be co-operation or constant suspicion, ill-will, and possibly sabotage?

The one hundred members of the orchestra are almost a collective personality when they face a new conductor, and if they and the maestro are competent, that is how they sound in public performances. If the conductor does not know how to cope with this personality or brings out the worst in it, it will sound indifferently or worse.

The men of an orchestra, almost by nature, take a show-me attitude. They respect a conductor who knows his own mind and how to get what he wants. They are indulgent with one who treats them kindly and does not ask too much of them. A conductor who drives them like a tough top sergeant causes them to gripe, to resent, and to behave. A conductor who patronizes them becomes a hated enemy. A conductor who is pretentious amuses them, and a conductor who does not know his stuff becomes the butt of their jokes.

Whatever the relationship between conductor and orchestra, it cannot be gauged precisely from watching them in action before an audience. The caliber of the performance may give a clue, but it may not be decisive. A well-intentioned, competent orchestra can make a poor conductor pass muster, just as a brilliant but ill-intentioned gang can make a fine conductor sound like a dub. As much depends on the disposition of the one hundred men in the ensemble as it does on the competence and character of the leader.

A fine orchestra like the New York Philharmonic-Symphony and a brilliant conductor like Stokowski could not seem to hit it off. In 1930, Stokowski was guest director for two weeks, and it was a hash. To hear the men tell about it, Stokowski picked on them, bawled them out unfairly, and finally kicked two men out of the orchestra for the duration of his visit. Stokowski's version was that they were unresponsive and insubordinate. Since he was a guest and had not the power to fire, they could get away with murder; the punishment of the two who were banished was merely a two-week vacation with pay.

Eleven years later there was a return engagement. For the centennial season of 1941-42, the board of the New York orchestra invited Stokowski to be one of a series of eminent guest leaders. The invitation was for four weeks, but Stokowski did not care to accept more than two. As the players describe the renewal of diplomatic relations, Stokowski had them on edge after several rehearsals. They were indignant that he saw fit to lecture them, and they reached a high in impatience when he convened them during a rest period to continue a dissertation. The situation became so aggravated that on the day of the opening of the season, some of the men said to an orchestra official, "If that guy delivers another lecture, or makes some crack after the concert tonight, he'll conduct without an orchestra tomorrow." For his part Stokowski was indignant, too. He told the official during the intermission of the first concert, "If they don't play any better during the second half, I'm through."

The official pleaded with the men, "This is our centennial. You have only two weeks with him. Please!"

The men responded to this appeal, and the performances improved. At the final concert of Stokowski's visit, the orchestra sounded as it should—like a first-rank outfit playing under a conductor of quality. But the fact remained that orchestra and conductor were not compatible, though it is probable that if Stokowski were their year-round boss, compatibility would be achieved.

Playing for another guest conductor, Koussevitzky, the same players wore their party manners. The conductor requested a rehearsal for Monday, customarily a free day in the orchestra's schedule, and the men assembled for it cheerfully. Morning rehearsals were shifted from 10 A.M. to 9:30 A.M., and afternoon workouts from 2 P.M. to 4 P.M., and while there may have been some grousing, the collective personality remained friendly. Benevolence irradiated the fortnight of Koussevitzky's stay. At the end of his last concert he went to the orchestra room to tell the men they were "one hundred great artists" and to promise each of them autographed photographs. The players, in turn, gave him a group picture signed by every man. Throughout the visit, the performances were excellent.

The one hundred men of an orchestra may seem to a harassed conductor to march, attack, and react with solidarity, and in the face of an enemy to close ranks. But they are actually one hundred men of widely differing backgrounds and points of view. Some are profoundly in love with music; some have their minds on the fifth race at Churchill Downs or on Joe DiMaggio's batting average. They are earnest, morose, prankish, and matter-of-fact; introvert and extrovert; impudent and reserved; industrious and indolent. There is a little of everything in a big orchestra, even, occasionally, someone who is not particularly fond of music.

When the men in an orchestra become playful, the conductor had better beware. Of course, they don't dare turn playful with a Toscanini, save on his terms, which means that they may laugh at his comments and gestures if he means them to. When they told him once that there was a strong man in the New York Philharmonic who could lift people by holding his arms outstretched stiffly and placing them under the other person's armpits, Toscanini wanted proof. The strong man lifted the maestro, and the boys roared.

Occasionally the boys make sport of a lesser man, either to test his capacities as a musician or just to be devilish. The tricks are as diverse as the resourcefulness of the musicians. A string player in the rear section of the orchestra will deliberately go through the motions of playing but actually will not play at all. A wood-wind player will make an entrance that is a split second late. A brass player will hold on to a note just a mite longer than necessary, or in a big, climactic passage will blow ever so slightly off key. If the conductor can detect crime and culprit instantly, the playful lads will subside and make music. You can't bait a conductor who is on to your gags. But if the poor conductor is incompetent or inexperienced, he is headed for some hazing. Of course, if he is incompetent enough, he never discovers that his leg is being pulled, nor does he become aware of the miserable performance he is giving. But most conductors know when a work is going badly or well. The problem for the conductor is to establish beyond question that he knows the score and intends to be the boss. It is best to establish this point without getting tough, but it is better to demand strict discipline than to go down through too much geniality.

Being blunt and independent, some of the orchestra boys do terrific jobs on a conductor. A conductor of the New York Philharmonic held forth didactically at one rehearsal, lecturing on musical theory with careful, hair-splitting detail. The men shifted restlessly in their seats, waiting to be told to play, but the lecture went on and on. Finally one of the oboe players reached his saturation point, and stood up and said, "Maestro, you talk too much."

The silence was deafening. A colleague whispered to the oboe player that he should not have said that to the conductor. But the independent oboist was defiant.

"With $75,000 in the bank," he said, "I should be afraid of that fellow!"

The instrumentalists are alert to every vagary of a conductor. They are like a class of small boys who take in shrewdly the strength and weakness of their teacher. They are also a group of artists who have ideas of their own as to how a piece of music should go, and they compare one conductor's ideas with another's. Thus they are quick to note that one maestro affects slow tempos and another fast; that one man makes the orchestra roar as if it were blowing for Judgment Day and another makes it whisper like a night-club singer without a voice. They know that one conductor takes four or five minutes longer to play the Beethoven Fifth Symphony than another. They have violent opinions as to which man and procedure are right, and will carry on endless disputes among themselves as to the musical rectitude of several approaches.

Most of the men in an orchestra know their stuff. When they achieve seats in a major symphony ensemble, they are generally experts. Some of them regard themselves as something more than specialists of one instrument. They fancy that they have talent for conducting, and they feel frequently that they know more about it than most of the conductors they have to work with. As a cellist, Alfred Wallenstein had conducting aspirations. He had a poker face and a habit of seldom looking up at the conductor. This distracted most conductors, but since the cellist was one of the best, conductors rarely complained. Bruno Walter was conducting once when Wallenstein was looking bored and when his eyes glanced about everywhere but at the conductor's baton. After the concert, Walter chatted with Wallenstein and asked him what his ambition was. "To be a conductor," said the cellist. "I hope," Walter said, "that you have no Wallensteins under you."

Orchestral players can break the morale and the heart of a conductor, but they are not without pride in their work, and they derive pleasure from the kind words of a conductor. Like the virtuoso who will remember verbatim a rave notice he received a decade ago, an orchestral player will treasure the commendation of a conductor he respects. There is a man in the New York Philharmonic who still talks about the time fifteen years ago that Toscanini stopped, nodded, and beamed at him during rehearsal for his fine playing of a tricky passage.

A good orchestral player does not get by merely by turning up at rehearsals and performances, doing his stuff and drawing his paycheck. There is an erroneous impression abroad about the amount of time a man in a major orchestra puts into his job. Thus the men in the New York Philharmonic receive a minimum of one hundred dollars a week for five rehearsals and four concerts. The time they put in officially is less than twenty-seven hours. But most players have to spend hours of their own time practicing, learning new works and reviewing old. Some practice more conscientiously than others; some need more practice than others. And a good many keep their hands in by playing in small groups privately for their own pleasure. Chamber music is one of the hobbies of many professional orchestral men.

The members of a good orchestra usually arrive at their rehearsal hall half an hour to an hour ahead of time. They get out their violins, horns, clarinets, oboes, and tubas and go over difficult passages. When a conductor like Mitropoulos schedules a flock of new and difficult works during his stay as leader, the men have to put in a great deal of extra time. They receive their parts a week or two in advance, and it is up to them to be familiar with their assignments before rehearsals begin, and these parts are often difficult to master.

A rehearsal of a major orchestra is not the occasion for the study of a new work from scratch. No conductor could keep up with the heavy schedule of a modern major orchestra if he had to teach the A B C's of a work. He takes it for granted that each man is acquainted with his duties. The rehearsal time is employed—at least it should be—to synchronize each man's assignment and to form of the isolated materials a unified and tightly made structure.

Usually the conductor arrives at the rehearsal hall ahead of time, too. If the men are puzzled by problems, they may visit his dressing room to seek advice in advance of the rehearsal. Occasionally he calls some of them in during the rest period in the middle of a rehearsal to make suggestions and criticisms. Toscanini's habit is to remain standing on the podium throughout a rehearsal. If there is a pause between numbers, they sometimes come up to him with their scores to discuss a question of phrasing. They are quick to adopt useful suggestions, and it occasionally happens that they can teach a conductor a trick or two. When José Iturbi was entering the conducting field, he engaged one of the French-horn players of the New York Philharmonic to give him lessons, so that he would know from personal experience what was possible or impossible on that instrument when he faced the orchestra.

Each instrumentalist has his own ideas about the best way of looking after his health, his technique, and his instrument. Some even have a philosophy of art, since many of them are theorists and composers and others have become members of an orchestra only because they could not quite make the grade as solo recitalists. A few, in fact, chose steady salaries rather than the uncertainties of an independent career, though they were capable of it.

Is the celebrated virtuoso or singer the only musician who under-goes daily tortures because of problems of health and diet? Consider the woes of a French-horn player. When the weather is un-duly cold or hot, he worries about contracting or swelling lips. In winter, he has a jar of vaseline handy and applies it to his lips before a concert, to be sure they will not get chapped. Throat irritations are an agony to him, as they are to a singer. He has to avoid gassy foods before a concert, and a brass player cannot risk discomfort at the wrong time, not if conductor and audience are to stay happy.

A wind-instrument player depends largely on his embouchure, the application of lips to mouthpiece. His talents as an instrumentalist are in direct proportion to his capacity to control delicately the pressure of air that he blows into horn or reed. That is why lips, lungs, and breath control are fundamental. The string player watches over his hands with the concern of a virtuoso. And well he might. I know of one fiddler who lost a year's work because he injured a finger of his left hand, and it took two operations to enable him to resume his work. Like conductors and virtuosos, orchestral players get occupational ailments. One of the most serious is neuritis in arm, wrist, or fingers. Then they are lost for months.

Orchestral players, especially those who have occasional solos to play, are subject to tension and nerves, like artists who face a huge audience alone. There was a trumpeter in a major orchestra who worked himself up into such a state when he had a solo passage to do that, several times after the concert, he fainted.

A first-desk string player will splurge on an expensive instrument. The concertmaster appears now and then as soloist, and since he is one of the highest-paid men in the orchestra, he may even acquire one of the choice old Italian violins. Each player is an expert on the maintenance of his equipment, and some must spend more than others to keep theirs in order. The chap who plays the double bass has to spend a dollar and a half for a G string and three dollars for an E string, whereas the violinist can replace his strings at a lower price. But the costs of string replacement even for a bull fiddler are as nothing compared with those of the harpist. There are forty-eight strings on the harp. Think of having to renew them all at once at a dollar a string and up. Fortunately, a harp player does not use the instrument as extensively as a fiddler in the course of a concert, and in many scores the harp does not appear at all.

Some instrumentalists own two or more instruments of their choice. Like the champion tennis player who carries at least two favorite rackets, the violinist may tote a case with two fiddles, and the horn player may have one or two horns at home in reserve. Probably the record is held by Anselme Fortier, the first double-bass player of the New York Philharmonic, who possesses seven bull fiddles. Fortunately, he lives in a house, not a city apartment.

The men in the orchestra hanker for self-expression, probably because they spend so much of their time expressing the conductor's wishes. Occasionally the urge for self-expression takes the form of written comments on the printed music, as the Am-Rus Music Corporation discovered whenever the music for Shostakovich's Seventh Symphony was returned after being out on loan to various orchestras.

A good many instrumentalists, seeking their meed of immortality, inscribed their signatures and the dates of performance on the back pages of the music. A hard-boiled player wrote not only his name but this comment, "So what?" Beside the last note of the seventy-five minute symphony, a violinist scribbled, "From here on you can relax, boys." There was a bloodstain on one page of music, with this apology and explanation jotted down by a player, "I killed this mosquito with my bow because it was bothering me. Stadium, July." Finally there was the bassoon player who thought it worth while to record his encounter with a conductor. "It was here," wrote the bassoon player on the printed music, "that the conductor begged: 'Come out, bassoon, let us hear you, come out, we love you.' "

Who can match the gusto of the California musicians who congregated every other Sunday morning in a high-school auditorium in Beverly Hills, without fanfare, pay, audience, or reporters, to play music they did not encounter on their jobs? They were mostly men engaged at the various movie studios—top-notch instrumentalists. They paid modest dues to cover the expenses of their sessions. The conductor was usually a guest, possibly a composer who led the men through a new work of his own, or a well-known conductor who directed some little-known composition. The men gave up their Sunday-morning games of golf and tennis, their trips to the beach or the hills, their gardens, their families and the luxury of staying late abed, and they even fined themselves for tardiness.

Being experts in their medium, the members of an orchestra can hold forth, not unlike a talkative conductor, about the requirements of their work. The flute player will tell you that "you must not blow the flute, you must play it." The oboist observes that composers are making increasing virtuoso demands on the oboe. The trumpeter says you need wind and endurance to do a good job. The drummer has to know how to count. What about the man who stands in the back of the orchestra, waiting for long intervals to give the triangle a gentle tap? Well, he needs at least patience.

The men in an orchestra, being of various ages, both actual and in spirit, act according to their tastes, on and off the stage. They play practical jokes on each other. Theodore Cella, the New York

Philharmonic's harpist, tells of a traditional stunt tried on the harp player. The harpist need not keep his foot on the pedal, which may be set in a notch and released when required. An opera harpist, who had a long rest ahead, fixed his pedals for the next passage and asked a musician who sat near him to wake him; then he relaxed and dozed off. The neighbor changed the position of the pedal, and when the harpist was awakened and plunged into his music, he heard to his horror—and the conductor's—some of the most fantastic sounds that ever came from a harp.

Recently an orchestra made a long tour across the country. Their nights on the Pullman were made hideous by a trumpeter who was about to be drafted into the army and who got up early to practice bugle calls. Touring with an orchestra is fun and a headache. The men don't get enough sleep. Dressing rooms in concert halls of some towns are basements, furnace rooms, gymnasiums, even men's toilets. The men swear about drafts, and they fear catching cold. But there are advantages on tour. Since there are concerts almost every day, there are no rehearsals, and there is nothing an orchestra player likes better than no rehearsal.

On tour, as at home, the boys engage in endless card games. They play bridge, poker, pinochle, and hearts, seldom, if ever, solitaire, for orchestral players are not lone wolves. Some of them are camera fiends; others draw. A good many are composers on the side and spend all their spare time writing and copying their own music. Occasionally a kind conductor schedules one of their works and invites them to get up on the podium to lead it; then the boys in the orchestra give all to make it a happy occasion for their colleague. Some of the men are chess players. In the club room of the New York Philharmonic, it is a standing order that no cleaning woman is ever to touch a chess game when it is left on a table overnight, for some of these matches have gone on for weeks. The card games here are also fabulous. Among the honored subjects framed and hung on the wall are a set of poker hands in which one player held a royal flush.

Within an orchestra there are as many jealousies as in an opera house. A violinist resents his neighbor. A trumpeter thinks that he should be in the solo chair. A cellist fumes because he is not promoted when the first cellist leaves for a better job, and his resentment is greater when an outsider is brought in to fill the post.

Though there may be internal quarrels, the men face the outside world as a strongly unified group. When a critic wrote that the members of the New York Philharmonic-Symphony were constantly forming cabals against conductors, the men met in angry conclave and dispatched an impassioned letter of protest to the publisher. When another critic wrote a piece condemning an orchestra and observing that some of the players should be discharged or pensioned, the men beefed. Later when a few were dismissed and pensioned, they insisted that they had the critic to thank, and it would not have gone well for that citizen if he had met up with some of the boys in a blackout.

The men in an orchestra no longer have the old-fashioned prejudice against women joining their numbers. As soon as the girls proved that they did not seek special favors but wanted only equality as musicians, hostility began to fall away. Female harpists were admitted to orchestras first, because there was a shortage of talented male players. But more recently there have been practitioners of almost every instrument of the modern orchestra, and as the war has drawn male players out of the symphonies into the army, there have been increasing calls for gifted women. The brasses, because of their demand for wind and endurance, are supposed to be most difficult for women, but Koussevitzky had two young ladies as first and second trombonists in his orchestra in the Berkshires in the summer of 1942, and he pronounced them excellent. An attractive group of girls was hired by Stokowski for his All-American Youth Orchestra in 1940 and 1941, and the boys in the orchestra joyfully welcomed the beauteous coworkers. The audiences were also delighted. When Stokowski took this orchestra to South America, he had to put up the girls in swank hotels in the center of town, because the inhabitants were clamoring to see and honor them. Maybe the next step will be to place the girls in the forefront of the orchestra, like the front line of a good-looking chorus.

The personnel manager and the librarian are listed as members of the orchestra and have duties beyond the playing of instruments, though they occasionally pinch-hit on an odd percussion instrument when a score requires an augmented ensemble. The personnel manager is the liaison man between conductor and orchestra and between orchestra and management, because he is the union spokesman for the players. It is his job to know symphonic players all over town, for at short notice he may need substitutes for absent members of his ensemble; good, experienced players are not too numerous. When Artur Rodzinski conducted a Shostakovich opera, he needed eighteen extra men, and Maurice van Praag, the New York Philharmonic-Symphony's personnel manager, was able to assemble them in several hours. He can find men who play Wagner tubas and E-flat cornets—species of musicians who are rare and getting rarer.

The librarian is a key figure in an orchestra. He has to supply the scores, properly marked, for one hundred players. No two conductors play a score exactly alike, and the librarian and his assistant must annotate every part according to each conductor's conception. The New York Philharmonic-Symphony has a library of 2000 compositions, which means a master conductor's score and dozens of parts for every composition. Moreover, about fifty scores are added to the collection each season. In the library are rare scores, and some that have become invaluable because of notations by a long line of conductors. Many scores are seldom used, like the large collection of music by Ludwig Spohr accumulated during the early years of the orchestra because one of its founders, Ureli Corelli Hill, had studied with the composer. Works like the Beethoven symphonies that are active season after season need special attention, for they wear out. Conductors have a habit of flipping pages of their scores violently and causing damage to the volume and pain to the heart of the librarian.

To hear them tell about it, orchestral players are a misunderstood lot. If the orchestra plays well, the conductor receives the credit. If it plays badly, individuals in the ensemble are roasted, not only by the conductor but by the audience and the press. But they are not always misunderstood to their disadvantage. Many years ago, when Mahler was conductor of the New York Philharmonic, he led the men on a tour. A good many of the players had frugal habits. Instead of going to an inn after the concert, they saved their hotel allowance and spent half the night playing cards in the waiting room of the railroad station and the other half sleeping on its benches. In one town Mahler spent a sleepless night and at 4 A.M. decided to take a walk. He summoned his assistant and they strolled through the darkened city until they came to the railroad station. Mahler decided to look in, but the assistant, fearing that he would be furious if he discovered that the men were not resting comfortably in hotel rooms, tried to dissuade him. The conductor insisted on entering. "Look, Sam," he cried to his assistant, as he recognized the snoozing members of his orchestra. "Such enthusiasm! They are so anxious not to miss the train for the next concert they are here hours ahead of time!"

11

THE AMATEURS, BLESS THEM!

Letter from an Amateur—Amateur Cellist—The Oratorio Society—Grand Opera in Raleigh—Doctors—Chamber-Music Fans—Amateur Meets Professional—Try It on Your Recorder—Al Smith Wonders.

ANY SOUND MUSICAL SOCIETY must have a large and well-informed body of amateurs as one of its foundations. They are firm and undeviating in their devotion. Their love of music has no coarse, mercenary motivation. Their behavior is based on that first Christian principle—love. The practice of their music bespeaks the great virtues—faith, hope, and charity.

Professional musicians are all right, in their time and place. They allow themselves to be photographed and interviewed; they accept piddling sums up to several thousand dollars an appearance, and they sometimes give inspiring performances. But they are the superstructure of the edifice. The rock-bottom base is the great public, and the binding agent is the corpus of amateurs.

Think only of their commercial value. They are immense consumers of printed music, instruments, and records. They are the most consistent purchasers of tickets for concerts in the big cities. In the smaller towns they are shining lights of leadership, organizing concert series, lectures, amateur orchestras and choruses. Out of their good works they not only draw nourishment for themselves but they help to provide gratification for their communities.

There are amateurs in every field of music. They play in orchestras, sing in choruses, function in local operatic productions, and meet for sessions of chamber music. In a large city, like New York, they are not fazed by the presence of exalted orchestras like the Philharmonic-Symphony, the NBC Symphony, and others of that

gaudy ilk. Like water rising to meet its own level, the amateurs
seek out their brethren and sisters in orchestras in settlement
schools, churches, social clubs, Y.M.C.A.'s, and unions. In a small
town that maintains only a scattering of professional instrumentalists, amateurs can be counted upon to pitch in and fill the vacant
seats in communal ensembles. A small ensemble in an Alabama
town needed a double-bass player. A youngster who played the bull
fiddle in a jazz band was asked to join the newly formed symphony.
He did not protest coyly, but gave it a try and quickly learned
enough about handling the instrument in symphonic music. In the
same town another lad, a clarinetist, undertook to learn the oboe in
three months, and carried it off.

All is not duck soup in these amateur organizations. I have heard
of a New England small-town amateur orchestra where the community's two best fiddlers refused to play with the orchestra because each thought that he deserved the post of concertmaster. The
conductor, a local musician, who understood small-town politics,
solved the riddle with a sad Solomon's wisdom by doing without
both. In another community an excellent amateur cellist and a good
fiddler refused to become colleagues in the same orchestra because
both were paying court to the same girl, and the poor conductor,
who had need of both, found that he was not only a *chef d'orchestre*
but a good-will court.

Newspapers receive a constant flow of letters from committees
promoting this or that local symphony orchestra, pleading for
recognition. Sometimes these letters provide a delightful insight into
the struggles and the passions that lie beneath the surface of amateur music-making. Here are some lines from an official of an orchestra in a small town in Indiana:

"Our organization, except for the three or four professionals, is
entirely amateur. The members receive no pay except the feeling
that they are accomplishing something worth while. And surely
they are. For this reason in times past, we have requested and received letters from Ormandy, Stock, and Stokowski praising, to
some extent, our efforts. Naturally not too much emphasis is placed

on the fact that the letters were requested. Pardon us these and other slight deceptions.

"The upshot is that now the town has become aware of our existence and would not consider an artist course without including the orchestra. Possibly the orchestra cannot and should not survive much longer, but the financial situation has certainly improved and the orchestra members will work diligently as long as their efforts seem appreciated. The audience is able to be rather critical of the orchestra.

"If I am out of order simply omit mention of the orchestra in your paper, but seven years, O Lord, is a long time."

Amateur musicians stem from every field of work, and their zeal has no relationship to their age or previous condition of servitude. Once they have made music their avocation, they are as devoted as the young neophyte about to take orders in the Church.

Anyone and everyone probably knows amateur musicians and meets up with them in home, church, club, or circle of intimates. Everyone, I am sure, could call the roll of delightful personages who give every moment of their spare time to music.

I know a distinguished New York lawyer who, at the age of sixty, began to study the oboe. As a youngster he had played the violin and had been in his college orchestra forty years before. But he found that the violin required supple fingers and agility he could no longer muster, and he could not hold his own in an amateur orchestra. He said quite equably that he expected to give the oboe two years of intensive study and he felt confident that he could then take his place in an amateur orchestra. "There aren't many oboes around, are there?" he said. I asked him how his family liked his oboe practice, and he grimaced. "They don't," he said, "especially when the fool reeds get out of control and I hit a note an octave or two higher than the one I think I am playing."

Russell B. Kingman, president of a factory in New Jersey, is an amateur cellist, perhaps *the* amateur cellist of America. His good friend is Pablo Casals, the greatest cellist of our time, and whenever Kingman went to Europe he would spend as much time as he could with Casals. As an official of the United States Lawn Tennis Association, he once sat in a box at Wimbledon with the King and Queen of England. When he returned to America he attended a luncheon of the United States Lawn Tennis Association and was asked to tell what was the most thrilling moment he had had in Europe. Everyone expected Kingman to say his visit with royalty. But he singled out a day spent with Casals.

Some of Kingman's experiences are remarkable even for the magnificent breed of amateurs. He was an extraordinarily good cellist and had even worked up a fairly extensive solo repertory under the guidance of his teacher, Leo Schultz, first cellist of the New York Philharmonic for many years. Since he had a sales job, he realized that traveling would impair his cello playing. He took a dummy instrument with him wherever he went so that he could practice soundlessly. He also took his cello.

Kingman came close to abandoning his amateur status. If we were to be as strict as the moguls of amateur tennis, we should probably have to bar him from this chapter. But amateurs who have tasted the tempting apple of some slight monetary return from their music, but who have in the end remained honest amateurs, claim and deserve indulgence. During his travels Kingman sent circulars to the women's clubs all over the United States and a letter saying that he was passing through their vicinity and would be able to give them a special price of fifty dollars for a program if they could supply an accompanist. Presently his musical engagements brought him more income than his business. He would go from town to town transacting his affairs during the day and giving concerts at night. Only once in all his flirting with the professional side of music did a business acquaintance find him out. A buyer in a department store happened to go—or was the poor fellow dragged?—to a concert at which Kingman played. The buyer was bewildered; couldn't figure Kingman out.

Kingman's essential amateurism prevailed. Tempted though he was to give up business for music, he held firm. His zest for music, of course, increased. He collected ancient instruments. He was the driving force behind the founding of a good local orchestra in Mont-clair and the Oranges in New Jersey, occupying the cello solo desk himself. He spoke with firmness about this amateur-professional dividing line. "Some of the amateurs are better than some of the professionals. The word professional in music is a misnomer. A man can be a professional and play jazz in a café, yet the player who has perfected his work by painstaking study is termed a mere amateur."

Look at the occupations of other amateur musicians. In the Vermont State Symphony Orchestra there was a bull-fiddle player who was a lawyer; a tuba player whose trade was paper hanging; a barber who played first trombone; a percussion player who drove a beer truck between Rutland and Boston; two brass players who were mail carriers; a second violinist who was a dirt farmer; female instrumentalists who were housewives, teachers, stenographers, and nurses. These amateurs played major symphonies, tone poems, and intricate modern works. This orchestra travels, merely for re-hearsals, up to seventy-five miles one way. Nor are these Vermont-ers unique. I have heard of comparable zeal in Arkansas and North Carolina, where some players travel from twenty different com-munities, one or two up to two hundred miles. Probably they could be duplicated in other parts of the Union.

Look at a big city outfit like the Oratorio Society of New York. This is a chorus of more than two hundred, which makes profes-sional appearances several times a season, but only the conductor and the soloists and, occasionally, assistant conductors are profes-sionals. The singers are amateurs, undefiled. Though they receive no money for their work, they attend fifty rehearsals a season, and they get more kick out of singing Bach's B-minor Mass than they do watching a world's series between the Yankees and the Cardi-nals. A survey of the members disclosed these occupations: thirty-six held secretarial positions; twenty-nine were schoolteachers; twenty-six were housewives; four were librarians; one was a dieti-tian; six were bankers; two were stockbrokers; one was an intern in medicine; two were carpenters; three were writers; three were artists; two were pianists (amateur); one was an archeologist; another was a traffic superintendent; four were interior decorators; one was a chemical engineer; four were chemists; there were also a dancer, a cement tester, a doctor, two nurses, two insurance men, two certified public accountants, a stone engraver, two architects, an actor, an allergy technician, a printer, a mechanical drafting supervisor, a dealer in precious stones, several social workers, two advertising executives, two bank clerks, and a dress designer. Was it good gray Walt who sang the song of occupations?

Is it only New York's amateur groups that can sing such a song of occupations? In an orchestra in Albuquerque, N. M., the conductor was William M. Kunkle, a member of the fine-arts department of the University of New Mexico. Like everyone else in the orchestra, he served without pay. The principal of the second violin section was a railroad engineer, the first French horn and the first trumpet were schoolteachers, and one of the cellists was a former New York lawyer.

In state after state we can find amateur ensembles refreshingly American in variety and gusto. In a town in West Virginia, an orchestra was started some years ago with nineteen people. It grew to more than fifty. The concertmaster was a talented little girl who held the job for years, during which she grew up, married, and bore a daughter. She was away from the orchestra only seven months while having her baby and then she came to rehearsals wheeling the baby carriage, with the violin case in the carriage beside the infant. Among the players were a soda fountain attendant, a steelworker, a glass-pane executive, an accountant, salespeople, farmers, clerks, bookkeepers, auditors, mill workers, insurance salesmen, newspaper people, small-business men, housewives and students, sign painters, and men on relief. The people in this orchestra typified democracy in action. They were representative of their community even as their community was representative of America.

Look at the faith and enthusiasm that put amateur performances of grand opera upon a stage in Raleigh, N. C. The singers were home trained—clerks and stenographers, postal employees, housewives, and students. The venture was homespun and indigenous, down to the laborious copying of the score and the gesturing of the heroine. Few in the audience had ever seen grand opera before, and even fewer of the singers. The conductor was an accountant. In a production of *Trovatore,* the tenor was a chap who read electric meters by day, the Leonore was a stenographer, the Count di Luna sold electric appliances from door to door, and the Azucena was the wife of a local capitalist.

The resourcefulness of amateurs in putting on local stage productions is axiomatic. Note how this North Carolina troupe prepared its costumes. They were designed and water-colored by an artist member of the group, and the sewing was done in the homes of the singers. To save money, the material was composed of bolt ends bought directly from adjacent textile mills. The wooden swords were turned out on a lathe by a singing carpenter. Coats of mail were fabricated from sheets of metallic scouring cloths bought at the ten-cent store.

Physicians seem to belong to the most ardent branch of the amateur musicians. I don't know why. Possibly it is because their work with the sick and the maimed induces them to seek forgetfulness, and music is better for them than pills for their patients. In any case, Manhattan and Brooklyn have doctors' orchestras of their own. Akron, Ohio, maintained such an ensemble for sixteen years until the war, when thirty per cent of its members went into the army and navy medical corps. For all we know, doctors may have classified themselves into ensembles made up of the specialties. If so, it might be entertaining to meet up someday with a psychiatrists' orchestra.

Amateur orchestras come into existence in singular ways. There were two New York amateurs who wanted to belong to an orchestra and had difficulty in finding the right one. They placed an advertisement in the Public Notice column of *The New York Times,* inviting others to join them in forming an orchestra. From one insertion they received enough replies to organize their cherished ensemble—and a respectable one it was, too—and within a year of the appearance of the notice they were giving concerts before an audience of friends and relatives.

Probably the most fanatical amateurs are the men and women who play in trios, quartets, and quintets. Some of them also double in orchestras, but their true passion is chamber music. They regard themselves as the elect among amateurs. There is no nonsense about their music. They keep in touch with three or four sets of players so that they may have quartets nearly every evening of the week. They have located their homes so as to be within walking distance of each other. They have changed the hours of their jobs and even the jobs themselves. No sacrifice—hardly any sacrifice—is too great for the inveterate quartet player. One man gave away his collection of records because he figured he would much rather play the music himself.

Have you ever sat in on one of these amateur sessions? The players arrive with their instruments so soon after dinner that they have scarcely had time to wipe the crumbs away from their lips. After the sketchiest exchange of small talk, the instruments come out, the stands are set up, the music is lovingly examined, and for a minute or two there may be some discussion as to the choice or order of works to be tackled that evening. An acid touch sometimes creeps into the conversation here, but the musicians do not stand on their opinions. The quartet player gives in quickly to the strongest-minded. He will play almost anything as long as he is permitted to play. The wives, if they have no movie to tempt them, sit on the side lines, chatting. If their conversation does not become intrusive, the players pay no attention to them. As soon as one quartet is played, another is hauled out and placed on the stands. The only pauses are to argue points of interpretation.

In the happiest amateur quartets there is always one musician who, because of his greater experience, is looked upon as a guiding spirit. After some moments of discussion, he gives his opinion on the moot point and the others go along. Stormy are the sessions where each musician fancies himself the most perceptive. More likely than not, such quartets do not function year in and year out. The players realign themselves with companions more to their taste, for bickering is not the stuff that the heaven of amateur quartet players is made of.

The saddest moments in the lives of these quartet players occur when, for reasons of illness or inescapable obligations of business or domesticity, a member of the quartet cannot appear, and his distraught comrades must hunt for a substitute. Until they find one they are despondent, their digestion goes bad, their work at the office sags, and their family life degenerates.

There are some amateurs who can share the work with their comrades. In such cases, and on stated evenings, extras are invited, and the make-up of the performing unit shifts, like a football team rich in substitutes. These are the more sociable amateurs who are willing to live and let live.

Amateurs react to professionals in various ways. Faced with an authentic celebrity, some are awed and tongue-tied. When they find voice, they mumble some inane remarks and then spend the evening in silent adoration. This is especially true of the love of an amateur for the great virtuosos of his instrument. A fiddler may give up an evening of quartet playing to hear a concert by Heifetz, Kreisler, or the Budapest Quartet; a cellist may sacrifice his comrades on the altar of Casals or Piatigorsky. But if it is a choice between making their own music and a concert by someone other than their divinities, it is hands down that their own music will win.

Other amateurs are the reverse of diffident. The minute they meet a professional they swing to the attack. They drag out their scores, they discuss editing, fingering, arranging; they launch on a dissertation of critical values. Their curiosity and their questions are endless. They will talk for hours about music. Eventually the professional leaves, his head bloody and his ears bent.

The renaissance of the recorder has been like manna from heaven to the hesitant who toyed with the idea of becoming amateur musicians, but who felt that they were too old or too busy to master a new technique. The recorder is one of the rudimentary instruments,

predecessor to the flute. It was revived by a group of British enthu-
siasts, and the vogue has spread to this country. One store which
had sold half a dozen recorders to antiquarians suddenly was
swamped with orders and at the peak was selling 4000 instruments
a year.

The nice thing about the recorder is that it takes no more than a
few hours to learn to play a simple tune. Quartets have been
formed, using four different sizes of the instrument. You will find
families playing in recorder quartets, and there have been chamber
orchestras made up entirely of recorders.

The sound of the recorder is all right if you don't have to live
with it. It is impecunious in overtones, but penetrating and persistent. There is certainly no harm in playing the thing, and there
may be advantage, for the recorder offers a simple medium for
learning elementary score reading and ensemble playing. Want to
play it at home? Fine, so long as the neighbors don't complain. But
in public places? Please, no.

While thousands of choruses in these United States thrive even
more lustily than the amateur orchestras, there have not been many
small chamber ensembles devoted to song, with madrigals, motets,
and other part songs read through of an evening for pleasure. However, when the English Singers, led by that sensitive and learned
musician, Cuthbert Kelly, toured the country and charmed it with a
vast repertory of old and new songs for an ensemble of six singers,
they stimulated the formation of amateur groups. Mr. Kelly became
a father confessor to these ventures. People from all over the land,
as they had in England, wrote him for advice and information.

Some of these small singing units probably still exist. If the dis-
appearance of the English Singers from the American scene dis-
couraged them, it may be that troupes like the Trapp Family, the
American Ballad Singers, and the Madrigalists will awaken a new
generation to the joys of raising one's voice in song. That is, the
song for an intimate group. It would not be fair to say that Americans are indifferent to the pleasures of amateur singing. You have
but to look around you and hear the glee clubs, choirs, and choruses

in schools, factories, white-collar occupations, and unions to know that our vocal amateurs are legion—and long may they thrive!

Many of the amateurs are gifted enough to assume the role of virtuoso soloists. One of the most eminent of amateur musicians is Major John A. Warner, New York State Superintendent of Police, and son-in-law of Alfred E. Smith, Governor of New York for many years. Major Warner could not spare much time for his piano playing, but occasionally appeared with a local orchestra. It was a chore —as well as fun—to play in public. He would have to rise early to practice before going to the office, and his wife would turn down all social engagements so that he might resume practicing in the evening. His eminent father-in-law, who would travel fair distances to hear Warner appear as piano soloist, made no secret of his preference of *The Sidewalks of New York* to Beethoven. Summing up what must be the feeling of thousands of innocent bystanders on amateur musicians, he once said to Warner, after a performance, "John, I don't know how you do it—or why."

12

ANY HOPE FOR OPERA?

The Metropolitan—Radames the Hero—The Prompter—Maestro Salmaggi—The New Opera Company—Nine O'Clock Opera Company—American Operas—Opera in English.

THE METROPOLITAN OPERA is not the only opera company in America. It would not and should not want to be. Nor is the species of opera that the Metropolitan stands for all we have or should have. There are stirrings on many sides. Companies are being founded on less glamorous names and budgets. Operas are being written with an eye to other stages and a different public, and they are being produced with an awareness of the changes and advances in stage technique.

However, the Metropolitan and the traditions it pursues and by which it is pursued still cast a long shadow. If anything, the shadow has grown longer in recent years, as the Metropolitan has gone out on the radio and has become familiar to the ears of millions who have hitherto taken it strictly on faith from newspapers, magazines, and books.

There are reasons why the Metropolitan has dominated the field. Under its roof are gathered the best-publicized names in opera, and these names join in performances that are often of a high order. The Metropolitan can put on a good show, though the old house and its management have been abused roundly through the years. When a fine cast is assembled under the leadership of a great conductor, you get an extraordinary *Don Giovanni, Tristan und Isolde,* or *Aïda.* You can still encounter great singing actors at the Metropolitan, like the bassos, Salvatore Baccaloni and Alexander Kipnis, or the lyric soprano, Lotte Lehmann, or the baritone, Lawrence Tibbett, or the contralto, Kerstin Thorborg. You can still encounter voices of the first order, like the baritones of John Charles Thomas and Leonard Warren, the contralto of Bruna Castagna, the sopranos of Astrid Varnay and Grace Moore and Helen Traubel, the tenor of Lauritz Melchior, and the bass of Ezio Pinza, and not so long ago you could have heard the magnificent voice of Kirsten Flagstad.

Of course, some of the performances at the Metropolitan are stodgy, routine, and slapped together like a quick supper out of cans. Of course, prices have been too high and some seats are located so that only a contortionist would be happy in them all evening. Of course, the Metropolitan's forte is not the new or experimental, and when it tries something radical, it is likely to end up by being merely ponderous. You can say these things and more against the seemingly complacent house that has lorded it over American opera for sixty years. And yet it has given opera steadily through the years. It has conformed to a tradition of grand opera. It continues to give a good many of the works that are as much a part of the operatic literature as are Shakespeare, Ibsen, and Shaw of the theater without music. It would be an unhappy museum that did not have its Millais, Luini, and Boucher, besides its Rubens, Rembrandt, Titian, and Renoir. And the Metropolitan, with its Wagner, Verdi, Mozart, Gounod, and Puccini, is like a catholic museum where the second- and third-rate rub shoulders with the authentic first-rate.

We would not cherish the Metropolitan as we do if it were not for the genial anachronisms of some of its procedures and the delightful aberrations of some of its leading lights. The Metropolitan owes us the tidbits that warm our hearts and cheer our depressed moments. That seems to have been one of its functions. If it gave only great performances and if its people were constantly discreet and temperate, this would be a duller world.

The Metropolitan Opera is a theater where the conventions of opera are maintained on a grand scale. The supersimplified heroes are impersonated in just that way. Gestures are ample, and voices opulent. There has been a tendency in recent years to cut down on the amplitude of gesture, and to make the voice respond to musical logic rather than to project it with the volume required to be over-powering in a huge auditorium. But though there are an increasing number of artists in the house, they have not replaced all the ranting egocentrics who act and sing as if every character were the same, or, in other words, themselves with or without caricature.

Would we be happy with a company staffed with artists only? What would become of a chap like Radames, the operatic hero par excellence, of whom Ernest Newman wrote in the London Sunday *Times*, "He is all hero, and Italian hero, from beginning to end, from the moment when his great soul is fired by the ambition to become commander-in-chief to that last pathetic moment when, realizing that even his 'strong arms,' as he describes them, cannot move the fatal stone that closes the vault, he resigns himself to a sublime operatic death in G flat major." Newman speaks of him as "the traditional Italian lyrical hero," and he is that, but he is also the traditional operatic hero. "On public ceremonial occasions he is the operatic warrior incarnate," Newman remarks, "brave to the uttermost limit of the high B flat, terrible as a Wolf of Tuscany, a speech-making, chest-making, attitude-striking simpleton, a sort of Mussolini *avant la lettre*." Newman ends his tribute with the sad prediction that "we shall not see his peer again in opera until some librettist and composer show us an Isolationist Senator charging the armored hosts of Germany at the head of five hundred picked Gallup surveys, and ending the long-drawn war in no more time than it takes to sound a gallant trumpet fanfare in the orchestra."

But we shall always have Radames and his tribe. The new devotion to restraint in acting and singing will not rob us of the grandiloquent performers. Nature will see to that, even though the Metropolitan may not be looking for them any longer. The Metropolitan, in fact, has developed other ideas since Edward Johnson became general manager. Note the six classifications under which young singers taking part in the Opera Auditions of the Air are judged:

voice, theater, looks and appearance, musicianship, language, and
extent of repertory. Most of the prizewinning singers are young—
the women in their middle twenties, the men in their early thirties.
The quality they lack most is assurance, but their personalities
emerge as they acquire it. The gesticulating ham is not wanted.
Observe, however, that the first requirement is voice. Whether the
Metropolitan finds its singers through radio competitions or other
methods, it must find notable voices. If the voice is beautiful, other
factors will be overlooked. We shall always have the kind of
Radames who will not be constrained in the presence of operatic
heroism.

That type of singer always carries on as if he has had no rehearsal with the other members of the company and wouldn't learn
from them if he had. The charge is often made, for this reason, that
the Metropolitan puts on shows without practicing them at all. But
the company tries to rehearse each opera, no matter how familiar
and routined its cast, at least once each season. The principals, as
well as the secondary singers, are asked to attend. Still, the management is not inconsolable if, in a work like *Die Walküre*, Lehmann
or Melchior is not present. Singers of this stature are so sure of their
stuff that they can skip a rehearsal without harm. If they are absent, young singers have the chance to rehearse a whole opera with
a cast that includes veterans, and the experience is invaluable.

Rehearsals, of course, do not cover every eventuality. If they did,
the opera would seldom be in trouble. There are always unforeseen
headaches. One evening a performance of *Don Giovanni* began before Ettore Panizza, the conductor, discovered that he had on his
desk the piano, not the conductor's, score. The cuts agreed on between the conductor and the Don Giovanni, Ezio Pinza, were not
marked in the piano score. It was a troublesome evening for the
basso and the maestro, with each trying to read the other's mind and
with quick thinking needed to save arias and scenes from coming
to grief.

You may not like the prompter who is, on occasion, in better
voice than the singers. He can be heard many rows back, and on the

radio he is as insistent as an announcer with an advertising plug. If the opera is capable of giving an illusion, the prompter seems to do his best to dispel it. But the singers treasure him, for they know his value. In *Don Giovanni,* there is a concerted passage for seven singers. A young American, making his first appearance in the opera, kept entering a measure too soon during the rehearsal. The prompter did not forget this little weakness. At every performance, the prompter, busily giving cues to six other singers in a rapid-fire scene, always remembered to hold up his hand as a cautioning gesture to the young singer to wait another measure.

The lavish literalness of some Metropolitan productions is a recurrent delight to its unquestioning and uncritical patrons and a source of innocent merriment to its belittlers. The spacious, solid sets, the plushy props and hangings, and the gaudy costumes have become quintessentially Metropolitan. Who but the Metropolitan would put realistic iron shoes on wooden operatic horses? In a scene of *The Daughter of the Regiment,* Baccaloni as Sergeant Sulpice patted a wooden horse standing in the stall, and the horse responded with a kick. Once the stage hand managing the kick was too fast, and the basso was rewarded with a long, jagged cut across his hand from a nail in the real horseshoe.

The attachment to lavish *décor* has precipitated serious difficulties. When the Metropolitan decided to put on Gian-Carlo Menotti's *The Island God,* a designer was engaged to plan the sets and, with the approval of the management, worked out an impressive scene with a huge temple dominating the stage. The designer was paid $1000 for his work, and then someone discovered that the scene with its immense solid temple could not be dismantled quickly enough. Since this was a one-act opera, the temple would have to be set up or dismantled in the course of a short intermission. Faced with this problem, the Metropolitan decided to cancel the *première* entirely. The composer was horrified. He had worked day and night to complete his orchestration in time for rehearsals. His publisher, the house of Ricordi, did not take kindly to this decision either. The Metropolitan was forced to reconsider, it sadly hired another designer to make fresh sets at new expense, and the opera was produced.

The Metropolitan and its people are not the only operatic folk who adhere to the traditions of another day. Chicago and San Francisco have companies that produce opera along the lines that the Metropolitan affects, and they too have their measure of fine performances and their share of the old-fashioned and ludicrous. In a lower-priced vein but on the same general level of tradition is a company like the San Carlo, which has been touring across America for more than twenty-five years under the knowing management of Fortune Gallo. The singers in this company are less illustrious, but their routine is similar. The orchestra is much smaller than the Metropolitan's and there is one conductor instead of the half dozen at the New York theater. But the Radameslike grandiloquence is carefully cultivated, and the customers adore it, even if it is not quite so polished or sumptuous.

If you want to see traditional opera in its baldest form, as it was undoubtedly practiced for many decades in the provinces of Italy, look in on the performances presented by Alfredo Salmaggi, who likes to be called maestro. He wears his hair long and flowing and affects a black string tie in the style of the maestros of old. Salmaggi's productions are in a class by themselves, whether he gives them in New York, Brooklyn, Randall's Island, or wherever he can assemble a company and an audience. His Brooklyn season in recent years has been the apotheosis of Salmaggi opera. At each performance he goes out on the stage to talk to the audience. He reminds his customers that they must keep coming if they want him to stay in business, because nowadays the singers have a union and must be paid. He appeals to the balconies, "Can you get better opera than this for thirty-five cents?" and they thunder, "No, maestro!" Continuing the catechism, he asks, "Have you ever seen anything better at the Metropolitan?" and they intone, "No, maestro!" Once he promised them a ten-year-old girl in a debut as Gilda in *Rigoletto,* and when she did not appear, they began to shout for her. Another time, he undertook *Tannhäuser,* quarreled

with the lady who was to sing Venus, at curtain time, and gave the
opera without a Venus. He has brought elephants on the stage, since
that is in the tradition of grand opera. The style is grand, even if
the sets and costumes are seedy. Salmaggi has capitalized on everything. Once he told his followers about his son who had been drafted
into the United States army and he read them snatches from his letters, whereupon communicative customers began to yell bits of information about their own sons in the army and navy.

Do you know of any audience that has been more thoroughly in
rapport with its entertainers, except perhaps the crowds that went
to the burlesque houses or the fanatics who live and die with the
Brooklyn Dodgers? Salmaggi's public knows its opera, too. Once a
violent dispute broke out between two customers in the gallery.
The party of the first part was singing along with the singers. That
irritated his neighbor, the party of the second part, who shushed.
The party of the first part subsided for a while, but presently began
to sing again. The neighbor demanded, "Why do you sing?" The
gallery singer replied, "Because I know the music." Half a dozen
voices in the vicinity cried out—all this while the show was going
on—"Shut up! So do we!"

There are a place and an immense audience for opera in the old
tradition. But there are also room and an audience for a new approach—for opera that is streamlined and made credible for sophisticated audiences. The New Opera Company, organized by Mrs.
Lytle Hull and a group of her friends, has been giving opera on
Broadway with young and personable singers in productions that
have been stripped of some of the fancy, empty trimmings. The
Philadelphia Opera Company has tackled the problem along similar
lines but without benefit of a $150,000 budget. Under the artistic
leadership of the American conductor, Sylvan Levin, and a youthful business manager, C. David Hocker, this company has plunged
into opera on a modest basis and emerged with more than a modest
success. Levin has gathered around him a permanent company of
young singers who are willing to work interchangeably at major and
minor roles. He has hammered out productions that are smooth,

modern, and believable. He has given the operas mostly in English, obtaining fresh translations and making some of them himself. He has put on new and neglected operas as well as some of the standard repertory works. In two seasons the company had established itself and could make a bid for national recognition, signing up for a tour of fifty American cities.

A cheer for the Nine O'Clock Opera Company is also in order. A group of young singers, fresh from the Juilliard School of Music, worked out a lively production of Mozart's *The Marriage of Figaro*. They gave it with a minimum of scenery. They dispensed with chorus and ballet, employing a narrator to bridge the places that require a large ensemble. They employed two pianos instead of an orchestra. Because the production had cohesion and sprightliness and the young Americans could sing, the show scored a hit in New York and went on to delight audiences all over the nation.

A youthful ensemble put on Gluck's *Iphigenia in Tauris* at Marot Junior College, in Thompson, Connecticut. The head of the music department of the school decided that he wished to stage the work. He organized a chorus of young women at the college and reinforced it with young men from near-by schools and with volunteers from local choirs. He recruited an orchestra of young players and obtained the collaboration of several professional singers for leading roles. Communities in the neighborhood heard of the production and invited the performers to repeat it in their local halls.

Opera need not be high-brow or elaborate. Marc Blitzstein was able to put on his operas, *The Cradle Will Rock* and *No for an Answer*, both of them original in conception and content, filled with driving power and engaging freshness, without much scenery or costumes. There was no charge for instrumentalists, since Blitzstein played the piano himself. Not that he conceived his works for one instrument, but because funds were insufficient, this had to do.

American opera, of course, is where you find it. Even if it is not produced at the Metropolitan with a gold-plated cast and with sets and costumes that cost $25,000, it may be authentic opera. Jerome Kern's *Show Boat* was opera, though it had its birth on Broadway.

Edna Ferber, author of the novel on which it is based, confided that she expects it to be produced at the Metropolitan someday. The Metropolitan could do worse. Gershwin's *Porgy and Bess,* Virgil Thomson's *Four Saints in Three Acts,* Aaron Copland's *The Second Hurricane* are other worth-while lyrical works that saw the light of night outside the hallowed walls of the Metropolitan.

Who shall say where musical theater ends and opera begins? It seems to me that *Of Thee I Sing* has the elements of opera. And a work like *Oklahoma!* is an American opera. Certainly it is as American as an imaginative Tin Pan Alley, even if hardly authentic Midwest. The singers, it is true, sing set numbers; for the rest they talk. But is it necessary that the story be developed in recitative to make an opera of a dramatic piece? Mozart and Beethoven did not think so; they wrote in alternating speech and song in *The Magic Flute* and *Fidelio.*

We need in American opera more youth, more adventure, more willingness to forget the strict rules of the form and the traditions of another school, time, and world. By all means, let us have opulent Verdi and slick Puccini and resounding Wagner and elegant Mozart, done to a turn by great singing artists. But let us not take for granted that this kind of opera is the form which American works must follow. Nor is it essential that opera should cost five and seven dollars a ticket to be regarded as grand.

Composers must be encouraged to write operas for modest groups. There is a movement of considerable proportion under way to do just that. The League of Composers has commissioned several operas, and the commissions mean that productions are assured when the works are completed. Ernst Bacon's *A Tree on the Plains,* thus commissioned, was done at Converse College in North Carolina. Randall Thompson's setting of Kipling's *The Butterfly That Stamped,* also commissioned in this way, was performed over a nation-wide network of the Columbia Broadcasting System. The radio companies have commissioned operas for use over the air. Menotti wrote *The Old Maid and the Thief* on order for the National Broadcasting Company. Serge Koussevitzky, through the

Koussevitzky Music Foundation, which he founded as a memorial to his wife, ordered operas by Samuel Barber and Benjamin Britten, to be produced by the opera-dramatics division of the Berkshire Music Center at Tanglewood in the Berkshires.

If only a portion of the works that have been and are being written have the theatrical and musical quality to attract an audience, we shall soon have a fair repertory of American operas. They will be designed largely for production on a modest scale, perhaps by amateur groups and in the colleges. But there will be nothing against having the professional companies produce them, if they like. In any case, they might be, as Douglas Moore—who has himself written *White Wings, The Devil and Daniel Webster,* and *The Fall of the City,* using in order themes by Philip Barry, Stephen Vincent Benét, and Archibald MacLeish—has said, "the nucleus of a new type of opera company, functioning in the small theater and playing to a more general audience than the conservative opera-house public."

The conservative theater like the Metropolitan has not commissioned many American operas in its time. Its most recent effort was fraught with irritants and counterirritants for all concerned. The Metropolitan persuaded the Carnegie Foundation to grant $5000 for the commissioning of an opera. Half was to go to the composer and half to the librettist. The two were to frequent the theater, get the feel of the stage and its problems, and be free to consult with experts in the company, Thus far, an excellent approach. Officials of the company studied a list of American composers and chose Samuel Barber. He was delighted to hear that the choice had fallen upon him, but he discovered that Christopher La Farge had been invited to write the libretto. Barber contended that though La Farge might write an excellent libretto, a composer should be allowed to work with any colleague he preferred. Barber finally withdrew. Another American composer, William Schuman, was offered the commission, and he accepted.

Some composers spend many months searching for a librettist. Werner Josten obtained permission from Irving Stone to do an operatic treatment of *Lust for Life*, the story of Vincent van Gogh. He approached a number of playwrights. Some were too busy. One was on the verge of agreeing but decided that the time consumed in writing the libretto might be used in doing a play, which might bring in some real money. The trouble with opera is that it is seldom remunerative for the authors. Moreover, the librettist, unless he happens to be a W. S. Gilbert, is rarely noticed. He must be the servant of the composer, and a writer with real talent for the theater is not likely to relish playing second fiddle.

Our own repertory will be, naturally, in English. I also favor having most, if not all, the operas of the traditional repertory sung in English. At least three productions by three different companies in recent seasons have high-lighted the validity of the contention that if opera were sung in English, it might have a chance with people now indifferent. Of course, if you hold that people now indifferent to opera have achieved a blessed state, you also have a point.

The Metropolitan did *The Magic Flute* by Mozart in English. Even though the singers sported a variety of accents, thick and thin, the humor of the story came across. The audience had a better time than it has had in many seasons. Comedy is a fragile thing, and it must be in the language of the audience if it is to make its best impression.

Debussy's *Pelléas et Mélisande* was sung in an English translation by the Philadelphia Opera Company. In the Philadelphia audience were many people who had never heard the score and for whom it should have been, by all precedent, a remote and difficult world. But text and story were comprehensible, and it was heartening to see how the audience was drawn to the drama. People sat forward and listened intently. They responded to the opera, as the subtle understatement of the drama and the evocative web of Debussy's music added up to tension and excitement in the theater.

Tchaikovsky's *Pique Dame* was done in English by the New Opera Company. The story is an old-fashioned melodrama with crude psychological trimmings; even uncritical fiction readers would not swallow it too easily. But it is a melodrama; it has action;

it moves from crisis to crisis. Even in a trite English translation, the story caught and held the audience.

When the libretto is understandable, the task of the composer is easier. The composer, of course, can dominate by the power of his genius. If he is great enough, his music may grip the listener without reference to story or action. But opera is theater, and even the operas we scoff at have their moments of sound theater. How is anyone who is not a linguist to get the full theatrical value of an opera sung in a foreign language?

It has been argued that English translations would make clear how ludicrous are the stories and situations of some of the operas. Agreed. Let them. If an opera is ludicrous, let us find out the truth in all its nakedness, and if we are adult and sophisticated enough to have none of it, let us laugh it off the stage. Would Wagner's long, philosophical dissertations become a bore and an irritation in English? It were better so. His music is puissant enough to triumph over his rhetoric. It would do the Wagner worshipers no harm to discover that their hero often talked rot, not profound philosophy.

I am not a fanatic about translations. Some operas present insuperable problems. Verdi's *Macbeth* is a taut, dramatic piece, and it would be more powerful in English to an American audience. But Shakespeare is here translated into Italian, and if the Italian were translated back into English to fit the musical line, it would not be the Shakespearean diction. *Falstaff* and *Otello* would pose the same difficulties. People know Shakespeare too well to accept dilutions.

In defense of the composers, often dismissed as adolescent in their feeling for drama, it must be emphasized that most of them have not been the fuzzy creatures that legend makes them out to be. The best composers for the theater have possessed better dramatic instincts than some dramatists. Wagner knew how to end an act with a thundering climax, even if he took a long time arriving at it. Verdi had a sure eye for what was effective in the theater of his time. He was bedeviled by poor librettists and he fought with them to simplify and tighten their stories. One of his best librettos, for *Macbeth,* was drawn in its first draft by the composer himself. Mozart

knew a good dramatic theme when he saw one, and, if he had any
choice, shied away from mediocre stuff.

If English translations would bring more people to the music of
these men, they would be well worth it. Far better to have a new
audience make the acquaintance of Mozart's operas than to worry
about the fine detail and perception with which he set a language
and its idiom to music.

As a practical matter, it would be helpful if standard translations
could be adopted for the major works of the repertory. The Committee for Opera in America conducted a survey of translations and
found that in eight productions of Smetana's *The Bartered Bride*,
six different translations were used; in six productions of *Carmen*,
three translations; in four productions of *Così fan tutte*, three
translations; in three productions of *L'Heure espagnole*, three
translations. Singers who have to work in different productions of
the same opera have to master different texts.

The very form of grand opera has always raised problems for
some people. They say, "Why can't those fools on the stage say
what's on their minds instead of bawling endlessly?" Or they ask,
"How does it happen that four people, who happen to be a soprano,
contralto, tenor, and baritone, think of the identical tune at the
same moment to make a rousing quartet?" Well, how does the
chorus in a musical comedy happen to think of the same hit tune at
the same time? We accept conventional patterns for our day-to-day
life, not to speak of our art forms. An art is entitled to its license.
The legitimate questions are: Does it succeed within its frame-
work? Does it convey an emotion? Does it teach, exalt, amuse, or
enrich us? If opera doesn't do these things for some people, they
have the democratic right to keep away from it, as those who are
fond of it have the right to support it.

13

ORCHESTRAS—AMERICAN
SPECIALTY

---

*Two Orchestras in One—The New York Philharmonic—The Mexican Way—Radio
Orchestras—Upkeep of an Orchestra—Endowments—Giving the Public a Voice.*

IF THERE IS any form of musical organization in which this country
has taken over the leadership, it is the symphony orchestra. America
has more symphonic ensembles—professional, amateur, and mixed
—than any other country in history. From exalted and world-
famous institutions like the New York Philharmonic-Symphony,
Boston, Philadelphia, Chicago, and NBC Orchestras down to the
modest ensembles in colleges, high schools, lodges, unions,
Y.M.C.A.'s, which are precious to their members and neighbors,
their number runs into the thousands.

Standards of performance are high. Our best orchestras are the
equal of, if not superior to, the world's best. The Boston Symphony
under Koussevitzky, the Philadelphia under Stokowski, and the
New York Philharmonic-Symphony under Toscanini have played
with such all-around excellence that even the glowing warmth of
the Vienna Philharmonic's pre-Hitler glory did not surpass or
match them. Our second-best orchestras, like the Chicago as it was
under Stock, the Cleveland under Leinsdorf, the San Francisco
under Monteux, the Minneapolis under Mitropoulos, the Pittsburgh under Reiner, the Cincinnati under Goossens, the St. Louis
under Golschmann, are not far behind our best in the quality of
their performance, not at all behind them in the liveliness of their
programs, and compare favorably with the finest of other lands.

Even among the minor orchestras, there is an abundance of talented players. If a gifted conductor directs them, they are capable

of giving stunning performances. New York City's WPA Orchestra played brilliantly under the leadership of Beecham and Klemperer. Since we have a vast pool of talented instrumentalists and since conductors are being developed to lead them, our standards should remain high and may go higher. The small local orchestras are reflecting this upward curve in standards. But even where they don't, the ensembles have their excuse for being in the pleasure that the players draw from making music together.

It is the urge to make music together that has prompted the formation of hundreds of symphony orchestras. Another factor is civic pride. A fine musical organization gives prestige to a community. An opera company might bestow as much, if not more prestige, but it is three or four times as expensive to maintain. A symphony orchestra is not only less costly but more accessible. Usually you can start one with local talent. In the past a moderate-sized city had to import players from Europe or the Atlantic seaboard, but today it may discover its first-desk men and women among its own citizens. Occasionally a home-grown conductor can be found to lead the ensemble. Does the community wish to step up the standards of its orchestra? It can go to our leading conservatories for talented instrumentalists. It can find a gifted conductor who will be willing to accept a salary in keeping with the town's ability to pay. Our own conductors are coming along, and in addition, many experienced men who have come to this country to escape oppression abroad are eager to contribute their expert services.

One city may share with another the cost and prestige of an orchestra, if what has happened in the Midwest becomes a precedent. The Kansas City Orchestra, when directed by Karl Kreuger, agreed to give a season of concerts in Wichita. But in Wichita it was known as the Wichita Symphony Orchestra. There was no change in conductor or personnel. It was a felicitous idea, giving the musicians more employment and providing two cities with an orchestra.

Our orchestral tradition has flowered within the past century. America's most venerable professional orchestra, the New York Philharmonic, began as a co-operative in 1842. Before that year symphonic music had been something of a stepchild in New York. There had been professional opera of competence as early as 1825. But the orchestras, such as they were, were amateur. The Euterpean was an amateur orchestra that, during the 1820's and '30's, gave each year a concert and supper at the City Hotel near Trinity Church, with professionals from theater orchestras to augment the ensemble. This orchestra played for a time without a bassoon, because there was no bassoonist in New York. Until the Philharmonic's arrival, there was only one double-bass player in town. Some amateur groups had done without oboes, and at various times flutes and clarinets had been substituted in performances that would not have warmed a composer's heart. Beethoven's "Eroica" was once played by an orchestra of seven instrumentalists!

A group of interested musicians met one evening in 1839 in the Shakespeare, a public house on Park Row, to discuss the formation of a professional orchestra. Other meetings followed. It took until April of 1842 to form a society, for as Thomas Goodwin, who played the viola in the first concerts of the Philharmonic, wrote in his reminiscences: "Considerable difficulty was at first experienced in bringing the best musicians to interest themselves in the enterprise, many looking upon the whole business as chimerical and bound to come to grief; so the meeting for permanent organization was for various reasons again and again postponed."

The organizers of our first professional orchestra were sturdy democrats, and they adopted a democratic constitution. The "professors of music" who belonged were required to pay a twenty-five-dollar initiation fee. Fines were levied for lateness at meetings and for premature departure, and the members were liable to assessments of twenty-five cents a month to cover the expenses of the organization. One article of the bylaws prohibited "all indecorum of the members . . . at all the Society's meetings, viz: smoking, the wearing of hats or caps, violent language, etc."

For twenty-five years the New York Philharmonic was a cooperative, and the men divided the profits each season. At the first concert, moreover, the best-groomed members of the society were selected to act as ushers. They wore white gloves and wands, and escorted friends and relatives and such curious but rare music lovers as were willing to look in on the early concerts to the church-like pews in the hall. The wands of office were not long in use. According to Henry E. Krehbiel, the society's golden-jubilee historian, the wand was ruled out "because of the opportunities for amusement which it afforded to some of the younger attendants whose ebulliency of animal spirits sometimes overcame their sense of decorum." The white gloves were abandoned by the fourth season, which gladdened the hearts of the economical-minded brethren, because there was a saving of $4.75.

Sixty-three players joined in that first concert. They marched in almost like a military unit, and all but the cellists stood throughout the concert, as was the custom of the day. A handful who owned dress clothes wore them; the others had on everyday frock coat, cravat, and tightly fitting trousers. They played the first American performance of Beethoven's Fifth Symphony as well as music from *Fidelio,* Weber's *Oberon,* Rossini's *Armida,* Mozart's *Belmont and Constantia,* an overture by Kalliwoda, and, of all things, a quintet by Hummel, then a notable composer.

The high standard of this and succeeding programs was later a source of wonder to condescending Europeans and Americans. In 1892 Anton Seidl, conductor of the New York Philharmonic, sought a suitable program to commemorate the fiftieth anniversary, and a son of one of the founders suggested repeating the first program. Seidl laughed at the idea, saying the public's taste had advanced in five decades. When he was shown the baptismal program, he observed, somewhat abashed, that it would have compared favorably with any European program of the period.

Indeed it would. Here is the program of a concert played in Vienna on December 1, 1844: Mozart's G minor Symphony; an aria from Donizetti's *Gemma di Vergy,* a concerto for flute by Heindl, a vocal chorus by Gottfried Preyer, and Spohr's *Faust* Overture.

Being a co-operative, the Philharmonic was conducted by various of its members for a number of years. It did not decide on a permanent conductor until 1866, when Carl Bergmann was named to the post. In due time his stipend was set at $1000 a season, and outraged busybodies clamored that this was a fantastic sum to pay a man who conducted an orchestra.

It was not until the twenty-sixth season that a nonmusician was elected president of the society. R. Ogden Doremus, an eminent chemist, who had been an associate member from 1846, took office. He put the men into uniform dress clothes. He invoked the support of the social and fashionable elements of the town, and the orchestra's concerts became Events of the Season.

It may be that the orchestra would not have endured and grown had not the fashionable and moneyed forces fallen into line behind it. But one might wish that the orchestra could have gone on as a co-operative run by musicians without the intercession of the *grande dames* of society and the wealthy men of the community. Society and wealth have dominated the orchestras of the land for a long time, and their influence has not always been wholesome. It must be conceded that some orchestras would have fallen by the wayside, had not this support been forthcoming, especially in the days when radio had not spread a taste for music among millions and when it appealed to a limited number of Americans.

The democratic forms which the founding of the New York Philharmonic took were not typical of the organization of musical institutions in the latter part of the nineteenth and the early decades of the twentieth century. The Metropolitan Opera House was built in 1883 by a syndicate of rich men who wanted boxes where they and their ladies could shine, and since the older group of wealthy citizens had pre-empted the boxes at the Academy of Music on Fourteenth Street, the up-and-coming crowd raised its own opera house way uptown at Broadway and Thirty-ninth Street. The Boston Symphony Orchestra was the creation of one man, Henry Lee Higginson, who supported it lavishly for many years. The New York Symphony, with which the name of Damrosch was long associated, could not have gone on so long as it did without the backing of Harry Harkness Flagler.

In the end, an orchestra lives by the suffrage of its public. If an audience is not secured, even a rich man may have to give up his largess, or he may die and leave the orchestra bereft of support. The Los Angeles Philharmonic Orchestra encountered heavy going for some time after the death of its prime benefactor, William A. Clark.

In recent years it has not devolved entirely upon men of wealth to found orchestras. The drive of young conductors to find orchestras to lead has stimulated the formation of a number of ensembles. Several men have reared orchestras out of the sheer magnetism of their leadership. The most notable example occurred not in the United States but in Mexico, where Carlos Chávez was the catalytic agent of the Symphony Orchestra of Mexico. Beginning from scratch in 1928, he trained his own players. In the summers, while American orchestras were vacationing, he invited several first-desk players occasionally to be guest members of his orchestra. By 1940, when I heard the orchestra at the Palacio Nacional de Bellas Artes in Mexico City, it had become a polished ensemble, ranking with our better orchestras.

It takes a musician of personality and flaming determination, like Chávez, to build an orchestra as he did. But it can be done. It has been done with smaller orchestras in the United States. Without money or influence, young conductors have gathered able young players, rehearsed them thoroughly, and given fine concerts. Some conductors, it is true, have used the money and influence of wives, parents, in-laws, and friends. It does not matter what strings they pull. What does matter is whether they have talent and whether the music they play is worth playing and the audience for which they play cares to hear it. What also matters is that, thanks to their ambition and initiative, orchestras are founded where they are of value.

Occasionally some of these young men—and women—merely come into a big town, engage players from a well-established orchestra, give the ensemble a distinctive name, and pretend that they have organized an orchestra. All they have done is to surround themselves with an experienced group so that they may get notices as conductors. Such orchestras have meaning only to the conductor, not to the community.

The conductor who plunges into the uncertainties and adventures of a small town to found an orchestra is doing a real service to himself and the town. Many such orchestras were founded during the '30's. Many of them also owe their existence to the Federal WPA Project. For the project sought to give work to unemployed musicians. It paid them weekly salaries, skimpy though they were, and the musicians worked in the community orchestras. In due time the citizens of several towns—one of them was Buffalo—took over. The players were put on regular payrolls and became permanent members of a permanent orchestra.

The radio chains have also formed and maintained crack orchestras, the most ambitious being the NBC Symphony Orchestra, which was organized to bring Toscanini back to America. The Columbia Broadcasting System has its own ensemble, and so has Mutual. These orchestras are business propositions. The radio consumes music as an army consumes bully beef. The orchestra, a necessity to the network, functions as a public service.

Though the upkeep of an orchestra is less than that of an opera company, it is not a trifling sum. The expenditures of a first-rank major orchestra run up to $1,000,000 a year. Here is how the Boston Symphony Orchestra estimated its costs for the 1942-43 season: about $600,000 for salaries of conductors, instrumentalists, and administrative staff; about $150,000 for music, soloists, travel, printing, and miscellaneous items; $86,000 to maintain Symphony Hall, including insurance, interest, and taxes. The Boston Symphony is about eighty-four per cent self-supporting—a high percentage, meaning that it plays to capacity or near-capacity audiences at all its concerts. Nevertheless, it needs help to balance its budget. For the 1942-43 season its operating expenses exceeded its income by about $150,000.

The operating deficit of the other first-rank major orchestras is about the same. The second-rank orchestras have deficits of about $50,000, while the most modest professional ensembles may go into the red for only $10,000. The small-town orchestras that have a large nucleus of amateurs, with a sprinkling of professionals at the first-desk positions and a professional conductor, have moderate expenses, and they occasionally meet their expenditures with receipts from their concerts.

Are you thinking of organizing an orchestra in your city? Here is how one town approached the financial problem. Baltimore, grown in size and means during the war boom, decided in 1942 to build a professional orchestra of high standards, and proceeded on this basis. It invited Reginald Stewart, who eventually became conductor of the ensemble, to survey the field. He obtained information from thirty orchestral associations throughout the country, finding that budgets in cities like Minneapolis, Pittsburgh, Cleveland, Cincinnati, Rochester, and San Francisco varied from $200,000 to $400,000.

This is the budget suggested for the Baltimore Symphony Orchestra: salaries for ninety players, a conductor, and soloists for a twenty-week season, $136,000; hall rental, $9600; publicity and advertising, $5500; administration, $14,000; programs, $1000; music rental, $1000; campaign expenses, $5000; miscellaneous expenses, $3500; contingencies, $1500; total expense, $177,100. It was estimated that regular, popular, and children's concerts—a total of twenty-nine concerts—would bring in $59,700 and that there might be other income of $5000, making a total of $64,700 and leaving $112,400 to be raised in other ways.

It was proposed that $62,000 be raised by private subscription, obviously from people of means in the community, and another $50,000 be contributed by the city of Baltimore. The city's subsidy would take the form of an agreement to purchase six popular concerts with tickets priced at thirty-five cents to one dollar and five children's concerts with tickets at twenty-five cents, the net proceeds of these concerts to be retained by the orchestral association.

Baltimore was reminded of San Francisco's unique method of helping its orchestra. The Pacific Coast city collects a half-cent tax specifically for music. With the receipts it buys ten concerts from the San Francisco Symphony Orchestra; these are sold at popular prices, and the orchestra association keeps the net proceeds from the ticket sales.

Most orchestras have to conduct private and public campaigns for funds to meet their deficits. There are no longer orchestras whose losses are covered by one man. In some places a group of men and women undertake the responsibility, and some orchestras have seasonal drives. In Detroit, where the symphony orchestra abandoned —temporarily, we hope—its public concerts in the fall of 1942, the management had put on special concerts with leading lights of jazz, the movies, and the radio to help out. In Philadelphia Kate Smith was once invited to sing at a concert to raise funds for the orchestra.

The major orchestras earn considerable sums toward their deficits through radio performances and making records. The New York Philharmonic-Symphony received a substantial sum, well over $50,000, for its Sunday-afternoon broadcasts over the Columbia network even when it was a sustaining program. Now that the orchestra has a commercial sponsor, the United States Rubber Company, it is on the air fifty-two weeks a year and its radio earnings are well over $100,000. The Philadelphia Orchestra at various times has had commercial sponsors such as the Liggett & Myers Tobacco Company and the Chase National Bank. Where orchestra and conductor are popular, their recordings bring in considerable annual royalties.

I know that the Boston Symphony Orchestra missed its receipts from radio and records when the American Federation of Musicians applied economic sanctions in its effort to organize the orchestra. By threatening that it would pull out all its members if the radio and record companies employed nonunion players, the federation forced the Boston Symphony off the air and out of the recording studios. Income from records was not reduced immediately, for there was a steady sale of what the orchestra had recorded in the past. But the pinch was inevitable. It brought action from the Boston Symphony Orchestra trustees when Ernest B. Dane, president, died in the spring of 1942. Mr. Dane each year had written a check—it went as high as $50,000—to cover the deficit. When he died, there was no one who could or would make similar gifts, and the trustees opened negotiations with James C. Petrillo, president of the Musicians' Union. Koussevitzky had argued, while Mr. Dane was alive, that the orchestra should not have to depend on one man and that it would be better to earn the $50,000 a year via radio and records.

Some of the orchestras have endowment funds, though orchestras and operas have not benefited often from munificent legacies such as those that have been left to the Metropolitan Museum of Art, the large universities, and the medical centers. One of the reasons is that an orchestra is made up of human beings and dispenses an intangible art, factors that do not appeal to some rich men. Another is that orchestra associations have not set their sights for such legacies.

Nevertheless, there have been bequests—their number is increasing—and they have helped to bolster endowment funds. Probably the largest in America was the bequest by Joseph Pulitzer to the New York Philharmonic in November, 1911—$500,000 outright and an additional contingent bequest not in excess of $500,000. The New York Philharmonic received $1,000,000 from the Pulitzer estate. Most of the other bequests to the New York Philharmonic have been small, ranging up to $10,000, although one of $300,000 will accrue at some time in the future.

The other munificent benefactors of the New York orchestra— Clarence H. Mackay and Mrs. Christian R. Holmes—made their gifts while alive. At one time Mrs. Holmes footed the bill of an extra rehearsal for the orchestra every week—a couple of thousands a week, or well over $50,000 for the whole season.

There is a fallacious belief abroad that Henry Lee Higginson, founder of the Boston Symphony Orchestra, bequeathed it a huge sum of money. The orchestra's total endowment fund is $403,000; obviously Higginson did not leave millions to it. The plain fact, as George E. Judd, manager of the orchestra, has written me, is that "Mr. Higginson in a period of thirty-seven years assisted the orchestra to the extent of about $1,000,000. He had expressed the hope that he would endow the orchestra, which unfortunately did not prove to be possible. In other words, apart from his gifts during his establishment and active leadership, the only material gift which the orchestra received from its great benefactor at the time of his death was the library of music—a very important gift, of course."

The Boston Symphony Orchestra has received legacies varying from $1000 to $100,000. The Pension Fund, now in the neighborhood of $200,000, has also received bequests. The other major orchestras have pension funds which have benefited from gifts and bequests, but these contributions do not affect the operating costs of the orchestra.

The Philadelphia Orchestra is blessed with a large endowment fund. For the first nineteen years of its life, a small group of patrons made up the deficit. A campaign for an endowment was begun in 1915, was interrupted by our entrance into the First World War, and was resumed and carried on with vigor after 1919. The first goal was $500,000; then it was raised to $750,000. After the war, the aim was another $1,000,000, and contributors were promised that they would not be bothered any more. The campaign for $1,000,000 took seven years, with interruptions, and during this time Edward Bok guaranteed the annual deficit so that contributions could go to the endowment fund. The annual deficit during this period averaged $60,000; Mr. Bok's assistance during the drive amounted to more than $400,000. The endowment fund, now approximately $1,750,000—probably the largest of any orchestra in the world—was compounded of many small gifts and a lesser number of princely ones—like those of Mr. Bok; his wife, Mrs. Bok, now Mrs. Efrem Zimbalist, who gave in her own right; her father, Cyrus H. K. Curtis; and Alexander Van Rensselaer.

There have been a fair number of legacies since the establishment of the endowment fund in Philadelphia—a recent one was $30,000 —and some of these have been divided between endowment and pension funds.

In New York a step in a helpful direction was taken in memory of Dr. Harlow Brooks, physician and amateur cellist. When he died in 1936, his friends and patients joined in raising a substantial sum to endow the first cello chair of the New York Philharmonic-Symphony Orchestra in the name of Dr. Brooks. The idea should be pursued. Why not endow chairs for other solo instruments? Why not endowments for conductors? And endowments to finance the commissioning, rehearsing, and performing of American compositions?

Even though most of the men of wealth who maintained orchestras did so because they were sufficiently altruistic and fond of music to believe in the value of an orchestra, some were autocrats in the affairs of the organization. It was inevitable. They were accustomed to running their businesses in that fashion. Sometimes the result was good; more often, not. Orchestras were kept under the leadership of conductors without any real gifts because directors in key places insisted on retaining them. Programs were circumscribed because a heavy subsidizer did not like novelty. Incompetent players remained because they had influential support. Soloists of no account were hired because they had social and business connections. Nor do I speak exclusively of the past.

Not all men of wealth have exercised their authority constrainingly, harmfully, or undemocratically. When Marshall Field became president of the New York Philharmonic-Symphony Society, he brought in some democratic ideas. In the days when Clarence H. Mackay was at the head of the society, there was a small executive committee which made virtually all decisions. If a new conductor was to be chosen, the committee canvassed the field, made the choice, and signed the man to a contract. Then the accomplished fact was ratified by the full board. Field suggested that the full board vote on major decisions, such as the naming of conductors. He also insisted on the addition of young men to the board.

Even this reform does not go far enough. Someday perhaps an orchestra board will take the public into its confidence and give it a voice in the affairs of the orchestra. Why not invite the public to have a say in the naming of a conductor? Then, surely, you would avoid the awkward situation that occurred when the New York Philharmonic-Symphony chose Wilhelm Furtwängler as Toscanini's successor only to discover that the New York public was outraged at the choice of a man who had worked for the Nazi government.

I am not under the delusion that letting the public have a voice would sweep away all problems. It might even complicate matters already sufficiently complex. Consider the problem of finding a conductor for an orchestra like the New York Philharmonic-Symphony, with its long and killing schedule. It is now conceded that the job is too big and exacting for one man. The biggest names among the conductors refuse to consider the post for more than a few weeks a season. They feel that it is too difficult, the efforts required of them are too great and the public and press too exigent.

Though the public has no voice in the inner councils of the orchestra, it can make its presence felt. It complains about stodgy programs and it kicks about novelties. One indignant subscriber rushed into the offices of the orchestra after a concert at which a long and, to him, raucous new score had been played. He flung his tickets on the nearest desk and shouted, "You can have them for that kind of music!" There have been complaints about the dress and looks of conductors. There are always protests about the absence of Americans among conductors, and then there are protests against hiring young Americans whenever one is given a chance. Even though the public may have conflicting views, it would not hurt to let such views into the conference room of the trustees. Certainly some boards of trustees could stand improvement.

I am not alone in viewing some trustees with a jaundiced eye. Conductors, players, and subscribers have reacted the same way when they have been privy to the trustees' actions or inactions. One conductor laced into a set of trustees one day with a vengeance. "If I conducted poorly," he cried, "you would fire me. And quite right. But you, you do nothing. You meet and you fight against progressive action. You run short of money, then you can think of nothing to do but cut salaries or appeal to the public. As trustees, you should do something yourselves. Or *you* should be fired!"

Amen!

14

CONCERT FOLKLORE

Concert Manners—A Singing Painter—Song with a Goose—Recorder Recital—Only Albanian Singer in America—Curzon and Paderewski—Cocktail Party in the New York Public Library—How to Make Chimes—Stage Fright—The Society of Timid Souls—Even the Doorman Knows Better.

OUR CONCERTS DO NOT constitute the sum of our musical life, but they are the average American's most frequent contact with it. As one who has heard and observed a rich diversity of concerts and concert givers, I have a little collection of suggestions for the corpus of our musical folklore. Possibly these observations prove that musicians really have peculiar customs and that an aura of delightful unpredictability surrounds them. So be it.

Lest you should think this chapter is aimed at the humble, struggling performer who has to be different to win attention, let us begin with the great and near-great. Have you ever noticed the emotional crises through which some musicians pass as they perform for their public, or at least the crises that seem to find outlet in their facial expressions and bodily movements? I am not referring to those opera singers who go through lavish gestures that they construe as acting, nor to the born hams whose grimacing is deliberately planned on the genial notion that it adds up to charm. I am talking of the honest, serious musicians. Their oddities of behavior may be unconscious and incurable, stemming from habits acquired over the years, but they are yours for the relishing. Here are a choice handful of mannerisms that have cheered me up through many concerts.

Have you watched Walter Gieseking play the piano? If he did not have a huge concert grand in front of him, you would think that he was weaving his way through a broken field, like a gifted halfback. He twists and turns, bobs up and down. At times he seems in peril of bashing his shining bald head against the keyboard, at others of taking a flier off the bench. All this time he is making the piano sing with subtlety and variety of color, since he is a magician of tone.

Joseph Szigeti, one of the finest violinists at large, has a habit of breathing in and out through his nose as if struggling for air. At the very moment his bow is tracing a tone of the finest-grained texture, he will begin to sniff. The sharp intakes of breath recur. After a while they weave their own fascination, and it requires will power to follow the music; otherwise, you sit like one hypnotized, waiting for each sniff and wondering whether it will come when the tone is most gossamer.

Artur Schnabel has trouble with a chair that has a way of sliding back, often as he poises himself for a fortissimo passage. He sometimes keeps you in a fever of suspense as he clutches the chair, hauls it back under him, and strikes the keyboard. You relax gratified, he plays on for a while, and then suddenly you are on edge again as he reaches back for that slipping chair.

Emanuel Feuermann, a great virtuoso cellist, looked as if someone were holding a sliced lemon in front of him. In profound or trivial music, his cheeks were always drawn in; his lips were open as if working on an invisible all-day sucker. Perhaps this habit went back to boyhood practicing reactions. This may be an occupational trait of cellists, for several eminent players look much the same way when they play.

Vladimir Horowitz has a weakness that one associates more with children who are still struggling with their piano lessons. His eyes follow his hands, and he looks like a typist who uses a two-finger, hunt-and-peck system. But Horowitz has one of the formidable techniques of our generation. In a prestissimo passage, his fingers strike the notes much more rapidly than the eye can see. You might think that he would go bug-eyed from trying to keep track of his prestidigitation.

Rudolf Serkin seems shy. He walks from the wings to the concert grand in the middle of the stage, with his head turned to the rear, as if averting his gaze from the audience. When he plays, he has a peculiar nervous gesture: whenever his hands have occasion to rest, they turn the knobs at the side of the piano bench which raise and lower the seat. You expect the chair to shoot up in kangaroo fashion, but its level never seems to change. Has the mechanism been dislocated?

Josef Hofmann is poker-faced. He seems to be utterly indifferent to what he is playing, which, of course, he is not. During pauses he sits back, lets his hand fall nervelessly at his side, and you wonder whether he is asleep or has filled an inside straight. At any rate, his attitude is restful, as is, in a way, the impassive countenance of Jascha Heifetz, who looks like a solemn judge or a bronze sculpture. Not many musicians have the benevolent air of Kreisler, who looks fatherly, mellow, and comprehending. His manner is a restful contrast to that of the fiddlers who weave back and forth like boxers, until you become absorbed more by their footwork than their music.

Wanda Landowska wears costumes in the old style, with billowing skirts that cover her feet. And with good reason. She wears no shoes during a concert; they interfere with her control of the pedals on her Pleyel harpsichord. She has specially knitted, thick woolen socks for her public appearances. Being one of the great musicians of our time, she can afford to consider comfort before fashion.

Percy Grainger, one of the most popular pianists playing in America, carries a knapsack when traveling; he figures a suitcase might hurt his hands. His favorite exercise is walking. When he arrives at a railroad station of a town, he hires a cab in which he deposits his trunk and knapsack, and jogs along beside it on the way to the hotel. He has also made unconventional entrances for his performances. At a concert in Brooklyn he strolled down the aisle, in full view of the waiting audience, stopped to hail a friend, and then ambled the rest of the way down the aisle, clambered up the platform, and calmly went to work at the piano.

Singers are in a class by themselves. Among my souvenirs are the warm, genial souls whose affection seems to embrace the entire audience; the manly, muscled gents who exude virility like Clark Gable, and best of all, the fluttering sopranos who quiver with girlish excitement but whose sharp eyes never miss a trick. Their delicate hands weave arabesques in the air, and their elegant handkerchiefs are crumpled and uncrumpled. Their actions seem to say, "I am a frail woman, but I have room in my heart for all of you. Can you resist me?" Can you? It is a touching moment when she receives her meed of floral tributes. Ushers bring them down the aisle at the end of the first half of a recital; flunkies and accompanist help to collect them. She keeps a handsome bouquet in her arms, supervises the arrangement of the other flowers on the piano and at the sides of the stage, not forgetting to smile and curtsy to the audience. You sometimes wonder, as she stands in her bower of blossoms to sing an encore, whether the lady has hay fever, and if she has, whether any of these plants are up her allergy.

I am also fond of the singers who carry notebooks with the words of the songs they are to sing, for their memories need fortification. A pianist can memorize a long Schubert sonata; a violinist can learn the Brahms concerto, but this kind of singer dares not trust himself with two or three verses of a song. Behold how he concentrates, but mark well how he chances all as he casts his gaze to the gallery and approaches a thunderous final high note.

The artists make you forget their mannerisms in short order, for they play or sing so persuasively that your attention is held by the music. But there are some performers whose foibles are not compensated by any musical satisfactions.

A screwball nightingale in New York who fancies herself a coloratura soprano gives a concert each year. Her concerts draw swank audiences that pay good money to hear her. She is a perfect caricature of the prima donna. Even Bea Lillie, whose take-off on the genus, coloratura soprano, is a classic, is not so funny. People guffaw, but our heroine keeps on singing. Lately she has begun to make recordings, paying a private company to immortalize her incomparable interpretations. Her records are collector's items, and they have a brisk market. She makes money out of the delusion that she is a singer and people pay to foster it. Who's loony, anyhow?

One season a singing painter or painting singer gave a New York concert. She had an easel as well as a piano and accompanist on the stage. She began by drawing a sunrise scene, and then sang a little number appropriate to the dawn. Her pictures and songs followed the sun in its course. As the sun was setting, she sang *The End of a Perfect Day*. The sun dipped beyond the horizon and she offered *Beyond the Sunset*. The program ended with the appearance of the first star, which was duly illustrated on the easel and in song with Wagner's *Song to the Evening Star*.

Another literal-minded lady chose to sing songs about certain animals and fowl, and she illustrated her chores by having a cat and dog and a tame goose on the stage. She sang a "complete performance" of *Cavalleria Rusticana* all by herself.

A sweet little lady who specialized in old English music, which she played on virginal and recorder, was so full of her subject that her recital turned into a Benchleylike illustrated lecture. The conversation was cozy and friendly; the music was distinctly unprofessional. Before beginning the performance, she leaned over the footlights to borrow a program from a member of the audience, explaining that she had forgotten the order of her numbers. As she picked up the recorder, she warned the audience that the instrument, if it were not sufficiently warmed up, might give off strange sounds. It wasn't, and it did. She played a composition on the virginal, paused midway in a repeat, and said casually, "And so on and so forth."

Henry Cowell, who has earned recognition as an American composer, goes in for tone clusters at the piano. Since composers have not written customarily for tone clusters, he has provided himself with a repertory. Tone clusters are what they sound like—a cluster of tones, stuck by the fist, elbow, or any other blunt and handy object. Cowell occasionally rises in the middle of a composition, sticks his head under the piano top, and twangs some of the strings.

It is axiomatic that you can find the queerest ducks among those trying to crash through to success; some, of course, will be obliged to keep trying forever. You have heard examples on the amateur hours. If you wish to make the acquaintance of others, just an-

nounce a contest for new talent. The Robin Hood Dell Sy
Orchestra of Philadelphia offered a prize of $250 and an
ance for an artist ready for a professional career. Among the four
hundred applicants who considered themselves ready for a concert
career were a hurdy-gurdy player who said he had the Tchaikovsky
and Grieg piano concertos in his repertory; a male coloratura
soprano who said he was also a "fair-to-middlin' hog caller" and
who claimed he could hold A flat above high C for three and a half
minutes while lying prone; a tin-whistle virtuoso who insisted he
was ready to hold his own with an orchestra, and a spoon player
who said he had a repertory that included compositions "specially
written for spoons by Schubert and Bach."

But even where the musical talent is channeled along less singular lines, you will find people with strange ideas of their capacities.
A young woman, in a private audition for a manager, began with
one of the difficult arias of the Queen of the Night from Mozart's
Magic Flute. Her next offering was the equally difficult but dras-
tically different *"Liebestod"* from Wagner's *Tristan und Isolde*.
The unimpressed manager said, "Can you sing a simple song?"

Then there was my friend, the Albanian tenor. He arrived at a
newspaper office one day, loaded down with publicity material and
photographs. He said he was going to sing at Carnegie Hall on
Saturday night and requested publication of his picture and a story
about himself, since he was "the only Albanian singer in America."
It developed that he was to be one of many singers at a political rally
at Carnegie Hall, and he was told that it couldn't be done. "Don't
you understand," he pleaded, "what this means to me? This is the
first time in my life that I shall sing at Carnegie Hall," and with a
tremulous voice, "and it may be the last time, because," and here
his voice fell to a sorrowful whisper, "because I'm really a crooner."

When the small fry of the musical world try to give the one concert of a lifetime at a New York concert hall, something often
happens to bedevil the occasion. Lack of funds is one of the major
obstacles. One poor chap, who was determined to give his recital,
assured the manager that he could swing the cost, but on the evening

of the concert, the prospective recitalist admitted that he had not raised the rental fee for the hall. The manager of the hall, who had been stuck for the rent several times in the days when he did not hold out for the full fee in advance, refused to open the doors. The would-be performer pleaded, but got nowhere. Suddenly he plunged out into the street, shouting that he would fix everything. It was feared that he was going to do violence to himself. But he returned intact—without the money. Again he pleaded, to no avail. In the meantime, a crowd of friends and relatives had gathered outside, clamoring for the doors to open. The manager came out to announce that the recitalist had taken sick. Someone in the crowd shouted, "The hell he has, I just saw him running by all dressed up in soup and fish." The manager said, "He's just had a seizure." A little while later the "seizure" had worn off, and the saddened fellow went out to join his audience.

An accompanist practiced a higher form of criticism by getting plastered just before the concert. The poor recitalist was in a dither, which made no measurable improvement in the accompanist's condition. The concert manager poured cold water over the accompanist, slapped his face, pounded his back, and finally stirred him to a semblance of life, so that he could walk out on the stage and precariously begin the concert. Fortunately for the recitalist, the accompanist sobered up as the program progressed; unfortunately for the accompanist, the music was of such a nature that he had to go out and get tanked up again the moment the concert was over.

Unexpected success can complicate things. Clifford Curzon, an English pianist, arrived in America one year and engaged a manager to put on two concerts, one for piano alone at Town Hall and another with orchestra at Carnegie Hall. Money was no object, for he had the funds to foot the bills. Since it is a difficult job to get an audience for a first appearance, the manager began to worry early about an audience for Curzon's second. Whether the newcomer turned out to be a modest success, the best that could be hoped for, or a flop, not unprecedented for a debutant, the second concert was almost sure to be a sore trial. Playing it safe, the manager distributed thousands of passes for the second concert before the first took place. Curzon played exceedingly well and received stunning reviews. And on the evening of the Carnegie Hall concert, it seemed that everybody with passes had decided to use them. By 8 P.M., reserve police had to be summoned to keep order outside the hall. The pianist, arriving to find that he could scarcely get into the hall himself, cried, "Me and Paderewski!" After the concert they broke the news to him. The box-office receipts were zero; those people who wanted to pay for their tickets had not been able to get within a block of the box office.

Some of the wildest things happen when an august institution decides to put on a show. During the New York World's Fair of 1939, the British appropriated $15,000 to produce two orchestral concerts in New York. The British government sent over Sir Adrian Boult, one of its noted conductors, and several composers and soloists.

The sale of tickets did not matter so much as the fact that the British government could not afford to squire concerts that were not at least a *succès d'estime*. The time was June, with a heat wave smothering New York, and the manager felt that people could be dragooned to the concert only through social pull. Annie Oakleys would not be enough. It was decided to drum up interest through a reception for the visiting artists. British businessmen here were induced to sponsor the reception. The roof garden of the British Building at Rockefeller Center was set aside for the event, but at the last minute it became unavailable. An official of the New York Public Library came to the rescue by obtaining permission to give the reception in the Astor Gallery of the library, and five hundred invitations to a cocktail party were sent out. Then another crisis developed. Two days before the party it was discovered that the municipal laws forbade hard liquor and smoking in the library. The invitations were out and they said "cocktails"; tea would not do. Five hundred cocktails and two hundred Scotches and sodas, plus the usual trimmings, had been ordered and paid for at Longchamps.

The party was budgeted at $2000, and it was uncertain that Long-champs could readily supply tea instead of drinks at short notice. Finally someone telephoned one of the trustees of the library, and in a faked Oxonian accent declared that the British government was miffed. The trustee said he would consult with the city fathers, and on the morning of the party he got special dispensation.

The party went on with hard liquor. A WPA worker, costumed in the livery of an impressive flunkey, stood at the door, calling off the names of the entering guests. Even when there were several hundred people in the gallery, the WPA man, having the time of his life, kept shouting names in the best Court of St. James tradition. Toward the end of the party, he was assured that his services were no longer necessary, but he declined to quit, and until the bitter end he bellowed out names as if at a royal levee.

Then there was the organist who wrote a piteous letter to the Organists' Guild in New York saying that he had worked in a church in a small town for two years, hearing little but praise of his predecessor because the latter had played chimes on an organ with no chimes. The organist explained that he had tried various combinations unsuccessfully. He feared that his position was being undermined, and that he had to learn how to get chimes from the organ. He listed the make and year of the organ, and wrote down every one of the stops. I hope he received advice that helped him out of his troubles.

Putting yourself out to be nice to the press occasionally produces unforeseen annoyance. Pierre Luboshutz and Genia Nemenoff, husband-and-wife two-piano team, arrived, weary from traveling, in a small university town one morning, and they had scarcely settled in their hotel room when someone on the phone was asking for an interview. They went downstairs, and an eager young girl took copious notes. The pianists returned to their room, and shortly there was a request for another interview. This time there were three reporters, two male and one female, and the musicians patiently answered their questions. Once more the phone rang when they got back to their room, and this time Miss Nemenoff begged off. Her husband went down to face another group of interviewers. After answering their questions, he posed one of his own, "This is a remarkable small town," he said. "How many newspapers does it have?" The interviewers explained, "We're in the school of journalism, and we're practicing."

Nervousness and stage fright are among the prize bogeys of musicians, young and old, unknown and famous. Lily Pons has an attack of the jitters in advance of every performance. Before an appearance at the Lewisohn Stadium in the summer of 1942, she suffered through one of the most violent. It left her so limp that she had to lie down. Her nerves were not pacified by the uncertainty of the weather and the recurrent bulletins telephoned by Stadium officials that the concert was off, then on, then off again. Finally a cheerful voice called to say that the concert would definitely be held. "It makes no difference now," Miss Pons said wearily, "but I would rather sing, I have already had my vertigo."

Rosa Ponselle used to go on a walking jag before every appearance. She would arrive at the Metropolitan Opera House a couple of hours ahead of time, pace up and down the street in front of the theater for many minutes, and then go to her dressing room for more pacing. Elisabeth Rethberg pinches thumbs—other people's. A friend who stood with her in the wings on an opening night discovered later that her thumb was black and blue from the soprano's pinching.

Frank St. Leger, now a conductor at the Metropolitan Opera, became unnerved during a performance of *Faust* at Covent Garden in London. As he entered the pit for the final act, he picked up his baton and whispered to the concertmaster, "Last act." The concertmaster nodded, but did not move his violin from his knee. "Last act," said St. Leger sternly. "I know," said the concertmaster placidly. "Well, what are you waiting for?" snapped St. Leger. "Last act, second violins start," said the concertmaster.

Sir Thomas Beecham turned up at the last moment for a Metropolitan Opera performance, threw off his coat, straightened his tie, and hastened nervously toward the pit. To the stage manager who was walking at his side, he said, "What opera am I conducting tonight?"

Harold Bauer got so jittery at a recording session that he walked away from the piano and requested an employee of the recording company to sit down and talk to him. A talented cellist worked himself into a state before every public appearance; once he left town suddenly, another time took ill, and ended up by quitting the cello. He took to playing jazz on the piano, and in this medium he had no psychological troubles. He filled engagements successfully, playing with the gusto of a man who loved an audience.

Possibly this chap would have been saved for the cello—not that playing jazz at the piano is a lower form of occupation—if the Society of Timid Souls had been functioning when he was having his troubles. This organization was formed by Bernard Gabriel, pianist and teacher, to help potential public performers out of their miseries of nervousness. A score or more of them gather at his studio periodically, pay seventy-five cents' admission, and receive refreshments, advice, and perhaps a cure. If the nervous musician fears noise, the crowd in the studio raises a racket while the victim plays. If silence bothers him, they make him play in a concentrated calm. If he fears loss of memory, he is encouraged to repeat a piece until he can get through it and that ghost is interred. If criticism is his bogey, he gets a blast of that.

It would be a healthy thing if someone organized, to balance this doubtlessly useful organization, a Society for Temerarious Souls. It is my experience that the hardy, fearless musicians, who will play anywhere, anyhow, anytime, outnumber the timid souls. The object of such a society would be to teach the overeager musicians timidity and humility. Like Spaniards who observe the convention of refusing food at least twice, these anxious Euterpeans would be taught to decline to perform even if the host asked only once. In fact, they would have to be taught not to thrust themselves on their friends and neighbors without being asked at all. Once such a society succeeded in keeping them from performing at private gatherings, it might be feasible to advance on the great reform—

keeping them from foisting themselves on the unsuspecting public.

There are almost no limits to the patience and resourcefulness of would-be careerists when they seek the attention and support of prominent artists. A young pianist who wanted lessons from José Iturbi sat for days in the lobby of Iturbi's hotel, waiting to beard the lion. Finally, he wore down the pianist's resistance and persuaded him to listen at least once. The young fellow had some talent, and Iturbi agreed to help him when he could. Since Iturbi was a busy man, the tenacious youngster spent endless days in the lobby of that hotel, waiting for an occasional lesson.

Some of the girls seek the assistance of famous musicians, usually men, after their own fashions. They send long, heart-rending letters, retailing their problems and tribulations, not forgetting to enclose attractive photographs.

Don't think that all of the wit, wisdom, and power of observation belongs to the musicians, managers, or newspaper people who deal with music and its practitioners. Some of the keenest observers are ushers, doormen, and backstage workers. There is a doorman at one of the concert halls who can talk as knowingly about music, its people and its audiences, as any professional. He knows the gossip, foibles, and aptitudes of all the conductors, and his favorite is Bruno Walter. He can analyze soundly the performance of Rosenthal, comparing its style, tone, and personal mannerisms, with those of other veterans like Hofmann, and he can compare each of them with his performances of several decades ago. He can tell at a glance deadheads in an audience from paying customers, and not merely by looking for punched tickets, but from their faces, clothes, and general demeanor. He talks sadly about the decline of artistic standards, makes recommendations for the job of permanent conductor of the town's leading orchestra, discants on why a permanent conductor would be better than a system of guest stars, and second-guesses the critics. Whenever I need the corrective of an undeluded and slightly ironic point of view, I have a chat with my doorman friend. If he were a writer, he could, I am sure, do a livelier chapter on the folklore of our concert life.

15

THE NEGRO IN MUSIC

IT HAS BECOME clear in the course of this war that our color lines, racial animosities, poll taxes, and accumulation of bigotries are being used against us by an enemy who does not mean to cure them. We may smile wryly when we hear the Japanese promising that they will protect their yellow-, brown-, and black-skinned brothers, for their record as protectors is less than brilliant. We may chuckle when we hear that a minor official in Nazi Germany has sent Marian Anderson an invitation to make a tour of fifty concerts, provided she can guarantee that she is one hundred per cent Aryan. But we know that the barbarism of weighing blood percentages of human beings is not a laughing matter. And knowing it, we have to concede that we have the mote in our own eyes to deal with. Fundamentally it is not a problem for music alone, but for the whole nation. Nevertheless, hatred and discrimination are evil wherever they exist, and an advance on any front is a gain for the entire battleline.

When you observe the success and public acclaim of Negro singers like Roland Hayes, Paul Robeson, Marian Anderson, Dorothy Maynor, Anne Brown, Ethel Waters, and others; when you see that a talented young conductor like Dean Dixon can be invited to lead the New York Philharmonic-Symphony at Lewisohn Stadium and the NBC Symphony over a nation-wide network; when you remark on the tremendous popularity of a long line of Negro jazz musicians like Duke Ellington, Louis Armstrong, Count Basie, Lionel Hampton, Teddy Wilson, Hazel Scott, and scores of others, you may well ask how anyone can claim that Negro musi-

cians in America still suffer from discrimination. They are successful, and their success has opened many doors to them and their
fellows. But they do not tell the world about the troubles they have
seen.

Occasionally a sore spot erupts so that its malignance is visible
to all. Have we forgotten about the segregation of Negroes in the
South as if they were an inferior race and condemned to Harlems
and concentration camps in the Nazi fashion? Paul Robeson reminded us the other day by speaking up in meeting in a Kansas City
concert hall. During an appearance there he told the audience, in
which the Negroes were segregated, that he had made it a practice
not to sing where his people were roped off and kept to themselves.
He had accepted this engagement on the insistence of friends, but
he wished to tell the audience that he was singing under protest.
Several of the white listeners stalked out; others followed as the
program continued. Whereupon Robeson added a group of songs
that cried out against the institution of Jim Crow.

Is the nation's capital above criticism? When you talk to people
who work in Washington, you learn that even in the midst of a war
for liberation, discrimination is rampant. You learn that at a time
when there is a shortage of skilled secretarial and stenographic help,
government agencies fear to employ Negro girls who have the requi-
site skill. But these things are under the surface. It takes a scandal
like the barring of Marian Anderson from the use of Constitution
Hall, home of the D.A.R., to remind the world that in Washington
there are people who neither understand nor observe the fundamentals of American democracy. In Washington, fortunately, there
were lower-case democrats who were outraged at this action of the
D.A.R. Men like Secretary of the Interior Harold L. Ickes and
women like Mrs. Franklin D. Roosevelt were not content to accept
this decision. Mrs. Roosevelt resigned from the D.A.R. Mr. Ickes
led in organizing a monster demonstration of protest, inviting
Marian Anderson to sing in Washington from the platform of the
Lincoln Memorial overlooking the sweep of green toward the Washington Memorial. Some 75,000 persons filled this unusual concert

hall on Easter Sunday in 1939 to express their living faith in the American ideal, for it was no longer a concert but a democratic manifestation.

In 1942, Miss Anderson's manager again asked for a date for a concert in Constitution Hall. The D.A.R.'s reply was an invitation to sing a benefit for war relief. Miss Anderson accepted this condition gladly, but imposed one of her own—that there be no segregation of the audience at her concert.

Negro musicians know about discrimination. Their success does not shelter them from it, and their path is the harder for it. Paul Robeson says that from the beginning, as a football player at Rutgers, as a student, as an actor, and as a singer, he had to give something extra because he was a Negro. It was only when he discovered the truth about his place in the world that the drive generated by his being a Negro turned into a consciousness of being a human being first. When he met men like G. B. Shaw, Sir Stafford Cripps, and Jawaharlal Nehru for the first time, he scarcely understood them. But when he realized that oppression and discrimination were virtually everywhere, and that it was not the Negro alone who suffered, he became militantly progressive. He spoke up boldly for the exploited and downtrodden. Though his uncompromising stand cost him some engagements, it won him others, as well as a new host of friends and admirers. After making several movies, he said he would never make another picture so long as the Negro continued to be represented as a servant, buffoon, or superstitious ignoramus.

The Negro artist is haunted by the fear of discrimination. Even where no semblance of it exists, he braces himself for it. When Marian Anderson, then twenty-one, took part in a contest of which the prize was a public appearance at the Lewisohn Stadium, she was the last of the candidates to be called on a hot August day. It was not surprising that she and her teacher were suspicious when they discovered that she was listed to wind up the competition. Fearing that she would be stopped before she had a chance to show what she could do, he warned her to keep singing even if the gong sounded. But the judges listened and gave her the prize.

As her award, she sang before a Lewisohn Stadium audience and proved that she had an extraordinary voice. There was reason to believe that her career was well launched. But her manager could scarcely sell her, and such engagements as came her way were at puny fees. She had done almost as well when engagements at church parties and other affairs in the Negro community would net her twenty-five and fifty dollars each. She decided to go abroad, and the Rosenwald Foundation helped to pay her way. She worked hard in Europe and presently became a celebrity, singing in many countries and establishing a formidable reputation. The news of her triumphs was published in this country. Did the American managers hasten to sign her up, as they jostled each other whenever a new star appeared on the European scene? They hesitated to take another chance on her. One of them, Sol Hurok, finally did, and made a fortune.

It is generally conceded that Marian Anderson is a great artist, but there have been dissenting voices, based, in some cases, not on the merits but on bigotry. I happened to be discussing Miss Anderson with a singer from the South, and I said that I respected her for achievements gained in spite of handicaps. The Southerner exclaimed irritably: "Handicaps, nothing. She's lucky! You boys and the public have gone out of your way to be nice to her because she's a Negro." (Only he didn't use the word Negro.) "If she were treated like the rest of us, she would be just an ordinary singer!"

Miss Anderson speaks of discrimination without self-consciousness, as if it were an ever-present phenomenon that had to be faced with intelligence rather than with bitterness. But she admits that it is distressing each time she is confronted with a new phase of it, no matter how firmly she has hardened herself. She recognizes, moreover, that, because of her position, she suffers from it less than other men and women of her race.

In most cities of these democratic United States, the first-class hotels are not open to her; in some, even the second- and third-class will not let her in. She has to put up at the homes of Negro families.

There have been one or two honorable exceptions, like the Algonquin in New York, run by Frank Case. The Auditorium in Chicago was another exception, but the busybodies would not let it be. After stopping at the hotel for some years, Miss Anderson discovered during one tour that she was no longer welcome. An executive, patently embarrassed, said that other residents of the hotel had objected. Miss Anderson requested that she be confronted with the objectors, but was refused. Then another reason was trotted out: her Negro friends, coming to visit her, had passed through the hotel and some of the white guests had objected to their presence. But, Miss Anderson explains, if she has friends in a town where she is giving a recital, she makes it a point to visit them at their homes, fearing that they will be turned away or be asked to use the service entrance.

She gave a concert in Atlantic City, N. J., singing to a packed house in a large auditorium. Her visit was turned into an occasion. There was a civic celebration, and an official of the town presented her with the keys to the city. But the hotels would not rent her a room for the night.

Negro musicians, when they are touring, have to be careful about where and how they eat. If they are permitted to stay at a good hotel, they consider it wisest to take their meals in their rooms. Miss Anderson, Dorothy Maynor, and others have had to be reticent about showing themselves in public places; Paul Robeson has been denied entrance to a fashionable New York eating place, though he came as the guest of a prominent white person, a valued patron of the place.

Being persons of sensitivity, these Negro artists do not relish trying to gain admittance where it is hedged about with restrictions. But they are conscious of their duty to their people and of the role they must play in helping to win simple, democratic equality. They take rebuffs, swallow their pride, and keep trying to open hostile doors.

Miss Anderson admits that when Roland Hayes, first of America's outstanding Negro singers, came along, there were fewer doors open to him. By the very fact that he could make a big career he broke down some barriers. Paul Robeson battered down a few more. She, in turn, has made things easier for the musicians who followed her. Thus Miss Maynor was permitted to occupy a studio in Carnegie Hall. But it took considerable pressure to get her the place, for the renting agent feared that other tenants would object. In the end, he signed the lease with Miss Maynor's manager.

Negro musicians are making careers as recitalists. But not one has been given a chance to sing in a major American opera company like the Metropolitan. Marian Anderson once confided that she would like to try her hand at opera, and there are several roles—Carmen, Amneris, and Erda—that would suit her in every way. In the popular-priced companies like those run by Alfredo Salmaggi, Negro singers have been given a chance. Thus Caterina Jarboro has sung Aïda several times, and splendidly, too.

How can we expect a hospitable approach to the Negro musician from the Metropolitan Opera House when some of its patrons will not even tolerate the presence of a Negro in an adjacent seat? At a recent opening night at the Metropolitan, several Negroes, dressed in white tie and tails, like the other customers, occupied ten-dollar seats. Some subscribers whose seats adjoined those held by the Negroes were annoyed. They complained to the box office, which explained that the seats were purchased through speculators. For the box office has to be tender about the prejudices of its quality trade. If Negro customers buy tickets directly from the box office, precautions are taken to give them aisle seats and to tear up the ticket for the neighboring seat, so that no white patron will have to rub shoulders with a Negro. Even when business is good, this practice is followed; an opera official explained, with a long face, that "the sacrifice had to be made."

One of the outraged subscribers who complained about the presence of Negroes in the audience at this Metropolitan Opera opening blamed their temerity on "That Man in the White House who encouraged them to be bold." It was probably the responsibility of That Man that Negroes demanded the right to work in our war factories, to serve in the country's armed forces, and, if necessary, to die for it.

But with unchanging bigotries in the paying customers, how can we expect essentially conservative institutions like the Metropolitan Opera or the New York Philharmonic-Symphony Orchestra to invite Negroes to become members of singing or playing personnel? I don't know whether there are Negro instrumentalists good enough to hold down a place in a first-rank symphonic ensemble, but I do know that none has ever become a member of such an orchestra. The chances are that Negro musicians, realizing that their avenues of opportunity in a good orchestra are slim, turn to jazz, where Negro ensembles can make good.

Not that the Negro jazz musician is better off than the Andersons, Maynors, and Dixons. He faces all manner of difficulties in obtaining commercial sponsors for his radio programs, and the commercially sponsored programs pay well. Only recently have the big radio networks promised to add Negro musicians to their regular personnel. Duke Ellington says that he has never had a commercially sponsored radio hour on a big network. The reason given him is that the Southern affiliates of the networks will not tolerate it. But Duke knows better about the attitude of Southern people. He and his band played in a dance hall in Atlanta for Negro dancers. There were 3000 Negroes on the floor, and in the galleries were about 5000 white persons who had paid their way in just to listen to the music. The Negro is invited occasionally, but not in strict proportion to his number and merits, to play at the fashionable, best-paying dance resorts. A few Negro bands do well by barnstorming, playing one-night stands at college proms, in movie theaters and dance halls of smaller towns. The younger people of America are open-minded about their jazz favorites; they don't worry about color if the musicians can deliver.

On records, the Negro jazz musicians get their best break. In this medium, their work is in open competition with the field, and it sells on its merits. As a result, a good many excellent Negro musicians have received a considerable lift in their profession through records and the juke boxes.

The picture is not unrelievedly somber. There are people, millions of them, who have no prejudices, and there are an increasing number of musicians who are getting a fair deal. Many white people have made it a point to help gifted Negro artists. Eleanor Roosevelt has made special trips to New York to be at concerts conducted by Dean Dixon. Dorothy Maynor was enabled to become a singer thanks to the support, both financial and moral, of several white women. John Henry Hammond, Jr., has done good work in hunting out and encouraging Negro jazz musicians. John Charles Thomas wrote to the officers of a naval training station to make sure that the Negro boys in training would also be admitted to the audience before accepting an invitation to sing there.

Negroes, of course, help their own within their limited means. I know of no more touching story than the way money was raised to enable Marian Anderson, then in her teens, to get her first lessons from a professional singing teacher. Her South Philadelphia neighbors, who were proud of her and who in later years always spoke of her as "our Marian," took matters into their own hands, since they knew that the girl's mother, who had to take in washing, could not afford to pay for lessons. The neighbors held church benefits; they contributed nickels and dimes. Finally there was a fund of $126, and she could take her first formal lessons. When this fund was exhausted, the community raised $500 more to send her to a more eminent teacher.

But the patronage of generous white people or faithful Negro neighbors is no real solution. The basic question is: are Anderson, Maynor, Robeson, Ellington, and Armstrong unique? I think not. The incidence of talent among Negroes would probably strike as high an average as among any other group, and possibly higher, for the Negro is musical by nature. But the first glimmers of talent are not always recognized in an impoverished environment. What chance has the scion of a sharecropper to show his talent? What chance has he to get it developed, if it is indeed recognized?

Negro musicians should not be restricted to isolated successes, nor to all-Negro ensembles like jazz bands and occasional Broadway shows like *Porgy and Bess* and *Cabin in the Sky*. Not that all-Negro shows are without their real uses. Through such shows we discover singers like Anne Brown, who was a student at the Juilliard School of Music when the George Gershwin operatic setting of Du Bose Heyward's *Porgy* was going into rehearsal. She wrote to Gershwin, asking for an audition. She got it and the job. What was more, Gershwin called her up one day and said, "What do you think Georgie has done for you?" She couldn't guess what Georgie had done. Georgie told her. He had changed the title from *Porgy* to *Porgy and Bess*.

Despite the opportunity that Anne Brown received through *Porgy and Bess,* she was for many years virtually a one-role singer, as far as public and producers were concerned. After the first run of the opera, she did little, and when the work was revived to immense success, she was again in the ascendant. The temptation was great to remain a one-role singer. The producers who wanted her to stay with the show through the New York run and the road tour offered her a two-year guarantee of $75,000. But she was determined to venture all on a future as a recitalist.

There are many fine potential artists among our Negro people. Given equal opportunities to grow, live, study, and work, they might take their rightful place, to the enrichment of the nation. But we must rid ourselves of the notion, symbolized by the moving pictures' consistent refusal to let a Negro be little else but a flunky or a comic, that the Negroes are an inferior race. Scientists of standing have said repeatedly that there are no inferior peoples, and within a democracy there should certainly be nothing less than equality for all citizens. It should no longer be necessary for the Negro to sing, as he did in the year of our Lord 1943, in an anti-Jim Crow song, "Give me some democracy to defend."

16

THE CHANGING SCENE

Radio—Background Music—Film Music—Jazz, the People's Music—Jazz in Carnegie Hall—Federal Music Project—The Four Freedoms—Music in the Armed Forces.

MUSIC PLAYS A PART, however small, in making our world, and our world plays a part in founding, altering, and renewing musical standards, audiences, and institutions. The world is changing; therefore, music must also change. The direction in a changing world, it seems to me, is toward music by the people, for the people, and of the people. There has been a great deal of progress, and possibly some retrogression, but the forward urge is unmistakable. The times have their own logic and dynamic; music has no choice but to come along.

The impact of the radio on music in less than twenty years has been incalculable. Some generalizations are possible: radio has brought music to more people than any other medium at any time in history; it has built a vast, new audience; it has stimulated people to make further acquaintance with music in the concert hall and opera house and through recordings; it has induced some people to develop skills of their own in music. All of these contentions are provable at least in part, but no one can tell how much of it is for good or ill.

The surveys that measure audiences claim that they can measure the size of the public for particular broadcasts. They probably make shrewd estimates, but they do not and cannot gauge the concentration of the listening, and the way the new audience listens is as vital as its numbers.

Radio has bombarded people with all sorts of music, bad, good, and indifferent. Much has been prettified and sweetened, and some has been served without sauce or garnish. Music has framed the reactionary rumblings of a W. J. Cameron and has been used as agent of good will for cigarettes, tooth paste, oil and gasoline, banks, automobiles, tires, celanese, and utilities. It has been employed as time filler when a studio could think of nothing else to put on the air. And a great deal in all forms, styles, and schools has been broadcast straight, with no apologies, ulterior motives, or sugar-coating.

Radio has so much time to fill that it is bound to turn to offerings of unsurpassed variety. Alfred Wallenstein, who conducts three or four radio programs a week, has said that he could not adhere to the familiar repertory year in and year out without stultifying himself and his audience. Even if his interests did not lay in exploring untrodden fields, he would be driven to it. His schedule gives him no alternative. Other broadcasters are in the same position. They have to be hospitable to the new and to the neglected past. The radio has introduced more new operas in a season than the Metropolitan has put on in a decade. What professional concert organization could undertake 103 Bach cantatas presented on the Sundays for which the composer wrote them? How could a true and valiant singer of the people like Woody Guthrie reach an audience in every part of the country without months of travel if the radio did not welcome him?

There is another side—a case against radio. It puffs up the stale, the mawkish, and the maudlin. It gives a preponderance of its time to things that are cheap and in bad taste. It trades heavily on the *status quo*, and dresses that up, too often, in lush sentimentality. It works too hard at selling its wares, in a way that is beneficial neither to the product nor to the buyer. But it is a new instrument, and we may hope that the times and the people will shape it to more useful purpose.

Radio, like the movies, depends on music to help out with programs not essentially musical. Background music is extensively employed by both mediums, but neither radio nor the screen has worked out and applied a sound theory for the use of music in dramatic productions. The failure is due to a misunderstanding of the power and function of music. The theater, or what is left of it, is apt to make a more intelligent use of music.

Music generates tremendous emotional power. Given a chance, it can overwhelm a story or a situation, or it can serve to heighten it. I, for one, am always irritated when I hear in a movie or on the radio a burbling of musical sounds during a scene in which actors are speaking. If the words convey meaning, I want to hear them clearly. I don't want them taking on protective coloring from the music so that I have to strain to catch them in flight, like a bird in thick foliage. If the music can add something to the drama, why not give it a chance to develop according to its own logic? Why confine a composer to a series of unrelated sounds that are no more useful than any other sound effects? If sound effects are all that are required, use them frankly. But let us have an end to the throbbing violins and the golden horns merely because they are pretty sounds.

Occasionally a film has used music knowingly, like its superb employment by Prokofieff and Eisenstein in the Russian film *Alexander Nevsky,* and now and then there have been pictures that have dealt with musical subjects, such as the stories that employed famous musicians of concert, opera, and jazz. These films have done their bit toward exposing a new public to music, but the movies have not probed deeply. I don't think that the movies need to be ambassadors of music. The sound film is a medium, for the most part, of telling a story. That is the source of its wide appeal. But Walt Disney has given intimations of his understanding of music, and I am not referring to *Fantasia,* which was self-conscious and over-laden. Many of the documentaries have gained from the adroit use of music, and since the best of them have been produced by independent, progressive groups, they have had the collaboration of composers who are alert to the potentialities of new forms.

Both the screen and the radio make extensive use of jazz. For jazz, more than any other form in this country, is the people's music. Our young folk have been brought up on it. Their responses are kinetic, and they are right, for jazz has, in common with other and older forms of popular music, a direct appeal to the nerves and muscles. Nor is the fondness for jazz confined to young Americans. Some of our best players traveled in Europe before the war and were received with tremendous enthusiasm. In France especially, *le jazz hot* was hailed as a great new force in music. The intelligentsia, abroad and here, have gone in for pretentious analyses of jazz. But the young people of Europe, like the young people of the United States, have not worried about theories and philosophies. Jazz has had a direct attraction for them. Jan Struther has told of her sixteen-year-old son who had to remain in England while his mother and younger brother sought refuge in the United States. The boy took the news bravely, but was obviously disappointed. His mother tried to cheer him up, telling him that they would soon be reunited. "I don't mind staying," the youngster said, "but I envy you hearing Duke Ellington and Benny Goodman."

No one can guess what the effect of good jazz will be on other forms such as symphony, opera, chamber music. It is too soon to tell. For jazz, as it has flourished in recent years, is relatively new; at least its acceptance by a wide public is new. I am speaking of the jazz by virtuosos of hot jazz or swing. Not the jazz without imagination or variety, but the jazz that has freshness of approach, audacity, and real variety. Perhaps this jazz is most clearly evidenced by the improvisatory spirit of the best players, but it is also discoverable in performances that are carefully worked out. It has invention, wit, pathos, and honest emotion.

Even if the future is unpredictable, it may be guessed that our best jazz will have an influence on other musical mediums. It is a sign of the times that the venerable New England Conservatory has established "a department of popular music." This is inevitable when you consider how it has penetrated our lives, and how musicians have moved from one field to the other, without violence to either. Benny Goodman is the best-publicized example of a player who has tackled both swing and Mozart. But there are radio orchestras who make symphony music their principal occupation and who can beat out a neat bit of jazz on occasion. William Schuman, the composer, did his first composing in jazz, and one may assume that the boldness and originality of his thinking were not impeded by this experience. Robert Russell Bennett, one of the shrewdest arrangers of jazz, has worked in other forms with an imaginative lift that has owed something to this work. Robert McBride's music, in its humor and economy of means, has also been indebted to his preoccupation with jazz forms and idioms. Fine symphonic players like Jan Savitt, the violinist, and Henry Levine, the trumpeter, have turned exclusively to jazz, and a jazz trombonist, Jack Satterfield, has taken a post with the New York Philharmonic-Symphony. Musicians like Szigeti and Iturbi have found stimulus and refreshment in jazz, while Heifetz delights in playing jazz privately, but on the piano, not the violin.

One of the immediate effects of jazz may stem from the stunning virtuosity of its best players. There are trumpeters, clarinetists, and trombonists in jazz bands who have an elasticity of technique and a command of nuance that make the achievements of good symphonic players seem tame indeed. Lehman Engel, conductor and composer, who had concerned himself largely with the so-called high-brow stuff, enlisted in the navy and was put in charge of a group of musicians for band and symphonic programs at the Great Lakes Training Station. The virtuosity of the jazz players was a revelation to him. They could do things that symphonic players considered impossible. Such prowess is bound to attract the interest of composers alive to the new possibilities in old instruments.

One of the recent tendencies in jazz has been to bring some of its players into the halls devoted to the illustrious symphonic organizations. The idea originated no doubt in the brain of some clever press agent, and in time it may prove to be worth while. But too often the jazz practitioners who have invaded places like Carnegie Hall have frozen up under the pressure of their surroundings. That has not been good for their music. "Fats" Waller appeared at Carnegie Hall, and sat at the piano like one transfixed, playing endless improvisations that did not reveal his work at its earthy best and that bored even some of his devoted followers. A jam session was planned for the end of the concert, but "Fats" sat so long at the piano that his colleagues, waiting in the wings, became irritated. Some had other engagements and left, and others were weary by the time their turn came.

The devotees of today's jazz take pride in their work. The believers have no doubt of the validity and integrity of their music. They practice it without fear or apology. But they need to guard against cheapness. For jazz is immensely marketable, and it is susceptible to easy commercialization. It is agreeable to make money out of music, but it is shameful to degrade its quality, whatever the milieu. It would also be a pity if jazz became too serious and self-conscious, for its most endearing qualities are its humor, gusto, and impudence. When it reflects these qualities, jazz has the precious tang of the American spirit at its best. Then it is truly a people's music.

Another movement of vital importance to the people has been the government's support of art in recent years. The support came about as a result of the depression. In seeking to make work for the unemployed, the government set up the Federal Music Project. The project has already left a mark on the people, though we cannot measure its depth or breadth. For the project brought music in the flesh to millions of Americans not reached hitherto. Only the radio could match it, and the radio remains after all a mechanical device, at best a substitute for the living sound of the real thing.

The Federal Music Project was responsible for the formation of hundreds of orchestras, bands, choruses, and chamber-music ensembles. It not only gave work to unemployed musicians, but it also brought music to new audiences free of charge or at admission prices that compared favorably with movie prices. Performances were variable, but generally gave the audience a fair idea of the music. The project's ensembles did not pretend to compete with glamorized names. They did their job as best they could, and it was a worth-while job as long as it lasted.

Nor was performance the only accomplishment of the WPA. It conducted classes for people who could not afford them otherwise, helped composers by providing copyists, enlisted the support of eminent musicians to work with young people, and maintained in various parts of the country a forum and laboratory where composers had their music played and discussed. Its units played an enormous amount of contemporary music, probably more, in sum, than all the other established institutions put together. It provided radio stations of limited means with ensembles for performance.

The Federal Music Project was helpful to composer, performer, and audience. But the reactionaries in and out of Congress, pounding away at the arts projects, succeeded in dissolving the Federal Theater Project first. The crisis in world affairs enabled them to peck away at, dispense with, or emasculate the others.

But the projects endured long enough to establish the truth that music and the other arts are not the province of the few, that the public has a still unmeasured capacity for them, and that the government has a duty to the people in the field of the arts as well as in economics and politics.

These are the things that we have been fighting for in the new World War. The Four Freedoms include freedom from want. This freedom means assurance of food, clothing, shelter, medicine, and education, but, as I read it, it also encompasses the intangibles. The people are fighting for the right to make and hear music, not at prohibitive luxury prices, but within their modest means. They are fighting for the right to a good and full life, which means the opportunity to know and enjoy art as readily as the limited group who always had the money and leisure for it.

Our new army and navy are another index to the direction in which the people are moving. Our armed forces have a large representation of men whose tastes run to the good things in art. The comparison with the First World War is striking. Walter Damrosch, who worked with our men in that war, has testified to the advance. He was called in 1917 by General Pershing to improve the caliber of army bands. He formed a bandmasters' school at Chaumont, in France. He examined about 250 band leaders; only five were equipped for the job. He obtained the co-operation of French musicians and gave intensive six-week courses to relays of prospective band leaders and players.

In the evenings, when schoolwork was done, the teacher-musicians would play chamber music and the students would listen for hours. The men who listened to the informal concerts in Chaumont were regarded a bit unusual for that day. But they would not be unusual today. Nor would there be a shortage of band leaders or bandsmen today. America has produced thousands of competent musicians in the last generation, and the army and navy brims over with them. In the ranks and among the officers there are young American conductors of considerable experience as well as men who have held important posts in symphony orchestra, opera house, and jazz band. The following gives the briefest kind of idea of the new attitude toward music in our armed forces:

Leo Orynwaka, aviation mechanic with a pursuit squadron, traveled day and night after finishing maneuvers in Louisiana, to reach New York in time to spend his furlough rehearsing and singing in the Oratorio Society's annual performance of Handel's *The Messiah*, which he had not missed in a dozen years.

When the Special Services Office of the Puerto Rico Department of the United States Army purchased a large record library, a difference of opinion erupted between the soldiers and the chief hostess of the Service Club. The plan was to rotate several sets of records throughout the various bases and posts on the island, and the chief hostess published a notice in the local army paper, *Caribbean Sentinel*, announcing the order of the programs. Sergeant Lawrence A. Goodwin of the Signal Corps did not like her juxtaposition of compositions, and wrote to New York to get a season's programs of the New York Philharmonic-Symphony broadcasts over the Columbia Broadcasting System to serve as a model.

In Kentucky the Louisville Symphony Orchestra made a lend-lease arrangement with the Fifth Armored Division at Fort Knox whereby the orchestra loaned the soldiers music and instruments in return for guest appearances of soldier musicians. The Eighteenth Infantry Training Regiment at Camp Roberts, California, formed its own twenty-five-piece symphony orchestra, using enlisted men, with Private Robert Pompeo, a Los Angeles pianist, as conductor, and the musicians' comrades attended the camp concerts with clannish devotion. At Fort Hancock, N. J., the enlisted men produced, sang, played, and designed a condensed version of *Carmen,* calling in only two guest artists—one of them Lily Djanel of the Metropolitan Opera, who sang Carmen. In Texas the men at Ellington Field, an aviation-cadet replacement center, were so eager to have a visit of the Houston Symphony Orchestra that overnight they turned a hangar into a concert hall and back into a hangar. The Dayton, Ohio, Philharmonic Chorus had its ranks depleted by the draft and the war industries, but it made good its losses with army personnel at near-by Wright and Patterson Fields.

The armed forces have a vast number of trained musicians in the ranks—composers like Samuel Barber and Marc Blitzstein, instrumentalists like Toscha Seidl, who has had to play the cymbals on parade in a navy band; Ossy Renardy, Eugene List, Gyorgy Sandor, Jacques Abram; singers like Arthur Kent, John Carter, Elwood Gary, and Clifford Harvuot of the Metropolitan Opera; conductors like Jacques Singer and Richard Korn. The New Manhattan String Quartet enlisted in a group so the foursome could stay together. Musicians in uniform are anxious to use their spare time to practice; this determination requires uncommon energy and spirit, for every musician has as his first duty the job of becoming a soldier, sailor, or marine.

By the very fact that so many musicians are in the armed services, there is bound to be an invaluable interpenetration of interests. The professional musician not only trains some of his colleagues to play and sing a bit, but also imparts something of his own enthusiasm for music. The enlisted man, who has the attitude of the layman, is giving the musician an intimate understanding of his point of view.

The U.S.O. has brought illustrious virtuosos to the camps, and they have been received by large, responsive audiences. Brailowsky began one concert with encore stuff, and presently the men were whistling for something more substantial. Feuermann gave a recital on the proportions of a Carnegie Hall appearance, and the service men found it to their taste. It is estimated that almost ninety per cent of the men who attend camp concerts have never heard a formal recital, concert, or opera. For this reason the name players have had the biggest audiences. There have been occasions when a morale officer felt that "this is not the type of entertainment the enlisted man enjoys." No doubt he prefers leg shows. But the army is not trying to uplift him or sell him culture. If he wants it, he can have it. One camp paper reported that Albert Spalding had a big audience and a fine time; it thought that he had played down to the audience very little, considering that on the theater marquee the billing was "Ann Corio and Albert Spalding."

Nearly each camp and station has its contingent of jazz players. Some of the jam sessions heard in out-of-the-way places in America could not be duplicated, before the war, anywhere but in the principal centers of the top jazz players.

The army and navy have discovered that there is considerable interest in singing, and they are trying to train men equipped to lead the boys in group singing at every camp and station. The men in the services generally prefer the old standbys of the uniformed man's song literature, but choruses have sprung up that devote themselves to more complex music.

What is true here holds abroad. The Red Army has an official chorus that ranks with the best in the world. Russians are outstanding singers, and in all divisions there are singing groups. Nor is the voice the only medium for music. There is a profusion of bands, orchestras, and other ensembles. The Red Army, in peacetime, was a prodigious commissioner of music in the Soviet Union, paying substantial fees to composers for symphonies, concertos, operas, as well as for songs and marches.

In the British Royal Air Force there are bands, official and unofficial, at all stations. Wing Commander Rudolph O'Donnell, director of music for the RAF, recruited an orchestra from among the best musicians in the force, and it grew to a strength of more than one hundred. When the Griller String Quartet joined up, O'Donnell called the men into his office and suggested that for the first evening of their service it would be pleasant if they joined with Howard Ferguson, British composer and pianist, also in the RAF, in the Brahms Quintet.

An RAF man in this country, attending a recital by Horowitz, sent a request for an encore by jotting down the opening of a Brahms waltz and adding these words: "Will you please play this? I heard it last in London in Queen's Hall, when there was a Queen's Hall."

Maybe music gets into a commander's hair now and then, like the time Ensign Richard Korn took over the coast-guard band at the Manhattan Beach Training Center in New York. Assuming that his first task was to prepare the national anthem, Korn devoted his initial rehearsal to it, starting, stopping, and starting all over again. Suddenly an officer strode into the band's rehearsal shack to order a halt. "I've been trying to drill my men out there," he said, "and for the last half-hour they've done nothing but snap to attention for *The Star-Spangled Banner!*"

17

ON BLACK DISKS

*Concerts of ,Recorded Music—Add-a-Part Records—Caruso Made It Respectable—
Two Highballs Make History—"Bugs"—Recording Technique—The Big Three.*

MUSIC ON RECORDS is a substitute for music in the concert hall, opera house, and home. Though they recognize that it is a substitute, millions of people have nevertheless gratefully accepted it. For music on records, even at its weakest, is better than no music.

Techniques of recording and reproducing recorded sound have progressed rapidly, so that music on records is steadily coming nearer to the sound of the living thing. The war has put a halt to the possibility of marketing advances, but when it has ended, there is likely to be greater progress. Reproducing apparatus will probably give you the sound of voices and instruments with more precise definition of tone and color. The records themselves may undergo changes. There may be longer-playing records. Or the shining black disks as we have known them may be dispensed with entirely and sound tracks on celluloid may come into use. The bulkiness of the disks has been one of the arguments against records, as have been the limitations of time and space of each disk.

But none of these factors have prevented the recording industry from having a renaissance in recent years. Record collecting has become a national pastime, practiced by some with a passion that absorbs nearly all their spare cash and a good part of their energies. Some collectors, if they have the money, buy almost everything. They pride themselves on the inclusiveness and catholicity of their collections. They have rooms devoted entirely to their record collections, they maintain card-index systems, like libraries, and they carry special insurance. I heard of one man who bought a larger house to accommodate his records. Another had to shore up his home because the weight of his records was a menace to its foundation.

However, the average consumer cannot afford an enormous collection. He buys what he believes will give him the most enduring satisfactions. He studies the record reviews and advertisements, spends hours at his record shop listening to the possibilities, and, when he makes his selection, hurries home to listen to it over and over.

Records are not used exclusively in the home. Universities, museums, and hospitals put on concerts of recorded music regularly. Individuals who own extensive collections do likewise. In West Chester, Pennsylvania, there was organized a series of outdoor concerts, attended by a large proportion of its citizens, by tapping the record collection of one man. Record concerts are held in private homes, with a group of modest collectors pooling choice items from their libraries to build special programs. Hundreds of schools and choruses use records for illustration—a vast improvement on old methods of talking about music instead of listening to it.

Radio stations, especially the smaller, independent outlets, broadcast recorded programs by the hour. In New York, Station WQXR has made and sustained a reputation on a foundation of recorded music. Scores of small stations throughout the country depend on records for the bulk of their program time. The value of these stations to the community and their reliance on records were among the arguments used against Petrillo and the Musicians' Union in their battle against the use of records in place of living musicians.

It may be impossible to turn the clock back—to throw out technological improvements and to return exclusively to living musicians on small radio stations and in modest, little bars and restaurants. But it is not impossible to pay the musician who makes records a royalty for its use on the radio and in the juke box. No radio station, however small, would dare to take the contents of a daily newspaper and read it piecemeal over the air. The newspaper owners would be up in arms, for the courts have upheld ownership in the news. If the radio stations sold to radio advertisers programs of news taken from a newspaper purchased for three cents, the protests from the publishers would be overwhelming.

I submit that the musicians who make records have a case that should appeal with special force to believers in private-property rights. It may be that Petrillo and his union were disingenuous or even foolish to make the technological improvements the object of their attacks. It would have been better tactics to insist only on a fair share in the returns from these devices. But the opponents of the union, despite their protestations, were not fighting for principles only. Most of them welcomed an opportunity to lambast a labor union.

The sales figures tell the story of how the ownership of records has spread in this country. In 1941 about 110,000,000 disks were pressed and distributed in the United States alone—10,000,000 more than the peak year of 1921. In dollar sales jazz accounted for about seventy per cent. But symphonies, operas, chamber music, songs, and the other materials of concert hall and opera house have been gaining steadily.

The record industry has been on the verge of disaster at least twice. The advent of broadcasting in the '20's and the depression in the early '30's seemed to be death sentences, but each time the battered patient struggled to his feet and went on to more robust health. The Second World War put another crimp into the business. No one can tell what will happen after the war, but it is a reasonable guess that recordings will thrive as never before. Certainly they will if the standard of living is raised for most people, for families with a little extra income purchase a combination radio-phonograph as one of their first extravagances. Once they have the phonograph, they are lost, for record collecting, even on a modest scale, is almost inevitable.

Music is not all you get on records. Thomas A. Edison forecast years ago that entertainment and instruction would be served by the invention, but even his most sanguine predictions have been surpassed. You will find on records poetry and drama, patriotic speeches and documents, voices of presidents and prime ministers, bird songs, bugle calls of the army, health exercises including a regimen for the restoration of the figure after the coming of a baby, dance and language lessons, card tricks, and sound effects of war, such as air-raid sirens and the roar of a dive bomber. Children listen to fables and fairy tales, animal songs and the adventures of Tarzan, Superman, and other heroes of the comic-strip mythology.

The lonely amateur or professional musician can share in music-making by means of Add-a-Part Records, in which the instrument he plays is missing, enabling him to be soloist with a symphony, a fourth in a quartet, or a singer with a ready-made accompanist. Even sales talks have been recorded and sent on the road, which is a big saving in traveling expenses and which might, if adopted widely, make the anecdotes of the traveling salesman fragrant posies of the past. Records even supply a touch of ribaldry, for there is a clandestine trade in off-color recordings.

Recording has come a long way since 1855, when a Frenchman named Léon Scott fashioned a machine that traced grooves on lampblack but failed to reproduce the sound. In 1877 Edison recorded and reproduced sound on wax cylinders. In 1888 Emil Berliner hit upon the idea of using flat disks and pressing copies from a master recording. In 1898 a machinist and experimenter of Camden, N. J., Eldridge R. Johnson, followed up Berliner's idea and set up shop to make commercial recordings; in 1901 it became the Victor Talking Machine Company. There was intense rivalry between the cylinder and the disk, but the latter, in its double-faced version with which we are familiar, triumphed. Antiquarians still collect the cylinders, and on them are preserved the only concrete mementoes we have of some of the great voices of the '90's.

Enrico Caruso helped to make records respectable. He signed with Victor in 1902 and gave the business its first great impetus. Everybody knew the name of Caruso, but since there was no radio, only a limited audience had actually heard him. The records satisfied a world-wide curiosity. Caruso became, and remains, the all-

time best seller on disks. If Caruso could make records, his contemporaries figured they could too, and presently other great
singers joined up.

When the awkward horn of the early talking machine was enclosed in a cabinet by Victor and called a Victrola, it became acceptable to fastidious housekeepers. Then electrical recording was perfected, and a new standard of reproduction became possible. With
this advance came the expansion of what was recorded. A symphony
orchestra playing a full symphony was tried out on disks, with
Stokowski and the Philadelphia Orchestra among the pioneers.
Complete symphonies, operas, and chamber works came into the
range. All the great artists began to record. Today you can hear
virtually every important musician on records. At least two, Rachmaninoff and Kreisler, who have remained aloof from radio, have
recorded entire repertories. The next generation will have an excellent idea of the style and musicianship of the artists of our day.

Here is an idea of how the consumption of records has expanded.
Horowitz, Toscanini, and the NBC Symphony made a recording of
Tchaikovsky's B-flat minor Piano Concerto, which was put on the
market in 1941. Within two months it sold 100,000 albums, more
than Victor had marketed of its entire catalogue of Masterwork
albums in 1933.

But there were extenuating circumstances for this remarkable
figure. A jazz version of a theme from the concerto probably turned
the trick. A band led by Freddy Martin made a record, called *Concerto,* which sold more than a million copies. People danced to it,
hummed it, whistled it, and listened to it from 100,000 juke boxes
and millions of radio receivers. Other band leaders made their versions of themes from the concerto. When the Toscanini-Horowitz
recording of the original came out, a lot of people were evidently
moved to investigate the composer's own conception of his music.

For the performer, making records has advantages and disadvantages. If he works better without an audience, the recording
studio is a pleasant place for him. If he feels constrained within the
strait-jacket of recording requirements, he is probably irritated

and below par. For recording is a split-second affair. A twelve-inch record side can absorb five minutes of music at the most. A movement of a symphony may take three or four sides, and the performers may have to pause three or four times in making one movement. They have to make sections of a work many times over when "bugs" or mistakes creep in. A blooper in a public performance is gone with the sound waves, but it is imprisoned on records.

In the days when the invention was young, the musician sang or played into a large horn. Today he works as if he were in a concert hall; microphones pick up the sound and channel it into the room where the engineers are operating the recording apparatus. Rallying round a horn raised its own problems. Members of an ensemble had to cluster near it as best they could, and no decent balance of tone could be established. The engineers recall one occasion when Caruso made a recording of the quartet from *Rigoletto*, with Galli-Curci, Perini, and De Luca. When the record was played back, only Caruso was audible. Caruso was asked to file down his powerful voice. The result was better, but he still dominated the quartet. Caruso was finally placed five feet behind the others, and at last the quartet sounded properly balanced.

The recording world has developed its legends and traditions. Old-timers recall that for Caruso's recording sessions a kettle and oil burner had to be handy. The tenor would not drink anything cold, and every time he worked up a thirst, he would knock off while the engineer boiled the kettle of water over the oil burner. He also insisted on having his own piano. Victor had to erect a derrick in its recording building to hoist that grand piano for Caruso's recording dates. The tenor was always accompanied by his valet, who brought along several changes of clothing for the great man. In the course of a long session, Caruso would change his costume three or four times.

Caruso worked with Farrar one morning on excerpts from *Madame Butterfly*. The session was not going well; Caruso took time off and trotted out to a neighborhood bar for a snifter. When he returned to the recording horn, Farrar caught a whiff of his breath. As she sang, she interpolated into the text, "Oh, you've had a highball." Caruso replied, also in perfect time to Puccini, "I had two highballs." That record is a collector's item.

The common "bugs" occur when a musician goes off pitch, makes an erroneous entrance or exit, drops a mute, scrapes a chair, rustles his music, or coughs and sneezes. When Bruno Walter was making the "Eroica" with the New York Philharmonic-Symphony for Columbia Recording, an engineer fresh on the job received an emergency call from Columbia Broadcasting to record an important news broadcast. He plugged in a wire and inadvertently crossed it with the line recording the symphony. When the "Eroica" was played back, a solemn voice appeared as a counterpoint to the first movement with these words, "The Japanese Embassy announced today . . ."

At an all-night recording session of a jazz band, the engineer heard a slight buzz during a take. He signaled the players to stop and try again, but the buzz persisted. The boys set down their instruments and began to scour the studio for the source of the buzz. Behind a curtain they found the driver of the band's truck—asleep and snoring.

In recording there is the equivalent of mike fright. A performer who worries about the necessity of being right on the first try is likely to tighten up. He flubs and the record has to be made over. A trombonist in Artie Shaw's band developed tightness at a crucial point in a piece, and eight times the band played the piece unsuccessfully. Shaw called a recess. The men exchanged stories, and one of the bandsmen did a funny jig. The trombonist relaxed and the piece was recorded smoothly on the first try after the recess.

When musicians record for the first time, the engineers try to put them at their ease to avert mike fright. A violinist reacted to the injunction to play as if he were at home a bit too literally. During the playing of a concerto, where he had a pause while the orchestra played, he took out his hankerchief and blew his nose. The recording supervisor shouted, "I said take it easy, but not that easy. Every time you blow your nose, it costs us fifty dollars."

One studio undertook to record the music of an American circus band. The musicians of Ringling Brothers, Barnum and Bailey were engaged, and they turned up in full circus regalia. They brought along the calliope, of course. It was set up in the studio to operate electrically, and as soon as the switch was thrown every fuse in the building blew.

A Scottish bagpipe band was making a recording on the seventh floor of a studio and the music was being sent down to the turntables on the sixth floor. The engineer noticed that the sound of the pipes faded out at intervals, and went up to the studio to see what was wrong. He found the pipers marching in single file in a circle around the mike. As they circled away from the mike, the sound of the pipes faded. The engineer suggested that the band stand still near the mike while it played, but the leader replied, "How can you stand still and play a bagpipe?"

During a recording session with Stokowski and the Philadelphia Orchestra in the Academy of Music in Philadelphia, the engineers worked from an enclosed booth offstage and had telephone communications with the conductor on the podium. To attract his attention they sounded a buzzer which happened to buzz in F sharp. During a rehearsal, an engineer sounded the buzzer to get Stokowski's attention. The conductor looked up in annoyance, but did not respond. The buzzer sounded again and again, and each time Stokowski's annoyance increased. Continuing to conduct, he looked around the orchestra and demanded, "Who keeps blowing that F sharp?"

Musicians develop peculiarities in making records, as they do in performance and in practice at home. William Primrose, the violist, a precise Britisher, practices in his shirt sleeves but before starting on the actual recording rolls down his sleeves, puts on his tie and coat, and smooths back his hair. Alexander Brailowsky ignores lights and the noise of engineers fussing around him while he is practicing, but when the take is on, everyone must leave the studio and all lights but one near the piano must be put out. Salvatore Baccaloni has a big, black cigar stuck in his mouth during recording sessions. He yanks the stogie out to sing a phrase or two, then clamps his teeth on it, and puffs away the moment he has a brief pause. Some singers, on the other hand, will not even enter a studio if someone has had the audacity to smoke in it.

When Toscanini makes records, he works with the intensity that marks his rehearsals and concerts. Supervisors, engineers, and all concerned with the recording seem to walk on eggs in his presence. Yet he is tame in the face of the technique's demands. I once watched him in a session. It took him an hour to make the Overture to *Mignon,* which another conductor would have batted out in one try.

Toscanini's recordings have been expensive to make, even though they have sold in large quantities. For the major expense of a recording session with symphony orchestra is the salaries of the players. They are paid fourteen dollars an hour or forty-two dollars each for a session of three hours in which they must have twenty minutes of rest in each hour. Actual playing time, then, is 120 minutes, or two hours. The scale is not unfair. Once the men are paid, they have no further interest in the completed record; they receive no royalties, whereas the conductor does, and their fee is the same for best seller or flop. When a conductor spends time in practicing instead of completing records, it is murder. A musician like Stokowski, who wastes no time or motion and whose average of satisfactory records for each session is higher than that of most other conductors, is held in especial esteem by the recording companies.

Musicians have the right to approve or disapprove their records before they are released, and thereby hangs a tale of conflicts. Some performers are never satisfied. They fret about one wrong note in a half-hour score. They try to remake a work each year. I know of one recording that was three years in the making. Representatives of the record companies are constantly pleading with eminent musicians to approve releases; then the musicians are apt to hear the most flattering evaluations of their talents.

Musicians employ recordings by eminent colleagues to study scores. Where commercial recordings are not available, they have

transcriptions of radio performances made privately. When Toscanini conducted the American *première* of Shostakovich's Seventh
Symphony, over the air, another conductor had a recording made
of it and studied it to make sure that his performance would be
different. "More authoritative," he privately pronounced his own
version.

A brief note on the recording companies themselves. There are
three big fellows in the field in this country—Victor, Columbia, and
Decca. Decca's principal interest is jazz. It has probably gone
farther than the others in building up a distribution system, since
the overwhelming proportion of its records are low-priced, and it
does not require a big store or a fancy neighborhood to market them.
Occasionally Decca issues bigger works, and in the past it has
imported impressive albums from abroad. Victor and Columbia
have also relied on importations heavily in the past, but the war has
shifted the scene of record-making to this country.

For many years Victor dominated the field. Then Columbia was
taken over by the Columbia Broadcasting System and turned into
a real competitor. Columbia led in the reduction of prices of the
Masterwork Records, and Victor followed. This move meant the
opening of a vast new market, for many more people could now
afford records.

Though the three big companies blanket the territory, there are
independents who put out occasional records in special fields, such
as those of a left-wing projection that Keynote makes. The small
companies perform a useful service. They record things that the
big fellows ignore, and sometimes drive the big companies to chance
unusual stuff.

Say this for records. They provide an enormous library of all
kinds of music for the listener who wants something fresh and unfamiliar as well as for the man who is just getting acquainted with
the standbys of the repertory. If you choose discriminatingly
among the records, you can travel along roads that the normal
concert and opera season never approaches. There is a brave old
world and even some of the new world on disks.

18

FOR THE CHILDREN'S HOUR

Music in School—Playing an Instrument—Concerts for Children—The Prodigy—Music Teachers.

Do YOU HAVE CHILDREN, grandchildren, nephews and nieces, small brothers and sisters or youngsters of neighbors and friends whose musical interests and future concern you? You are not alone. There are people all over the United States who have wondered about this problem and have consulted all manner of experts for advice and guidance.

Whether you want the child to be a musician or an intelligent listener with perhaps a little skill at making music himself for his pleasure, it is a problem to know how to proceed. If you are a musician or have sound counsel close at hand, you know where to turn. If not, you are likely to be at a loss. It might cheer you if the public schools in your community handled music discriminatingly as an integral phase of the curriculum. An increasing number of them do, but they are still in the minority. Many schools, pursuing rudimentary methods in music, teach a few songs, patriotic and otherwise, and consider the job done.

The job is not even begun. It should be started before the child is of grammar-school age, possibly in kindergartens or private classes. The first grades of grammar school are not too late, however, provided that a proper curriculum and expert teachers are employed. For music is a language, and a child can learn it as easily as English. By sharing in the making of music, children learn part of its vocabulary more easily, and in time they may feel at home with a wider vocabulary and the intricacies of grammar and syntax.

That sounds pretentious and difficult. It is neither. Some of the schools with progressive ideas about the uses and place of music have worked out excellent techniques for teaching children. Methods may vary, and I cannot pretend to be familiar with all. But here is one approach that has proved reasonably successful.

Since rhythm is the root of man's musical responses—the motor impulse probably led man to music by way of movements of his body, which became primitive forms of the dance—children are taught to recognize and repeat rhythmic patterns, to which most of them react from infancy. They are asked to beat out simple rhythms with their hands and feet, possibly to accompany them with other movements of the body. The rhythms are then clothed in simple melodies. As the children learn to recognize and repeat rhythms and melodies, they are taught the routine symbols which man has evolved as the best means of writing down the equivalent of musical sounds. The simplest symbols will do for a start, and children learn to hear in their inner ears the sounds suggested by these symbols and to translate what the inner ear hears into sounds audible to others as well as themselves.

In time they learn to recognize and sing more difficult patterns. From simple rhythms and melodies they may move on to music with two melodies running through it simultaneously, and later they graduate to three and four. They also learn to recognize the presence and effect of harmonies.

In this country sight singing and ear training are rarely taught in the average school; it was even rarer years ago. They should be in the curriculum of every school, in the earliest grades. For these accomplishments are not only basic but easier to come by in childhood. They become much more difficult as the child grows older, and they sometimes pose almost insuperable problems for adults.

The best opinion holds to the belief that it is not necessary to begin a child's musical education by teaching him to play an instrument. If the child shows an interest in an instrument, by all means let him have instruction on it, as soon as he has the physical capacity for it. The overwhelming majority of children of three or four are too young to begin wrestling with pianos or small-sized violins.

Even though you may hear of Ruth Slenczynski, who began studying the piano at the age of three, don't make your child start that
early. Little Ruth was an exception in any case, but her father, who
had made up his mind that his child would be a musician even before she was born, probably forced her interest. He once assured me
that she had insisted on playing the piano when she was three and
that she had refused to drink her milk if she could not deploy her
pudgy little hands over the keyboard. I was not there, and I have to
take his word for it. Children should wait longer before being
allowed to play wind instruments, for only an unusually developed
youngster has the physical equipment as early as the age of six.

Children should not be compelled, either in school or at home, to
like music—or else. If the youngster does not respond to music,
even when it is offered to him intelligently, don't brood about it. He
may get around to liking it later. And if he never gets around to
liking or making music, that is no tragedy. Wasn't it General Grant
who knew only two tunes: *Yankee Doodle* and everything else?

We should avoid the self-conscious approach of the music-
appreciation courses, and that should hold for adults as well as for
children. The formal music-appreciation approach is one of the
abominations of our popularization of the art. It has done much to
confuse honest people. It has often set up words as a medium for
understanding music, and words will not do, for music begins where
words leave off. Children—and older people—are asked to read too
many words and to listen to excessive talk as part of the music they
take in. There are not many surer ways to discourage interest.

A healthy attitude toward the performance of music for children
was evinced in the concerts put on for five- and six-year-olds at the
Horace Mann School in New York recently, under the direction of
Emma D. Sheehy. It is possible that other educators have developed equally sound methods. Here were a few of the fundamental
ideas:

"Recognition of children's interest in good music without its
being sugar-coated.

"No talking about music—it speaks for itself.

"Informal and intimate atmosphere; concerts to be held in large, attractive kindergarten rooms.

"Attendance limited to one hundred (children and adults).

"All children to have front seats.

"Artists to be on same floor level as children.

"Children to have seats which fit them—no dangling legs.

"Concerts limited to half an hour."

Good musicians were engaged for these concerts. There was a soprano at one; a string quartet at another; a flutist and harpist were at a third. The music ranged from folk songs to short pieces by Mozart, Gluck, and Brahms. During a brief intermission, the children were free to talk to the musicians and to examine the instruments. Printed programs were not distributed until the end of the program. Mrs. Sheehy reported that "these concerts proved to be brimful of satisfactions and enjoyment," and she added that similar programs could be planned for children in smaller communities by employing good local talent.

When there is ample music in the home, the child will probably develop an interest in listening to music without attendance at concerts. Gregor Piatigorsky's two-year-old daughter was fond of trotting into her father's study to command him to play. Obediently he would get out his cello and play unaccompanied Bach. After an interval of listening, the little girl would say, "Enough!" and the private recital would end.

There is always the danger that concerts for young people will be patronizing and tedious. Some of the series run by our major orchestras leave something to be desired. A big hall is filled with youngsters of varying ages. The concerts are led by a good musician who may offer a hash of information, pallid philosophy, and stale jokes. The lads and lassies sometimes listen; often they launch paper airplanes or fidget in their seats until the ordeal is over, as they would during a sermon. The experience of the sound of an orchestra may be salient and some of the youngsters probably develop a taste for music, but on the whole I doubt the value of these catch-all affairs.

You cannot prove or disprove a point with one example, but this incident is worth the telling. A friend of mine looked in on a young people's concert at Carnegie Hall one Saturday morning. He slipped into an unoccupied chair, prepared to be delighted with a glimpse of youngsters reacting to the finer things of life. The seat near him was vacant, but there was an envelope on it, left by a youngster who had departed early. Picking up the envelope, my friend glanced at its contents. It was filled with off-color picture postcards.

If some of the youngsters who come to these concerts are precocious, some of their parents seem to be a little less than bright. A mother dispatched a taxi driver to bring her daughter home from a young people's concert of the New York Philharmonic-Symphony. To make sure that the cabby would get the right girl, she provided him with the location of the girl's seat and a photograph of a six-year-old child. The cabby pulled up at Carnegie Hall and gave an usher the ticket and the picture. The usher, after a safari down the aisle, reported that he could not find any girl who looked like the picture. The cabby knew the girl's name, and the usher went off to page her. A young lady of sixteen answered to the name.

Possibly the happiest way to expose youngsters to music is to let it creep up on them casually. Even here you might get mixed results. One afternoon Flagstad decided to test the acoustics and rehearse a bit of her program in the ballroom of a hotel in Des Moines. She sang some passages from Wagner, while several young bus boys set the tables in the next room. She overheard one saying, "Me, I'll take *St. Louis Blues* any time."

The American Ballad Singers encountered another reaction. At a concert in Sault Sainte Marie, Michigan, a small boy served as stage manager, taking charge of the lights and curtain. As the singers began their program, he settled down in the wings, with a book, paper, and pencil, resigned to do his homework. But the Ballad Singers sang folksy stuff. The lad glanced up, permitted himself the luxury of a smile, a giggle, a guffaw. He put his lessons aside and sat fascinated, his head on his hands and his elbows on his knees.

Neither reaction really proves anything. Boys differ, and so do music and musicians. We can be sure of only one thing: some music will appeal to all youngsters but the tone-deaf. If we could find the means to reach them and to hold their attention, it would be easier to arrive at the point where we could expand the area of their interest. *St. Louis Blues* is a good tune and can be as useful a point of departure as Wagner, if not more useful.

Where the child is gifted, a little compulsion, or shall we say persuasion, will not hurt him. When he grows up possessed of a musician's skill, he may be grateful that someone had been strict. John Barbirolli, whose father and grandfather were musicians, was provided with a fiddle as a small boy, but he was restless. He would walk around the house while practicing, and his practice sessions were not profitable. His grandfather, who was determined to make a musician of him, decided to teach him the cello, since that was one instrument he could not practice and meander through the house at the same time. Now the lad had to stay put and in time he became a fine cellist.

Accident may play a big part in the kind of musical skills youngsters develop. As a small boy, Benny Goodman was sent to a settlement music school in Chicago with two older brothers, where they received free lessons. Instruments were apportioned according to size. The oldest of the lads was equipped with a tuba; the middle boy was taught the trumpet, and pint-sized Benny was provided with a clarinet. If Benny had been an overgrown kid, he might be today a virtuoso of the sousaphone.

When a child is extraordinarily talented, there is a more serious problem for parent or guardian. Obviously, such a youngster must be given the opportunity to follow his bent. But he should not be driven. He should not be fawned upon until he becomes spoiled. And he should not be exploited.

It is a wise parent who sees the musical aptitude of a child with a sense of proportion. I have run into my share of fond parents who construe normal reactions to music as sure signs of genius. They hurry to find teachers for their offspring, high-priced teachers if they can afford them. Or they turn heaven and earth to obtain financial backing. If they are wrong about the child's talent, they are heading for disillusionment and heartache, and they will make their youngster's days a trial.

Even if they are right in judging their child's talent, parents should think a thousand times before plunging the youngster into a public career. The temptation is great, especially when parents are poor. But the way of the prodigy is hard. José Iturbi recalls that he was working for a living when he was seven. In Valencia, his home town, he was hired to pound the piano in a theater. The hours were long and dreary, and there was little time for the tot to rest or relax. There were days when little José kept banging the piano as his father shoveled dinner down his throat.

Some public performances will not hurt a healthy youngster. But these performances should be limited and well spaced. Parents who must raise funds to support a prodigy may have to let him play publicly. But they are wise if they keep the youngster from sensing that his talent is strictly for money. Yehudi Menuhin's parents, who kept him well sheltered as a prodigy, sought to teach him that the achievement of musicianship was an aim in itself. He feels now that as a lad he did not know the strain of worrying about himself as a public performer. His object was to make music, and his problem in time became the improvement of his art. His parents, he says, did not spoil him with adulation. They gave him neither more nor less than his younger sisters. He grew up in a normal family environment.

Joseph Szigeti, who was also a prodigy, but not sheltered, believes that he gained from being tossed out into the wide world before he reached his teens and from meeting with all kinds of performers and audiences. He was constantly aware of his need to earn enough money to support himself and his father. Yet he did not grow up with a distorted sense of values. Possibly because he did not have a long succession of triumphs at the start. Possibly too because he had a tough constitution that became tougher from being exposed to the harshness of the world.

Unvarying success is bad for a prodigy. It may give him a swelled head and in the end, if he does not regain a sense of balance, it may lead to the deflation of his reputation. Feuermann, who was outstanding even among prodigies, confessed once that he went through a period when his playing deteriorated because he had distorted notions of his gifts. People, he said, made the mistake of telling him repeatedly that he was wonderful, simply because he had remarkable technical facility. At sixteen, he was a professor at one of Europe's famous conservatories, and that did not help his sense of proportion. One night he played a Bach concerto in Zurich, and an acquaintance came backstage to tell him that Toscanini had been sitting near her. Expecting to lap up further praise, Feuermann wanted to know what the maestro had said or done. The acquaintance reported that Toscanini had muttered, *"O, il porco, il porco!"* The cellist was outraged at first, but Toscanini's reaction shocked him so profoundly that he began to think about himself and realized that his complacency was injuring his art.

But parents will not learn. One father decided that his six-year-old son was a conductor. He trotted the child around to amateur organizations, inducing them to let the boy conduct patriotic numbers. He brought him to newspaper offices, seeking interviews. He wrote letters hymning the lad's genius. He was having a fine time, but was he doing the child any good?

A woman wrote that she had never attempted to publicize the ability of her seven-year-old pianist son. But she wondered whether she could induce critics to come and hear him, since she wanted to be sure that the praise of audiences and instructors was deserved. But note that she had exposed the lad to audiences in formal programs. What does she think publicity consists of?

If a youngster has talent, parents or guardians have the obligation to find the right teacher. There are many good teachers as well as poor ones. A teacher may be good for one child and bad for another. The problem is similar for adults, save that presumably they can decide for themselves whether they are working under proper guidance. You have but to listen to the sad tales of grownups to

realize that finding the right teacher is a provoking quest. Here is
the cry of outrage—not unusual—of a young woman who studies
singing: "Love of the almighty dollar," she says, "has taken the
place of the teacher's sincere interest in his pupil's progress." She
complains that rates are five dollars a half-hour, and some teachers
ask as much as twenty-five dollars for thirty minutes, and she wants
to know how many American families can afford such expenditures.
Her savings lasted for eight months and then she had to take a job
as a waitress.

Among teachers you will find disputes about rates for lessons.
The famous teachers who command high prices are limited. But
even those who get moderate fees are up in arms at colleagues who
undersell them. Nor are they enamored of the habit of some teachers
of giving scholarships as a way of enticing students away from other
teachers. Private teachers complain about the big institutions, and
the conservatories will tell you privately that some teachers do less
than a rounded job of musical instruction. Teaching music is a
highly competitive profession, not only as to fees, but in terms of
systems and short cuts practiced by the teacher.

Where does all this leave the bewildered parent in search of a
teacher for a gifted child? He is lucky if he can get a judgment
from a musician not interested in teaching or from an honest
teacher who declines pupils without talent or hope.

For the student whose family has no money, there are scholarships in the conservatories, but they are reserved usually for older
boys and girls. If your community has a music settlement school
with provisions for teaching younger children, it is a good place to
take a youngster, for he is likely to receive well-rounded musical
instruction.

At some of these schools the youngsters are taught not only music
but an orderly approach to the business of beginning and ending
their performances. They have to be neat about putting away their
music and music stands, and they have to move the chairs back
where they found them. One little boy, who had been soundly indoc-
trinated, played in a trio at his school's Town Hall concert in New

York. At the end of the performance, he carefully dismantled his music stand, picked up his music and chair, and walked off the platform. The audience applauded, and the trio came out for curtain calls. As our little hero marched on and off the stage, he kept toting his fiddle, music, music stand, and chair.

19

PATRON AND PATRONESS

A "People's Opera"—The Public Chips In—Constructive Patronage.

THE PERSISTENCE OF PATRONAGE high-lights one of the fundamental errors of much of our thinking, whether in art or economics. The notion that economic security can be percolated down from the top still has its fond upholders, but it is becoming clear even to the so-called classical economists that there must be purchasing power for all if there is to be any health in the social system as a whole. In the same way music and the other arts will not achieve health until the paradoxical system of propping them from the top is ended. And in music, the propping is not even done from the top of music but from the top of the social and financial worlds.

Individuals and institutions need money to be launched properly in music. Since musicians as a class have not the money, it must be provided by people of means. Some are motivated by good will; others by a desire to gain publicity, flattery, and social advantage. The intelligence of the patron may determine the quality of a musical enterprise, and unless the patron has excellent taste, he is not equipped to set up standards. The wise patron must be willing to let competent musicians attend to that task, and wise patrons are rare.

Women are most active in patronizing art, while their men earn the money that enables them to be patronesses. Being a patroness gives a woman something relatively useful to do. And as our musical and social systems are geared, a patroness has a function of importance. A good many institutions in this country owe their existence to the hard work and persistence of devoted patronesses. These women give much of their time to the work. They keep after their friends for contributions. They organize committees. They hold teas and bridge parties. They make their pet institutions an excuse for considerable social activity, and considerable social activity an adjunct for their pet institutions.

The system of patronage is bound to produce incongruities. We find a group of rich and prominent women organizing what they call "a people's opera." As an opera company, it is a well-considered organization, with able conductors and singers and a lively repertory. But these well-intentioned women get support for their "people's opera" by inducing the fashionable world to turn out for the opening night. The newspapers are dragooned into giving long lists of names of people who attended the opening and the swanky dinner and supper parties before and after. The costumes of the first-nighters are described in detail. The people, yes! Where are they?

The patronage of the social world has little meaning or value today. It may have been of use, in years gone by, for an artist to have a list of fancy names, drawn from diplomacy and the *Social Register*, as patrons. But no one, certainly not the large paying audience, pays attention to social patronage today. Two or three society editors, several social climbers, and a few naïve souls may be impressed. Otherwise, it is a dead technique. The best patronage is that of a paying audience of thousands of average citizens or, failing that, of people who give money rather than names.

Our august musical institutions were kept alive for decades by generous patrons. Now, we are told, they are becoming more democratic. But they have not carried the democratic idea much farther than inviting the general public to contribute to their upkeep. Our most venerable organizations have conducted nation-wide campaigns for funds, and have accepted donations of one dollar and less. The public has contributed, but is there any change in the direction of the institutions? Is the public invited to elect representatives to the boards of directors? Is the public told exactly how the money has been spent? Has the public a voice in the disposition of the money it has donated toward the survival and democratization of the organization?

The public has been wheedled into making gifts of cash, but the old methods remain. Now the patron is in a fortunate spot. He can have a voice in deciding the course of a musical organization without contributing money for the pleasure of making decisions. But the only justification for patronage is that the patron is willing to supply money or influence that leads to support by others. If the patron merely gives his name and acts, usually with caution and conservatism, as a director or trustee, he is doing music scarcely any good. It would be far better to have a good musician in his place on the board.

Of the patrons who really patronize, some contribute their money because it is an easy way to climb socially. A rich couple put up a large amount of cash for an elaborate musical entertainment to get on the dinner list of one of the most influential ladies of fashion in town. Some people become patrons of music because they wish to push the career of a particular artist, and they donate money to organizations that will employ that artist. Opera companies have been kept afloat because a rich man wanted to give his soprano wife or friend a place to sing. Several women have contributed large sums to the treasuries of symphony orchestras because they have been interested in getting appointments for favorite conductors. One man organized a concert series, in part, to give his wife, a musician, an outlet for her talents.

Some patrons, of course, support musical institutions and talented individuals not to aggrandize themselves or to push some friend or protégé, but because they feel it to be their duty. One lady aided a young pianist without even letting him know her identity. Many men and women have made substantial gifts to composers, singers, virtuosos, and conductors privately without seeking or desiring public recognition. There is an element of self-preservation in some of the modest patrons, for if they make their gifts publicly, they are besieged for aid by hundreds of prospects.

Many patrons do useful work. A talented young pianist was enduring agonizing troubles. Her husband was in Europe and could not get permission to come to this country. She had a three-year-old daughter, and had to be housekeeper, cook, and nurse. Since the piano was her only means of earning a livelihood, she had to find time to practice and to seek engagements. She had to begin by establishing her existence, which meant a debut recital in New York. She gave the recital and spent virtually all her savings. Her notices were first-rate, as was her playing, and she received a few engagements. To fill a date with an orchestra in the Midwest, she traveled by bus; otherwise there would have been no profit from the engagement. A generous person promised her a weekly allowance of twenty-five dollars so that she might hire a maid and find time to practice. That was constructive patronage.

There are people who make it their business to tap the sources of constructive patronage. They bring well-meaning patron and good cause together. I know a man who is virtually a walking encyclopedia of patrons, and a father confessor of committees and individuals needing assistance. He has wit and suavity, and it is amusing to hear him discussing the possibilities of a situation with a committee. He will mention a prominent lady and say, "She will give her house only for certain kinds of parties, and we cannot ask her for too many." He is annoyed with a young man who has inherited a huge sum of money, observing: "That boy is fat, absolutely rotten with money, but won't spend it." He knows virtually how much money every patron in town has and how much he is likely to shell out for any cause. If he were to publish a compendium of his specialized knowledge, it would be more useful than the *Social Register*.

Wealthy individuals are not the only patrons. Foundations make grants to talented individuals for one purpose or another, but there is nothing capricious in this aid. A fixed amount is granted, either for a debut or for living and traveling expenses during a period of composing. The awards are made by juries of peers. The artist does not need to beg or to employ personal guile. Some private patrons are equally alive to the personal equation and grant their aid with as much forthrightness.

Occasionally you will hear of people who as individuals have only modest means but who as a group can and do assist artists. Towns and villages have raised money to send favorite sons and daughters to conservatories here and abroad for seasoning. A small group of friends, the congregation of a church, a club, or a lodge may chip in to help out. A Negro tenor was able to give a debut recital because the tenants of a huge apartment house where he was employed bought several hundred tickets in advance. A young pianist received help from a group of Hollywood actors, directors, and writers who set aside a certain amount out of every pot in their periodic poker games—the kitty—as subsidy.

A mass base for the support of talented performers and composers would be the sensible procedure. If the Federal government will not set up a system for the encouragement and development of our best talents, perhaps our states and municipalities might undertake a program. The trade-union movement could become another source of aid and comfort. The unions of musicians have a stake and responsibility. There can be no gainsaying that their first task is to maintain sound working conditions and minimum wages. But once these are established—as they are becoming established in every branch of music, save composition—they might well turn their attention to promoting artistic standards. There are not many sounder ways than giving a hand to the new generation of musicians of talent.

The obnoxious patron or patroness wants to dictate the protégé's life and art. One who supported a young violinist for many years tried to veto his choice of a wife. Another turned a talented youngster against his parents. A third succeeded in irritating managers, press agents, critics, concert-hall directors—in short, virtually everyone concerned with the young artist's career. A fourth took over the management of a protégé herself, and made an omelet of it, causing her protégé to become a laughingstock. This particular protégé had enough talent for a modest career, but the patroness saw to it that virtually all doors were barred to the young musician.

This type of patron merely emphasizes how outworn the system is, while the decent patron makes it palatable temporarily. In neither

case is it defensible as a means of supporting art. Musicians and
other artists, who give content to our democratic ideals, ought not
to be dependent on largess. The Federal Music Project and the
other WPA art projects were a step in the right direction. But they
set up a means test. When a system is developed which leaves out
the requirement of poverty and which assumes that an artist is entitled to the food, shelter, and clothing he needs to do his work, the
hit-or-miss methods of patronage will be interred without tears or
elegies. Our artists have the vision to give depth and breadth to our
democratic ideals, and, like other workers, deserve economic security—not as a matter of chance but as a right.

20

HAIL, THE AUDIENCE!

The Initiated and the Uninitiated—Big Names—Applause—Program Notes—"The Five Wise Apples"—Nelson Eddy, Ladies!

AUDIENCES ARE THE LIFEBLOOD of music, as it is practiced today, as it was practiced yesterday, and as it will be practiced tomorrow. Like the theater, movies, radio, baseball, football, and murder trials, music thrives because of its audiences. Amateurs play for fun, and so do professionals, and occasionally they seek to amuse only themselves, but even amateurs are constantly rounding up people to listen to them.

The paying audiences make possible such professional music as is purveyed in these United States, and fortunately for the musicians the number of customers has been growing steadily. Among older people, there may still be a predominance of women over men in our audiences, for there was a time when it was unmanly to be fond of music. There is little doubt that the ladies of America have kept alive many of our musical institutions, for better or for worse. But among the younger generation, the notion that music is sissy has all but gone. The war, with its absorption of millions of young men into the armed services, may have upset the equilibrium once more, but only temporarily. When the men return, they will take up where they left off. For music is no longer an ornament for the few; the radio has made it accessible to the many, and, praise be, the many like it.

Audiences are as diverse as the people of this democracy. The least important, if not the least amusing, are the musical and social snobs. They patronize the shows that are regarded, in the best circles, as the cream of the moment. In New York, for a time,

Toscanini and the New York Philharmonic reigned supreme; then Stokowski and the Philadelphia Orchestra became fashionable; later the Boston Symphony Orchestra and Koussevitzky were *de rigueur*. In each case the snobs shifted their favors to the orchestra and maestro in fashion. These people also subscribed to the Metropolitan Opera on the flossy Monday evening, when the best people usually came. Possibly they derived some pleasure from music, but, more important, it was the thing to do. They came to be seen, and to stare at those who had come to be seen.

The great majority of our audiences pay their money because they want to hear music. You can divide this majority into two sections: the initiated and uninitiated. But general classifications are merely a short cut to discussion, for among the initiated and uninitiated there are many variations.

The initiated may be regarded as the people who have experience and judgment in music. They choose their programs and performers with care; they pay to hear music and performers that are worth while but not necessarily glamorized. They do not bow the knee to current idols, nor do they turn away from great musicians just because they happen to be celebrated. They are not stampeded by rave notices, nor are they turned away by disdain. They are true connoisseurs. They are wonderful.

The uninitiated are prey to what is popular and puffed up. They do not discriminate; they accept current standards. If a big name happens to be a great artist, they hear a great artist. If the big name is a pretentious phony, they patronize a phony. They are as likely to have a swell time listening to the phony as to the great artist. They are the mass buyers in the new mass production of music. They may not be connoisseurs, but they are wonderful.

Anybody who pays good money to hear music is wonderful, if you ask the trade. Even audiences of deadheads that turn out to listen to newcomers have their uses; to the particular performers and managers, these audiences are also wonderful. In a word, all audiences are wonderful.

The public as a whole loves big names. It is customary to charge this amiable predilection of the paying customer to our vast apparatus of publicity and our habit of glamorizing the virtuoso. American audiences are constantly being castigated for their susceptibility to high-pressuring. The lofty souls who do the castigating forget that it has been thus for more than a century wherever audiences gather to hear Western music. Horowitz, Kreisler, Heifetz, Anderson, Flagstad, Toscanini have drawn packed houses whereever they have gone. In any town on any continent, the situation is about the same. Moreover, people remain faithful to their heroes and heroines. For decades they will continue to patronize the same big names. They will take a chance on a new figure with reluctance. Only as the newcomer is built into a star and accumulates his own tradition and folklore does he entice the cautious and conservative public.

It is a pleasant parlor game among the high-brows to flail American audiences for lack of discernment. Some musicians turn up their noses at our tastes and tell us that elsewhere people are more discriminating. Take it from a man like Horowitz that this high-brow pose is the bunk. He is quite willing to play Tchaikovsky, if that is what the public likes, and he sees no reason to be patronizing about it. "Some musicians keep telling us that in Europe audiences have higher tastes," he says. "Well, I made more money in Germany playing Tchaikovsky than some of the stuffed shirts playing Beethoven and Schubert. And the German audiences loved Chopin, too—another composer who was not for these high and mighty musicians." Does the public like flashy arrangements? "Let them have them. Didn't Bach, Beethoven, and Brahms make plenty of them?" he wants to know.

Szigeti is another musician who has a good word to say for American audiences. He recalls that as a famous virtuoso in Europe he was restricted to the top-price circuit. That meant the big cities—Paris, Berlin, Rome, London, Vienna, and the like. He once wanted to play in Cracow, the Polish town which has a fine, old tradition of civilization, or had before the Nazis desecrated it. But Cracow was on the lower-priced circuit, and Szigeti's manager would not book him

there, admonishing him that if he played Cracow, it would hurt his
standing in the bigger cities. When the violinist came to the United
States, he was surprised and gratified to find that small towns considered themselves quite as good as large, that if a community of
15,000 could raise the money to pay for the highest-priced musicians, they heard them.

It takes all kinds of people to make an audience. Nearly always
there are the late-comers who have a constitutional inability to
arrive on time and who think they have a constitutional prerogative
to climb over everybody else. There are people who have to show
themselves off in their finery. There are chatterers and dozers, program rattlers and fidgeters. There are the scholarly folk who bring
their scores to concerts and operas; they seldom have enough light
to follow their bent and they aim flashlights on printed pages to the
vast annoyance of their neighbors.

Among my favorites are the fervid applauders. I don't mean the
professional applauders—the claque, relatives, or manager of the
artist—but the amateurs who have paid their way and who express
themselves by wild beating of the palms. They sometimes set up a
terrific clamor, and frequently they cannot contain themselves until
a piece of music is over. At any promising point, at any cadence
that sounds like the end, their hands are poised to start beating. No
one begrudges them their innocent pleasures, but the place where
the insistent applause gets you down—provided you are not the
artist on the receiving end—is at song recitals. A scientific observer
once kept a stop watch on the time elapsed at a song recital in applause and acknowledgment of applause and compared it with the
time spent in singing. Fifty per cent more time was devoted to the
amenities than to music.

The public is bewildered and bewildering. There are people who
want everything fitted into neat compartments and who bother
musicians and writers to give them opinions that will arrange themselves precisely and unquestioningly. They want lists of the world's
ten best pianists, singers, violinists, and conductors. Usually they
have made bets with their friends on the correct order, and anyone

timid enough to suggest that musicians cannot be classified like the best tennis players, the all-America football teams, or the best-dressed women in America is a low, lazy, lying lout.

Some of the simple souls expect musicians, newspapermen, music publishers, or librarians to know the answers to all their questions. They will phone you late at night, while you are working, to sing and whistle a tune and to ask what opera, symphony, movie, musical comedy, or radio show it comes from. Sometimes these tunes seem to stem from the imagination of the whistler on the other end of the phone. A friend of mine in a newspaper office has developed an efficient technique for dealing with these insistent questioners. He tells them, as he hangs up the phone, "I'm only the janitor."

Bewilderment may arise out of too much reading of program notes. Schnabel was once approached by an angry lady after she heard him play a Beethoven piano concerto. "The program notes said that Beethoven was in love again when he wrote this concerto," she cried out indignantly. "I did not find that love in your interpretation."

Or people are literal-minded. Gian-Carlo Menotti wrote an opera called *The Old Maid and the Thief*, spoofing spinsters. At the end of a lecture at a university extension course, he was confronted by a middle-aged lady, who bawled him out. "And remember," she concluded, "not all old maids are lovelorn."

Or people are just plain befuddled. At a concert devoted to the music of Orlando di Lasso, the program clearly indicated that the composer was born in 1530 and died in 1594. After one number, the conductor led forth a young man from the ranks of the chorus to take a bow for his singing of a solo passage. I heard an old gentleman whispering to his companion, "Is that the composer?"

Or people want exact information. A man went to a concert by a well-known violinist and enjoyed it. He also liked the review that one critic wrote about the event. He wrote the critic a letter, complimenting him on the review, since it agreed entirely with his own judgment. Could the critic tell him, he ended, the precise location of his seat so that he might compare it with his own?

Or a customer is outraged that Ettore Panizza, conducting a performance of Mozart's *Marriage of Figaro* at the Metropolitan Opera House, permitted a baritone to hold the last quarter note of an aria for four additional measures. He writes a threatening note, signing it Hector Berlioz, Jr., and saying, "If at the next performance of *Figaro* this shameful exhibition is repeated—if at the next performance the American public is to hear what Mozart did not write, I shall rise from my seat and in a loud, clear tone will shout, 'Who has dared to correct Mozart?' "

I hope he does, and I hope I'm there when he does. Nothing would surprise me in a member of the audience. There is a tradition that Americans take their music politely, compared with the hissing, booing, shouting, and cheering of European, particularly Latin, audiences. The tradition is based on the fact that people seem to sit through anything, bad or good, and give it the same measure of polite approval. But that describes only a portion of the audience, which holds no strong views and has no marked reactions to what it hears. It is certainly not true of a section of the audience which is increasingly independent in its judgments and growing bolder in displaying its feelings. The audiences that have heard Toscanini in recent years have known how to shout and cheer. The gatherings at the Berkshire Festival have been almost as demonstrative as a Latin audience. The audiences at the rarefied chamber-music programs know when they are getting value and they can be stiffly indifferent when receiving less.

The people who take their jazz seriously do not hesitate to state their feelings, and they make quick decisions as to whether an outfit is good or bad. I am not talking of the exhibitionistic jitterbugs who dance in the aisles for their favorite bands, but of the critical listeners who can relish the music without self-display. These audiences reserve the right to hoot and catcall, if they are not satisfied, and they refuse to be short-changed. Some time ago Erskine Hawkins and his band arrived at a dance hall in a Midwestern town to find a huge crowd in the street and only three or four people in the hall. When the band entered, each man was looked over critically,

because the young jazz fanciers had been bilked once too often. Big-
name leaders had arrived with makeshift bands. The youngsters
knew the personnel of their favorite bands, and they decided to
check up on Hawkins before parting with their money. Once the
word was passed along that the regular outfit was on hand, the boy-
cott was canceled.

Musicians, in all branches of the art, are discovering that they
can't get by with lesser stuff in the hinterland, which is a tribute to
the growth of a knowing audience. Springfield, Massachusetts, objected when several visiting orchestras gave programs without a
single American work. The managers of musicians, and the musicians themselves, occasionally receive letters from outraged customers in the so-called sticks. The big city newspapers receive them
too, and we know how keenly people are listening. The comments
are cutting, and they do not spare the illustrious. Toscanini's "sense
of proportion" is condemned, Stokowski's "virtuoso manipulations"
are lambasted, Serkin's "program was hackneyed and the performance something he should be ashamed of." To one listener Jan
Kiepura was simply "Dizzy," like the pitcher known as Dean; this
listener would rather hear "a singer with visual appeal than one
with mere vocal perfection." A new pianist is damned with faint
praise in the press, and an irritated listener argues that the pianist
was not entitled to any praise, even faint. When a young conductor
objected to the arrangements for the seating of orchestra and audience at a free concert with a WPA orchestra, some of the listeners
shouted that they were not interested in him but in Beethoven.

When you are patronizing with this new audience, you get slapped
down, and rightly. In reporting a festival of contemporary music at
Yaddo, Saratoga Springs, one year, I noted that five young maids
in the audience had squirmed through the serious stuff but had
perked up when a work by Robert McBride, written in the jazz
idiom, was played. I soon received a letter that put me in my place.
It said in part:

"At first we did not recognize ourselves as the five young maids
at Yaddo, perhaps because we are not accustomed to being de-

scribed by such nineteenth-century adjectives as 'prim, modest, and well-bred.' We hope that you will not consider us ill-bred if we describe the conditions under which we squirmed. Even if you were not the restless man behind us who kept prodding us with sharp kneecaps and practicing well-shod arpeggios on our spinal columns, you must have been near enough to observe how crowded we were. The crowd there in the afternoon seemed almost double that of the morning session; perhaps none of the critics got up in time to hear the morning concert.

"You were near enough, at any rate, to see how we perked up at Bob McBride's *Wise Apple Five*. It is only fair to tell you that our interest was not evoked by the introductory remarks about jazz, but was only the natural interest of five who have been playing Bob's music from manuscript for three years."

The letter was signed, "The Five Wise Apples." If the girls had given their names I should have been glad to apologize. Anyhow, dear Apples, those were not my kneecaps.

The days of adulation are by no means over. It is difficult in these times—it was difficult even before the war—to engineer enough enthusiasm to get up marching and chowder clubs in honor of a musician. A generation ago the friends and admirers of Geraldine Farrar could organize the Gerry Flappers and they made quite a to-do at her farewell to opera. More recently a hard-pressed press agent tried to promote an adoration society for Lily Pons, and the idea died in desultory fashion shortly after it was spawned. But you can always get the devotees mad by saying a harsh word, merited or not, about their gods and goddesses, even the dead whom they worshiped long ago.

If you mention the fact that a contralto's figure is plumpish, which it is, though no gentleman should harp on it, you will get a sharp reminder that you are probably no Apollo yourself, and since when are opera singers supposed to look like Hedy Lamarr? A lady who heard that the members of the New York Philharmonic-Symphony, her favorite orchestra, were being handled with ironclad discipline by several guest conductors wrote this heart-rending appeal: "To have players sweat in fear for my enjoyment is equivalent to sweatshop labor in industry. The men who give us such joy, I contend, should love their giving. I'd rather have Barbirolli with any imperfections he may have but with his keen human interest in his work with the men—co-operation rather than slave-driving—than all the conductors who may wring wizardry out of their instruments but wear the men out and warp their souls in the doing!"

If you don't mention the favorites of the devoted, you will hear about that, too. An admirer of Flagstad, saddened by the news that she was not returning to America, wrote to a newspaper, "Even though Miss Flagstad will not be here we can console ourselves by talking and writing about her, so please let's have many stories about her." A lady who read that Kreisler would not be able to play for many months because of an accident said she consoled herself by playing his records, summing up her thoughts with the observation that "while Heifetz and Menuhin were merely miraculous, Kreisler was superlative."

There was the chap in Evansville, Indiana, who wrote Szigeti, "Thought you might like to know that there is quite a large group of local Szigeti worshipers who are particularly thrilled that you are finally coming to our city for a concert. I claim to be the original local Szigeti fan. I have traveled several hundred miles to hear you play, twice to Chicago and once to Louisville. My friends say that I remained a bachelor until I found a girl (she's from Buffalo) who admires Szigeti as much as I do. Of course, she had the extra-attractive quality of playing the violin in tune and she is pretty."

Astrid Varnay had her admirers even before her debut at the Metropolitan. They were a group of young girls who had sat with her in the upper reaches of the house to listen to other singers. They knew that she was studying to be a singer, and they were on hand the night she made her surprise debut as Sieglinde, substituting at the last moment for Lotte Lehmann. One of these girls was standing in the lobby near the box office before the show, and she heard a disappointed customer say that he wanted his money back because Lehmann was not singing. She approached the customer and, speaking rapidly and heatedly, urged him to give the young singer a chance. The man was amused and decided to stay. Later he wrote Miss Varnay a note, telling her that he got his money's worth and that he applauded the loyalty of her friend.

If there is any musician who has his legion of hero-worshipers, it is Nelson Eddy, and they are mostly young women. Even before he became the darling of the movie fans, his power was clear. In February, 1934, he gave his first New York recital at Town Hall. He had made a modest career as a radio singer, though he was far from being a star. At that debut recital, the hall was packed, and most of the glamour girls of 1934 were there. The first appearance of the strapping young man with the handsome face and the blond, wavy hair induced a wave of admiration that was palpable to a toughened concertgoer. After the recital, a throng of girls overran the backstage quarters, and the stage manager, a hardened veteran, ducked across to the other side of the stage and stayed there behind the lighting switchboard until the charge of the debutantes was over.

When Eddy became a Hollywood idol, the number and devotion of his admirers multiplied incalculably. Two girls turned up one day at New York's Town Hall to buy tickets for a Nelson Eddy recital eleven months before it was to take place. They were told that tickets for his concert were sold as part of a series. The girls didn't want the series. They threatened a sit-down strike if they did not get the tickets. They had made it a practice to follow Eddy on his journeys. They had traveled to Philadelphia, White Plains, and even to Chicago to hear him sing. They were not to be denied in New York. I am sure that Eddy will agree that audiences are wonderful.

21

MIDDLEMEN OF MUSIC

*Managers—"Twenty Per Cent Was Not Too Much"—First Concert—Press Agents—
Critics—Mary Garden on Criticism—Asleep in Town Hall.*

IF THE ACTIVE AGENTS of music are the composers, performers, and audiences, what would you call the managers, critics, press agents, and other middlemen? Musicians have many names for them, some flattering but most of them resentful and contemptuous. A consensus would show that these middlemen are regarded as a necessary evil. Whether you like them or not, they exist and function, and as long as our music is geared as it is, they will continue to play a role.

Managers are like teachers; they are great if they have great artists. If they have mediocre musicians to manage, their shrewdness and skill will help them only to keep their losses low. The history of successful managements in this country is a review of the men who were lucky or wise enough to get under contract big or potentially big artists. With the artist of solidly established reputation, the task is to sell him judiciously and to keep him happy. More work and imagination are required to raise a gifted musician to stardom.

Only a few of those who undertake the management of musicians succeed at it, and each year it becomes more difficult. The chief obstacle to the newcomer today is the dominance of two large agencies —Columbia Concerts Corporation and the National Concert and Artists Corporation, formerly the NBC Artists Service Bureau. These major companies have several hundred musicians under their management, and their lists embrace most of the famous names in the trade. Each company, furthermore, controls an organization that helps communities throughout the nation to give a series of concerts each season. In this way they have a hand and a voice in a vast majority of American concerts.

The chief advantages of the system are that new towns have been opened up to music and that musicians who are not well known get a chance to appear in a series where the local budget does not admit of buying the biggest names exclusively. The value to the two major managements is obvious: profits. The disadvantages are that competition is limited largely to the two big companies, and occasionally it is perfunctory; that the small, independent manager has a hard time selling his artists and that the artist who cannot get onto the list of the big companies is restricted to the relatively narrow field that his manager's ingenuity can pry open.

But if you think that the two big corporations have sewed up most of the virtuosos and singers, consider the dominating influence of one man on the conductors in this country. Arthur Judson manages most of the well-known conductors. The principal exceptions are Toscanini, Koussevitzky, and Stokowski. Toscanini has been his own manager, and so has Koussevitzky. Stokowski and Judson were once closely associated, but they parted some years ago, and not amicably, if the stories current at the time are to be trusted. Otherwise, most of the well-known names are under Judson's management. Judson is also manager of the New York Philharmonic-Symphony Orchestra, and people in the business are constantly marveling at his ability to earn a salary from the orchestra and to receive commissions from conductors from his own stable of maestros who are hired by the orchestra.

Judson may be one of the big money-makers among the managers. But he has his troubles, too. When you manage a large number of artists, you are bound to run into ticklish rivalries. If Conductor B feels that he ought to have a shot at conducting in New York and if he thinks he is the equal of Conductor A, he may have a tantrum when he learns that Conductor A has received a call to direct in New York. The manager who has both Conductors A and B under his wing may explain patiently to Conductor B that the board of directors decides on the choice of conductors, but Conductor B will scream that he has been hornswoggled out of the big chance. Don't think that this is just a hypothetical case. It has happened more than once.

Virtuosos eye each other jealously, and the manager is the goat if one thinks that a colleague is getting breaks that rightfully belong to him. Performers, who may have decided and exaggerated notions as to their worth, hold the manager responsible if they do not receive engagements and fees to match their rivals. They quarrel over billing, check up on expenses, and demand personal attentions. The relationship between artist and manager is seldom, if ever, a cut-and-dried business affair. If the manager tries to establish it on that basis, he hears from his clients. I know one musician who was sorely put out because his manager was not at the railroad station to greet him on his return from a tour. I know a fiddler who threatened to leave a manager if he signed up an up-and-coming young fiddler.

Artists complain now and then that the fees they pay their managers are not warranted. Grace Moore decided to manage herself in the fall of 1942 and told reporters that she was doing famously and that twenty per cent was too much to pay a manager. From Frederick C. Schang, who had been her manager for twelve years, came this telegram:

"Just read story that Grace Moore claims twenty per cent too much to pay a concert manager. As Gracie's manager for the last twelve years I can tell you definitely—oh, so definitely—that twenty per cent was not too much. No, indeed it wasn't! Only the U. S. Internal Revenue Department is going to know accurately the difference between a professional concert agency managing La Moore's affairs and this artist going it on her own. After one season Gracie will charge herself fifty per cent for handling her own business if she can afford it."

Try as he will to keep his affairs on a business basis, the manager cannot get away from the fact that musicians are the most rugged and self-centered of individuals. Not many are content to fill their dates, accept payment, and live their own lives, letting the manager live his. Their ailments are the manager's concern. Their wives, sweethearts, children, accompanists are the manager's affair. Even the matter of what a musician shall play can be a problem to the manager. A concert committee in a distant town wants certain works, but the artist will play only what he likes. The manager has to mediate. A star usually plays what he likes, and the local concert committee grumbles. If the committee wins its way with a less prominent musician, the latter complains. The manager is caught in the middle.

Managers have their share of excitement. The thrill of discovering a new artist and watching him build into a sensational draw is warming to the heart as well as the purse. The manager makes a contribution, even though some musicians would deny it. If he knows his craft, he spaces engagements shrewdly, takes dates that have prestige value even at lesser fees, advises on programs, and helps out with such factors of showmanship as dress, bearing, and walking on and off the stage. Only a limited number of musicians become stars overnight strictly on the strength of their first appearances. The manager helps considerably, though one or two musicians could not be kept from the top even by incompetent managers.

Of the hundreds of musicians that a major management sees through a first concert, a small percentage returns for a second, and a small percentage of the small percentage is able to make a career of concert giving. Why, you will ask, do the major managements put on so many debuts? They have special recital departments to handle this service, and they charge a fee of $150 for managing a single concert. Since they must maintain the recital department for the New York concerts of their money-making artists, they figure that they might as well earn a little extra with a setup already in operation. The hopefuls, young and old, who insist on giving a New York recital debut persist no matter how many stories of misfortunes and difficulties they hear. They feel the call and will not be dissuaded.

In fact, some independent managers earn enough to stay solvent by handling only these sad debutants.

Some managers hold auditions and try to talk the hopeless cases out of spending their money for concerts. But they seldom succeed. The prospect will find someone to manage his debut, and if he can't obtain an established manager, he'll manage himself, or enlist a member of his family. An experienced manager can usually obtain a good idea of a young musician's chances from talking with him. The musician's training, experience, ideas for programs, and general attitude are fairly reliable clues. If the manager is doubtful about these, he may resort to an audition. It may turn out that the hopeful who performs brilliantly at an audition before a handful of people is a washout in public performance, and the artist who does poorly at the audition acquits himself brilliantly in the hall before an audience.

Even a brilliant performance is not conclusive. Managers have discovered that there are such things as one-program musicians. A young pianist who dazzled New York at her first recital tried again with a fresh program six months later and flopped. The intention of that second concert was to add to the fine impression of the first, which had not been enough to produce engagements throughout the country. Perhaps the manager hurried this young artist. There is such a thing as overmanaging. A talented young pianist was introduced to New York by a zealous manager who did such a thorough job of obtaining an audience that his charge had an overflow crowd on the stage. The young fellow became jittery and played poorly.

Good managers will not permit newcomers to be puffed in advance of a debut. They will not make extraordinary claims, and will advise the musician to be reticent. They insist, rightly, that public and press are likely to be suspicious of a musician who makes grandiose boasts in advance and that they prefer to find out for themselves.

You would think that a manager, like an artist, would like nothing better than praise in print after a debut performance. Actually, the manager does not sing hallelujahs if a musician receives kind notices. The useful reviews, as far as the manager's tastes are concerned, are outright raves or roasts. The manager can use a rave if the artist is really exceptional. If the musician is less than that, the manager does not want a meed of praise. He may not thank me for giving away this trade secret, but he much prefers a thorough roast. When a musician receives reasonably good reviews, he is certain that the way is open to him for a respectable career. He does not expect seventy-five engagements at $2000 each, but he would be content with twenty-five at $300. The manager is embarrassed. He cannot sell the artist at all, nor can he suggest that the critics were being polite.

There are all kinds of managers. Some carry on quietly, others flamboyantly. Some take the bad with the good philosophically, and some flare up at every injustice, real or fancied. Some are strictly businesslike, even hard-boiled, and some are emotional and excitable. Some care about music, and some don't give a hoot. Musically one of the most accomplished managers I have heard of is Fred M. Gee of Winnipeg, who in October, 1933, took over in place of the suddenly indisposed Stewart Wille, and played accompaniments for Lawrence Tibbett, reading through a full concert's compositions at sight.

Some managers employ all manner of resourcefulness to push their artists. One manager caused a singer under his wing to make a recording of one of her best numbers, and he sent copies of it to local concert managers throughout the country, on the theory that the voice itself would be more effective than all the printed encomiums. Another had an artist who appeared as soloist with an orchestra which, as a matter of policy, never permits encores. The soloist made a big hit, and his manager demanded that he be allowed to offer several extras, but the manager of the orchestra would not agree. The manager of the soloist ranted, and finally he dashed off to a telephone booth to notify the local papers that his artist had not been granted the privilege of being generous.

Managers, even within the same organization, watch each other like opposing generals. One man who managed a prominent soprano was resentful when a rival soprano was signed up by another man in his corporation because he feared that his own artist might lose some dates.

Managers have their good and bad years, like Wall Street brokers. In depressions their wares do not sell, and like the musicians, they suffer. Some years they strike it lucky, and other years they have their share of misfortunes. Look at what happened to the NBC Concert Service within twelve months. Kirsten Flagstad did not return to America; Fritz Kreisler was put out of action by an automobile accident, and Emanuel Feuermann died.

The large corporations can weather misfortunes of this kind. They have reserves of money and of big artists to cushion the shocks of sudden disaster. But the little man who is running an office on his own cannot withstand such shocks. The defection of one artist may put him out of business. As it is, he has to fight to keep his head above water. And we need the independent managers. They are good for music and musicians. They add variety, sparkle, and audacity to the scene. Unfortunately, the times are against them, though a few manage to thrive. I am sorry that there are so few.

There is never a shortage of press agents, however. Here competition is wide open. You don't need capital to go into business. All a press agent requires is a client. His office can be under his hat, though a typewriter and a telephone number where someone will take messages are useful, and a pleasing personality will help. There are some high-powered press agents with large offices and batteries of helpers. But press-agentry in music, as elsewhere, is a precarious field. If musicians change their managers from time to time, they are really fickle about their press agents. Some try a new press agent each season. The big managements maintain their own press representatives, but some artists are not content with the identical services their rivals get. They want special attention, and they are willing to pay for it. Of course, if the musician is tight, a serious conflict arises in his mind. Shall he pay a private press agent or shall he do without one but perhaps suffer from less notice? One musician resolved the dilemma by trying to hire a press agent on a piece-work basis—so much for an article, so much for a picture, so much for a mention in a gossip column.

The press agent in music, like his confrere in the other pursuits of America's much ballyhooed life, knows a hundred dodges to get his client's name or picture published. He tries, first of all, to get the musician some attention on stories of musical interest. But he will invade the society, garden, food, and fashion pages. In his client's name, he organizes contests, forms foundations, commissions works, writes letters, manufactures anecdotes. Presently a musician who is really articulate only through music has become a great public figure, whose views are canvassed on every subject.

Some artists are difficult for press agents. They expect miracles and they harry the press agent if they don't get them, while other musicians will refuse to co-operate. Vladimir Horowitz agreed to have a *Life* photographer come up to his home to make a series of shots of him. When the photographer arrived with an automobile full of equipment, the pianist refused to let him into the house. He had changed his mind about the pictures.

Press agents can perform a useful function. They can save the artist from personal annoyance, and give the mediums that reach the public smooth service. It is only when the press agents resort to meretricious stunts that neither the musician nor the public is well served. Of course, the press agent is making a living, and who are we to complain about a man trying to earn his daily bread?

For that matter, so is the critic, but in earning his daily bread, he is influential in deciding whether others shall do likewise. The critic is a brilliant, perceptive fellow to performer, composer, and public if they agree with what he writes. He is a crude, ignorant nincompoop if they hold opposing views. Since few human beings, even critics, belong to the extremes of greatness or smallness, let us assume that most critics fall somewhere between, though there have been one or two men close to the heights or the depths.

I interviewed Mary Garden some years ago, and it was difficult to get her to talk about anything but critics and criticism. What she said represents the feeling of many musicians.

"I think criticism can be very useful," she said. "Very useful. But," she brought her hands together, so that the palms were tightly pressed against each other, "criticism and rudeness are as close to each other as my hands. It is a gifted critic who can stay on the decent side of his craft.

"Not that it has mattered to me," she went on. "I have not cared about criticism. I have lived my characters on the stage, and if the public has responded to them, that has been enough for me. I have never forgotten the advice of an old French artist—always remember when you go out on the stage that someone in the audience has made sacrifices to be there.

"But I have known artists, good artists, who have suffered because of tactless writers and who found it that much more difficult to make a go of it in this country."

Miss Garden spoke of the fact that her voice had not always found favor with critics in America. They had maintained, in fact, that she had no voice at all. Her most eloquent admirer, James Huneker, had spoken of her voice as a "sonorous mirage." Miss Garden recalled these judgments without rancor.

"It has its advantages, being accused all one's career of having no voice," she said. "At least they cannot say now that I have lost it."

Critics also have their crosses to bear. They are assailed as scoundrels by those they censure and hailed as heroes by those they praise. They generally prefer neither attack nor approval but only a realization that they are doing their jobs, honestly and without prejudice.

They don't want sudden friendships thrust upon them by musicians who have a concert coming on, and they could probably survive without copious invitations to cocktail parties, teas, dinners, and suppers. They are especially suspicious of the musicians and friends of musicians who cultivate the acquaintance of managing editors and publishers; nothing so crass as a direct attack on the critic. I know one gentleman who has irons in several musical fires. He once had a chat with a young critic, telling him in the nicest way that he and the young critic's boss were close friends. The publisher, it seemed, relied on this gentleman to tell him how his critics were doing. It was clearly to the advantage of the young critic to be agreeable to this influential citizen, unless, of course, the young critic were skeptical enough to have his own thoughts.

Some people regard reviewers as men and women whose chief utility is to help them out in their difficulties. Students request critics to give them material for essays and theses. Ladies ask them for information with which to address their local discussion clubs. Teachers and parents want private auditions for their charges. A woman sent some sappy verses to one critic with this request: "Please send these lyrics to a good music writer to set music to the words. Please choose one whose music is more on the classical side."

Writers, however, have their little moments of fun. In a record-review column for *The New York Times* I devoted the first half to an album of bird songs and used a photograph of a woodcock to illustrate it. I needed another photograph and wondered whom I could tease by coupling him with a woodcock. I decided that Cole Porter was a likely prospect, and ran his picture near that of the woodcock. Was Porter amused or annoyed? I don't know. I do know, however, that the day after the pictures appeared in print, he phoned his record shop and ordered the bird-song album.

A famous Metropolitan Opera conductor died a while ago and a writer went through the clippings in his newspaper's files to find a paragraph by the paper's leading critic to be quoted as a tribute to the deceased conductor. But the critic had not been fond of the conductor, and the obituary writer could not find, amid scores of clippings, any paragraph of undiluted praise. Being resourceful, the obituary writer solved his problem after his own fashion, composing a paragraph of complimentary criticism and attributing it to the critic.

The unflattering occasionally does find its way into a respectable journal, and even sacred cows get a pummeling, if only by accident.

A letter savagely attacking a new opera company appeared in a prominent paper, written by a man who was a friend of the sponsors of the company. The letter created a furor. The writer of the letter had meant it to be a private note, but the critic, perhaps without realizing this, had published it. The letter drew an indignant reply, but its author stood by his guns. The critic was grateful; at Christmastime he sent his correspondent a magnum of champagne.

The detractors of critics sometimes say, "No wonder their notices are rotten, they're always asleep." I can assure you that generally they stay awake, through the thick of the performance and the thin of the music. Once in a while a critic, however, does catch a nap. My favorite scene of snoozing critics occurred some years ago at a Town Hall recital. Three of the fraternity sat in a row in aisle seats. One in the last row rested his head against the rear wall and dozed peacefully. The man in front of him had his elbow on the arm of the chair, his head propped in it, and he too was dozing. The third was nodding; occasionally his head jerked up, as if he were suffering from an unpleasant dream, or possibly it was just the music. Another critic who had a tendency to drop off now and then made light of his weakness with the comment, "I've left a call with the usher to be awakened at 10."

A critic wrote a severe condemnation of a cadenza played by a well-known violinist and was reminded by the violinist that he had praised the cadenza when he had played it for the first time several years before. That was why he had kept it in his repertory. The critic called up the man who had accompanied him to the concert at which the cadenza had been introduced. "Did I say I liked that cadenza?" he demanded. "All I know is that you slept through it," his friend replied.

There was the time that a press agent sent out a story that a baritone, making his New York concert debut, had invited a group of chorus girls, with whom he had worked in a movie theater, to occupy the first few rows at the concert. One reviewer spent some time demanding to know where the girls were. The press agent, who had planted the story, was indignant that the writer was checking up and cried out, "Look at that fool! A man is singing his debut recital, and this fellow is looking for chorus girls!"

Managers also take cracks at the critics, as who does not. A manager saw the chief editor of a leading newspaper at a recital of one of his artists. The editor was obviously having a good time. During the intermission, the manager made it his business to greet the editor. "I am delighted," he said, "that, after reading your critics, you still enjoy music."

For the information of the manager and other doubters, I should like to add that the critics still enjoy music, too.

22

IN THE AFFAIRS OF MEN

The Difference Between Busch and Furtwängler—The Adventures of Vaughan Williams—Toscanini and Fascist Italy—Casals and Fascist Spain—Enemy Art—Social Significance in Music—The Musician in the Community.

WHEN HITLER CAME into power in Germany, hundreds of artists, eminent and unknown, were driven out of the country. Indignant people exclaimed, "What beasts the Nazis are to exile men and women who never mixed in politics and who concerned themselves only with their art!"

What an epitaph for the artist! Is he so saintly that he must remain aloof from the world around him? Is it a mark of credit that he has been so far above the battle that he has given no thought to politics, economics, and international relations? As musicians, painters, writers, architects were hounded out of Germany, one felt profound sorrow for those who had been uprooted from their native soil because of the accident of birth, but one was proud of those flaming human spirits who had recognized the enemy from afar and had refused to temporize with him.

Consider those excellent German musicians—Adolf Busch and Wilhelm Furtwängler, both acceptably Aryan. Busch understood what the Nazis were up to; he packed up and left for good. Perhaps Furtwängler understood, too. Former associates brought reports from Germany that he was uneasy about many things and that he had fought to keep in his orchestra musicians who were, according to Nazi precepts, tainted racially. But he stayed on the job, helping, whether he meant to or not, to give an aura of respectability to a predatory gang.

There were non-German musicians who, before the Nazis began

their open aggressions, tried to minimize the nature of the evil. If they were not outright believers in Nazism or appeasement, they wanted, apparently, to keep their engagements and their public in Germany. Others simply followed the lead of their Foreign Offices which maintained diplomatic relations with the Nazis. Those who were men of good will recognized their error in time and confessed it openly.

The adventures of Ralph Vaughan Williams, dean of British composers, with the Nazis are illuminating. In 1938 he was awarded the Hanseatic Shakespeare Prize, set up by the Nazis when they were trying to keep on good terms with the British and when the British government, led by Neville Chamberlain, was seeing and hearing no evil in Naziland. The prize went to Vaughan Williams for the most distinguished artistic contribution by a Briton, and he accepted. Progressive voices in England were raised against the acceptance. They wrote to him that the Nazi record of brutality was written in letters big enough for all to read. In the summer of 1939, when I was in London, I happened to see some of this correspondence. Vaughan Williams explained that he had accepted the prize because it was from "the German nation."

Vaughan Williams learned shortly that "the German nation" did not relish an honest opinion or an independent thought. Being a man of good will, he signed an open letter addressed to the German government, protesting against the outbreak of new brutalities. That finished him with the Nazis. The British Council, working in the cultural field of international relations, had been planning several concerts for Berlin by a British orchestra in 1939. Naturally, a composition by Vaughan Williams was a must for such an occasion, but when the programs were sent to the Germans, they demanded that the Vaughan Williams score be eliminated. The British Council replied by canceling the concerts. Another group of respectable Englishmen had learned that there was no dealing with the Nazis except on their terms; for the Nazis would not conform to the code of English gentlemen.

Arturo Toscanini reacted to the Nazis more decisively. When

they came into power, he turned his back on Germany. He had seen the face of Fascism in his own country, and had found it evil. It is true that he returned to Italy for his summer holidays during the years of Mussolini's dominance and that he even conducted there from time to time. But he hated the Fascists, refused to play the *Giovanezza*, the party's hymn, and, when he appeared once in Bologna and rejected an order to preface the concert with the tune, was assaulted by a band of Black Shirt ruffians.

The renunciation of Italy was difficult for Toscanini. He is passionately fond of the land of his birth. Its colors and landscapes, its very odors, are dear to him. It has been a wrench to be away from it for long. After the United States entered the war against Italy, he was in a turmoil of excitement, thinking that at last Mussolini's days were numbered and that he might soon go home.

His break with the Nazis was also a sacrifice for him. As soon as they took power, he quit the Bayreuth festival, though Bayreuth, he felt, was the consummation of his career as a conductor. He used to say, "I conduct without being seen, since the pit is out of sight. I don't have to wear formal clothes. The atmosphere is perfect. It is the only way to make music." He did not take a pfennig for his work at Bayreuth. The management sent him checks and he returned them indignantly. "I can't," he explained; "it's like taking money from Wagner."

When he quit Bayreuth, Toscanini turned to Salzburg, just over the border from Germany, as a protest and an affirmation, and proceeded to make the Salzburg Festival the most important in the world. The day that Hitler's legions marched into Austria, Toscanini renounced Salzburg.

Toscanini, who knew the enemy in whatever land he bared his fangs, was on the side of the Loyalists in Spain. A friend who was with him the day the news came that General Mola, one of Spain's Fascist leaders, was killed reported that the maestro was jubilant. He clenched his hand and he cried, "Soon they will all get it!"

The maestro would not play the *Giovanezza*, but is not against all anthems. He has been proud to lead *The Star-Spangled Banner*.

He made a recording of it and gave the proceeds to the Red Cross. At the recording session, though there was no one in the hall, he ordered the men to stand during the performance—even when they were rehearsing it. When he was touring in South America with the NBC Symphony Orchestra, they arrived in one town on July 3, after a long haul. The players expected a couple of days of rest, but were dismayed to hear that the maestro had ordered them to assemble the next morning. They thought that another rehearsal was on the agenda and they had been rehearsed to the ears. But orders were orders; grumbling, they arrived at the appointed hour. The maestro came out on the stage, asked them to rise, and led them through *The Star-Spangled Banner* in a deserted theater thousands of miles from the United States. "Today is the Fourth of July," he said. "That's all."

Paderewski took his stand for his country and his people, acting for a time as Premier of Poland, and later, to the day of his death, giving what strength and money he had to the cause of his nation's freedom. Casals did not waver as to where his allegiance belonged when Franco revolted against and destroyed the legally elected democratic government of Spain.

Casals sacrificed more than most musicians for his convictions. He had to leave Spain when Franco and the Axis triumphed. I shall not forget my visit with Casals in the summer of 1939 in a hotel room of Lucerne. A little baldheaded man, wearing a gray sweater buttoned down the front, he looked like a puttering old granddad. But when he talked, his eyes took on intensity, his face became mobile and expressive, and the man of alert mind, quick perceptions, and warm heart shone through.

In those days Casals made strenuous efforts to help the Spanish exiles who languished, in misery, in the prison camps of France. He was virtually a godfather to all. When they needed help, they wrote to him. He did not ask for a means test; knowing they were in sore straits, he helped. His practice was to send two hundred French francs to an unmarried man, four hundred to a man with a wife, five hundred if he had a child. Casals told how these valiant fighters for democracy had not changed their clothes since the exodus from Spain! Some were wounded; others were sick. He tried to send them money for medicine. He collected funds from friends. He went on concert tours to raise money.

Casals begrudged any day he had to spend away from the Pyrenees, where the prison camps were located. He felt it his duty to be near his people. He spent all his time among them, trying to give them a small measure of courage and faith that life was still worth living. He talked with deep emotion of his beloved fellow Catalonians. He told how they had tried to make life gracious in the camps; publishing a little newspaper, painting and drawing on miserable materials and holding a small exhibition, giving concerts, organizing a chorus and teaching their fellows old and new songs.

Casals could not continue. His eyes filled, and he said, "It is beautiful, is it not?"

Casals spoke without rancor of his fellow musicians who remained in Franco Spain. That was their home. Where could they go? He was not even bitter about his former pupil, Gaspar Cassado, a brilliant young cellist from Barcelona. Cassado stayed out of Spain during the Civil War but worked for Franco. Casals remarked, with a gentleman's understatement, that his behavior was "limited." What is more, it endangered his mother and sister, for feelings were strained in Barcelona and some people were prepared to act against the relatives of their enemies. It was Casals who intervened in behalf of Cassado's family.

Casals had ample opportunity to leave Europe while there was time. His friends in America pleaded with him to come here, but he declined. He deprecated the tendency to call him a hero. His chief concern was that of a human being for other human beings. He had merely helped his countrymen when they fought for their independence and their right to run their country in their own way, without the help of Nazis and Fascists.

For his own part, he said, over and over, he was not a political animal. By that he meant that he belonged to no party. But what does it matter whether an artist wears a party label? By his acts,

not by his tags, shall ye know him. In his very way of life, Casals
performed his function, not only as a musician, but as a moral and
cohesive force in his community.

Not every artist has the means or the opportunity to be useful
on so vast a scale as Pablo Casals or Ignace Jan Paderewski. But all
—big-time virtuosos and humble practitioners—should know what
is going on in the world. The simple truth is that what happens in the
world affects the artist at every turn.

In wartime the issue is so apparent that there is no mistaking it.
The effects and changes rush upon us. In the first few months of the
war, events were swiftly altering the habits of musicians, like those
of other artists. Members of symphony orchestras were worried lest
their subsidies from wealthy patrons disappear in the face of the
tremendous increase in taxes and the demands of innumerable
worthy charities. Bookings for concert artists had to be shifted, because of airplane travel priorities, and it was no longer an easy
matter to make long jumps overnight. Railroad travel was develop-
ing restrictions. The Metropolitan Opera had to get a special dis-
pensation from Washington to complete a tour, because it needed
sixteen freight cars for its sets and costumes and other para-
phernalia and a special train for its personnel. For future tours, it
may be impossible to get railroad accommodations, and trucks will
be used, if trucks are available.

Musicians, of course, have rushed to help where they could be of
use. The younger men have been called to the colors. The women
and older men have played benefits for war-relief societies, have
appeared in army and navy camps, and have done what they could
to aid morale.

Long-standing antagonisms have been forgotten. Russian-born
artists who have had no contact with the Soviet Union have come
forward to raise funds for Russian War Relief. Rachmaninoff gave
the proceeds of a Carnegie Hall recital for medical supplies to be
sent to the Soviets, and for a musician of the old school whose wealth
and home had been taken by the Soviet government, this was an
extraordinary gesture.

One or two could not forget what they liked to think was their importance. A tenor, notorious for his egomania, was to appear at a benefit at Madison Square Garden amid representatives of the United Nations. Before the performance, he conferred with the organizers of the rally. He was amenable to the program arrangements. Then he glanced over the printed announcement and pointed to his name, which was in small type, placed alphabetically among the names of the other artists on the program.

"For myself," he said grandiloquently, "I do not complain about the size and place of the printing of my name. I do not care about such things. But my people—it is an insult to my people."

War produces not only enemy aliens, unfortunate enough when many are men and women of democratic convictions who merely were born in a hostile country, but it once made a category of "enemy art." In the First World War, Wagner's operas were excommunicated from the Metropolitan and other American opera houses. In the new World War, there has been sanity, but not without rumbles in the distance to show that some people are intent on having "enemy music" interned for the duration.

It is true that Wagner's circle, toward the end of his life, included preachers of the gospel that Hitler made his own. It is true that Wagner spoke and wrote similar nonsense in his declining years. It is true that Hitler loves Wagner beyond all other composers, and has seen to it that Bayreuth has been maintained as a going concern. There is little doubt that Winifred Wagner, widow of Siegfried, Richard's only son, has not found Nazism unattractive; she has certainly welcomed its arch proponent.

But even on the purely personal question of family convictions, there has been dissent and division. Friedelind, daughter of Winifred and Siegfried Wagner and granddaughter of the composer, would not compromise with the Nazis. She left Germany and made her home in Switzerland. When the war broke out, she would not go back to Bayreuth. Her mother came to Switzerland and ordered her home at once. Friedelind asked for twenty-four hours to get ready and used this period of grace to flee to England and out of reach of her mother's Nazi friends. She had tough sledding for a time. She was interned in England as an enemy alien. Finally she was released and managed to depart for South America. She met Toscanini there, and he helped her to get permission and passage to come to the United States.

Friedelind alone cannot atone for the sins of her family. Nor can her family's actions, or the preferences of Hitler, in themselves, make Wagner's music poisonous and revolting. I can understand the feelings of many sensitive musicians who are not fond of Wagner's music, but their objections are on musical grounds. It is for this, in small measure, that we fight—for the right to have our own opinions, for the right to like or dislike Wagner, for the right to like or dislike Mendelssohn, Meyerbeer, Beethoven, Bach, or Brahms, for the right to read Heine, for the right to admire Hokusai, for the right to be individuals, not robots taking orders from some ignorant functionary.

When the artist is alive and working in Naziland, the problem is more difficult. What about Richard Strauss, who remained in Germany? Or a pianist like Walter Gieseking, who went back to Nazi Germany each year after tours in this country? It has been contended that we should not tolerate them and their works. I agree, if tolerating them meant giving them our dollars to take back to Germany, where the foreign exchange helped the Third Reich to buy food and war materials abroad. Certainly it has been wrong to patronize a recitalist who, by deed or by silence, condoned Nazism. Certainly it has been wrong to heap money on him to take back to Germany, and it has been stupid to buy his records so that his overlords could lay their hands on further exchange.

Our enemies have not been so generous. You will remember that the big industrialists in Germany made patent agreements with our captains of industry that gave the best of our inventions to the Nazis, who were rather coy about disclosing their own latest developments. You will remember that, even before the war broke out, foreign artists traveling in Germany or Italy had to spend what they earned in those countries. The Japanese, after the start of the

"China Incident" in 1937, did not bother to pay just debts. I know that no royalty payments whatever were made to musicians whose records sold in large quantities in Japan. Joseph Szigeti has estimated that the Japanese owe him $25,000 for a five-year period, and it is likely that other musicians have also been gypped.

But what about a creative artist like Richard Strauss? I believe that those of us who like Strauss' music should have the right and opportunity to listen to it. But I agree with Erika Mann that we should not, in the pursuit of our tastes, have supplied Germany with desperately needed foreign exchange. And that is what we were doing before we went to war with Germany, even after our friends, the British, had engaged in the struggle. We were paying royalties to Strauss and his publishers every time an orchestra played one of his tone poems, every time the Metropolitan put on one of his operas, every time we bought a recording of one of his works. When we went to war, these funds were impounded, and we could listen to Strauss' music, if we wished, secure in the knowledge that we were not giving concrete aid to the enemy.

Just as music in itself is not automatically a foe, so it does not become a precious thing merely because it is the work of an ally. I happen to admire the work of Shostakovich; others do not. So be it. We should be free to hear it, and each man should have the right to dislike it if he chooses. We need not expect that Shostakovich's music will have for us the meaning it has for the Russians. Shostakovich wrote his Seventh Symphony during the siege of Leningrad, while spending part of his time on the roofs of his city, serving as an auxiliary fireman. He dedicated the work to the heroic potentialities of the people and he proclaimed the symphony the measure of his belief in victory. Naturally, the Russians would respond to such a work with deep feeling. During a performance in Moscow, there was an air-raid alert, and a warden came down the aisle of the theater to halt the performance and get the audience moving to shelters. But neither performers nor audience noticed him. The work was played to the end.

This music has tremendous social significance for its people.

Music can have such significance. It may be explicit, or it may be implicit. The magnificent songs sung by the International Brigade in the Spanish Civil War are towers of strength for the democratic spirit, and if you don't know them, I suggest you obtain the album *Six Songs of Democracy,* recorded by members of the brigade in bomb-shattered Barcelona. The dust-bowl songs of a folk musician like Woody Guthrie have obvious implications, as have the Jim Crow lyrics and other songs of Negro protest. You can tell that they have by the indignation they arouse in the forces of reaction. Woody Guthrie wrote me a note after his dust-bowl records appeared, and he told me of the derision heaped upon him.

"They called me everything from a rambling honky-tonk hitter," he said, "to a waterlogged harmonica player. One paper down in Kentucky said what us Okies needed next to three good square meals a day was some good music lessons. You can get some pretty fair music lessons down in Oklahoma, and in some parts of the country about all you got to do is just set around and play music and sing. I didn't come up here to New York to show you how good a music we got in Oklahoma or the whole dust-bowl states, but I intended to call your attention to the dust that's in the music, and the folks that's in the dust."

Woody's philosophy is worth further quotation: "When Oklahoma talks to New York, New York hadn't ought to get restless and nervous, and when Chicago says something to Arizona, that ought not to cause trouble. I ain't mad at nobody that don't get mad at me. Looks like whatever you try to do, somebody jumps up and hollers and raises cain—then the feller next to him jumps up and hollers how much he likes it."

We live in a democracy. There are still many good people, however, who hold to the theory that an artist should concern himself with his art and should not bother his precious dream-filled head with opinions on affairs of state. You will recall the outrage of some Congressmen that a moving-picture actor, Melvyn Douglas, and a dancer, Mayris Chaney, should be invited to help the government in the war effort. You will recall that the first economies proposed in the WPA were on the artistic front. "Now that we are at war," these Congressmen shrieked, "let's throw the bums out!"

When artists are attacked, they may defend themselves. But why should they be on the defensive always? I am glad to say that a good many musicians are acting as if they need not be.

A start has been made in the right direction toward integrating the artist in the large affairs of the nation, but it has not gone far enough. A man like Koussevitzky, who is aware of the forces at work in the world, maintains that a conductor is not merely the head of an orchestra, but should be one of the leaders in his community. In a talk to a group of young American conductors, he reminded them that they must set an example in their behavior, their speech, even in their dress. They owe it to the community to use their position for the greater good, and to speak their minds honestly.

Musicians can and should be effective in the broader realm of policy. As individuals, only a handful of men have the influence and the prestige to make a dent on the public consciousness. When Koussevitzky says that he thinks music must be geared so that it will be available to the great masses of the public, performed at its best at moving-picture prices, he is making a good point. But one voice cries alone in the wilderness. If there were a union of conductors proclaiming the same principle, the effect would be greater. If all the musicians in the land—conductors, singers, virtuosos, orchestral players, jazz musicians—were to unite in a program of action designed to make real the talk about music for the masses, then we might begin to make headway. Think of the pressure that could be brought to bear by a strongly united army of hundreds of thousands of men and women.

But that concerns a field in which musicians work. I have in mind larger issues. The artist is a highly sensitive and cultivated human being. His education has been extensive, his perceptions should be penetrating, and his design for living should be lofty. It follows that he should have something farsighted and ennobling to give to his community.

By the very nature of his art the musician must spend endless hours perfecting it and keeping his technique fresh, but he must find time for other things. He should be in the forefront of enlightened movements; he should join with his fellows to organize a concrete program for the integration of the arts in our society. He should be following not merely the trend of the battleline on the Eastern, Western, and Pacific fronts, but should be studying the underlying forces that precipitated that battle. He should be aware of the darkness and prejudice about him; he should lift his voice in angry protest at all oppression. If that means getting into politics, so much the better for politics.

A great writer, Romain Rolland, sent greetings to the American Musicological Congress in the summer of 1939, and in his message was this ringing statement: "In the field of art there is not—there should not be—any rivalry among nations. The only combat worthy of us is that which is waged in every country and at every hour between culture and ignorance, between light and chaos."

The artist—not one or a handful, but a community of fine spirits —must be in the vanguard of this combat!

INDEX

Abram, Jacques, 197
Add-a-Part Records, 203
Aïda (Verdi), 25
Akademie der Tonkünstler-Societät, 9
Albrechtsberger, Johann Georg, 9
Alda, Frances, 115
Alexander Nevsky, 191
All-American Youth Orchestra, 30, 73, 128
American Ballad Singers, 140, 214
American Federation of Musicians, 45, 163
American Guild of Musical Artists, 36, 45
Anderson, Marian, 28, 35, 105, 180, 181-185, 187, 228
André, Johann, 10
Andreozzi, Gaetano, 10
Anfossi, Pasquale, 10
Armstrong, Louis, 190
Ashe, Andrew, 10
Asioli, Bonifacio, 10

Baccaloni, Salvatore, 46-47, 105, 111-112, 142, 146, 207-208
Bach, Johann Sebastian, 5, 8, 9, 11, 13, 228
Bacon, Ernst, 150
  Tree on the Plains, A, 150
Baltimore Symphony Orchestra, 162
Barber, Samuel, 13, 21, 151, 197
  Essay for Orchestra, 21
Barbirolli, John, 80, 215, 234
Barlow, Howard, 30
Barry, Philip, 151
Bartered Bride, The (Smetana), 154
Bartók, Béla, 12, 23
Bauer, Harold, 178
Beecham, Sir Thomas, 31, 43-44, 58-59, 68, 78-80, 84, 102, 156, 177-178

Beethoven, Ludwig van, 8, 9, 10, 11, 13, 29, 43, 150, 158, 228, 230
  "Eroica" Symphony, 157
  Fidelio, 150
Benét, Stephen Vincent, 151
Bennett, Robert Russell, 193
Berg, Alban, 2, 61, 97
  Wozzeck, 61
Berkshire Festival, 62, 67, 231
Berlin, Irving, 15
Berliner, Emil, 203
Bergmann, Carl, 159
Black, Frank, 30
Blitzstein, Marc, 25, 149, 197
  Cradle Will Rock, The, 25, 149
  No for an Answer, 25, 149
Bloch, Ernest, 12
Bodanzky, Artur, 44, 78, 82-83
Bok, Edward, 165
Boston Symphony Orchestra, 29, 62, 66, 155, 159, 161, 163-165, 227
Boult, Sir Adrian, 175
Borovsky, Alexander, 101
Brahms, Johannes, 8, 11, 102, 228
Brailowsky, Alexander, 52, 99, 100, 197, 207
Britten, Benjamin, 151
Brooklyn Symphony Orchestra, 80
Brooks, Harlow, 165-166
Brown, Anne, 111, 180, 188
Busch, Adolf, 33, 47, 88, 248
Busoni, Ferruccio, 21
Butterfly That Stamped, The (Thompson), 150

Calvé, Emma, 113, 115
Carmen (Bizet), 154, 197
Carmichael, Hoagy, 15
Carnegie Foundation, 151

261

Carnival of Animals (Saint-Saëns), 75
Cartellieri, Casimir Anton, 9
Carter, John, 197
Caruso, Enrico, 28, 34, 40, 50, 71, 203-204, 205-206
Casadesus, Robert, 33
Casals, Pablo, 34, 47-48, 97-98, 101, 133-134, 251-253
Cassado, Gaspar, 252
Castagna, Bruna, 143
Castelnuovo-Tedesco, Mario, 71
Cella, Theodore, 126-127
Chadwick, George Whitefield, 12
Chaliapin, Feodor, 28, 32, 34, 115
Chamberlain, Neville, 249
Chaney, Mayris, 257
Chávez, Carlos, 13, 21, 52, 160
Chicago Symphony Orchestra, 31, 155
Chopin, Frédéric François, 13, 228
Cincinnati Symphony Orchestra, 155
Citizen Kane, 19
Clark, William A., 160
Clementi, Muzio, 10
Cleveland Symphony Orchestra, 155
Columbia Broadcasting System, 30, 161
Columbia Concerts Corp., 236
Columbia Records, 209
Committee for Opera in America, 154
Copland, Aaron, 5, 13, 150
  Second Hurricane, The, 150
Cordon, Norman, 111-112
Cowell, Henry, 172
Cradle Will Rock, The (Blitzstein), 25, 149
Creston, Paul, 81
Crooks, Richard, 28, 34
Crosby, Bing, 36, 114
Curtis, Cyrus H. K., 165
Curzon, Clifford, 174-175

Damrosch, Walter, 80, 85, 159, 195-196
Dane, Ernest B., 163-164
Debussy, Claude, 12, 13, 72, 152
  Pelléas et Mélisande, 152
Decca, 209
Delius, Frederick, 12
De Luca, Giuseppe, 205
Devil and Daniel Webster, The (Moore), 151
Disney, Walt, 29, 59, 65, 88, 191

Dittersdorf, Karl Ditters von, 9
Dixon, Dean, 180, 187
Djanel, Lily, 111, 197
Don Giovanni (Mozart), 46-47
Donizetti, Gaetano, 158
Doremus, R. Ogden, 159
Douglas, Melvyn, 257
Drechsler, Joseph, 10
Duke, Vernon, 15, 16
Durbin, Deanna, 64

Eddy, Nelson, 28, 34, 235
Edison, Thomas A., 202, 203
Eisenberg, Maurice, 97-98
Eisenstein, Sergei, 191
Ellington, Duke, 7, 180, 186
Elgar, Sir Edward, 12
Elman, Mischa, 28, 33, 99-100
Emmett, Daniel, 7
Engel, Lehman, 193
English Singers, 140
Essay for Orchestra (Barber), 21
Euterpean Society, 157

Fall of the City, The (Moore), 151
Falla, Manuel de, 12
Falstaff (Verdi), 107, 153
Fantasia, 29, 59, 62, 65, 191
Farrar, Geraldine, 28, 57, 205, 233
Federal Music Project, 161, 194-195, 225
Ferber, Edna, 150
Ferguson, Howard, 199
Feuermann, Emanuel, 34, 47, 52, 88, 169, 198, 217, 242
Fidelio (Beethoven), 150
Field, Marshall, 166
Fire Bird, The (Stravinsky), 16
Fitzgerald, Lawrence, 91
Flagler, Harry Harkness, 159
Flagstad, Kirsten, 28, 34, 35, 40, 45, 50, 105, 115-117, 143, 214, 228, 234, 242
Foote, Arthur William, 12
Foster, Stephen, 7
Fortier, Anselme, 125
Four Freedoms, 195
Four Saints in Three Acts (Thomson), 150
Franco, Francisco, 251, 252
Frijsh, Povla, 106

Fürtwangler, Wilhelm, 102-103, 167, 248

Gabriel, Bernard, 178
Galli-Curci, Amelita, 28, 113, 205
Gallo, Fortune, 147
Garbo, Greta, 83
Garden, Mary, 28, 115, 243-244
Gary, Elwood, 197
Gatti-Casazza, Giulio, 63, 78, 105, 115
Gee, Fred M., 241
Gershwin, George, 7, 13, 15, 16, 150, 188
  Porgy and Bess, 150, 188
Gesellschafts-Concerte, 10
Gieseking, Walter, 168-169, 255
Gilbert, Henry F., 12
Gilbert, W. S., 152
Giovanezza, 250
Glière, Reinhold, 14
Gluck, Christoph Willibald von, 149
  Iphigenia in Tauris, 149
Godowsky, Leopold, 100
Goebbels, Joseph, 116
Golschmann, Vladimir, 155
Goodman, Benny, 192, 215
Goodwin, Lawrence A., 196
Goodwin, Thomas, 157
Goossens, Eugene, 155
Grainger, Percy, 170
Grant, Ulysses S., 212
Greinert, Emil, 58
Griller String Quartet, 199
Guthrie, Woody, 190, 257
Gyrowetz, Adalbert, 10

Hammond, John Henry, Jr., 187
Hampton, Lionel, 180
Handel, George Frederick, 8
Harris, Roy, 13, 25
Harvuot, Clifford, 197
Hasse, Johann Adolf, 10
Hawkins, Erskine, 231-232
Haydn, Franz Josef, 9, 10
Hayes, Roland, 180, 184-185
Heindl, 158
Heifetz, Jascha, 28, 33, 35, 45-46, 49, 88,
  94, 96, 99, 100, 103, 170, 193, 228,
  234
Herrmann, Bernard, 19
Hertz, Alfred, 105

Heure espagnole, L' (Ravel), 154
Heyward, Du Bose, 188
Higginson, Henry Lee, 159, 164
Hill, Ureli Corelli, 129
Hindemith, Paul, 12
Hitler, Adolf, 17, 248, 250, 254, 255
Hocker, C. David, 148
Hofmann, Josef, 28, 35, 52, 100, 170
Holmes, Mrs. Christian R., 164-165
Horace Mann School, 212-213
Horowitz, Sonya, 86, 88-89, 93
Horowitz, Vladimir, 28, 31-32, 33, 50,
  52, 86, 88, 89-90, 93, 95-96, 99, 100,
  101-103, 169, 199, 204, 228, 243
Horowitz, Wanda, 89, 90
Houston Symphony Orchestra, 197
Huber, Thaddeus, 9
Hull, Mrs. Lytle, 148
Hummel, Johann Nepomuk, 158
Huneker, James, 244
Hurok, Sol, 183

Ickes, Harold L., 181
Iphigenia in Tauris (Gluck), 149
Island God, The (Menotti), 106, 146-147
Iturbi, José, 97, 124, 179, 193, 216

Jacobi, Frederick, 105
Jagel, Frederick, 79
Janiewicz, Felix, 10
Jarboro, Caterina, 185
Johansen, Henry, 116
Johnson, Edward, 51, 63, 109, 144
Johnson, Eldridge R., 203
Johnson, Evangeline, 83
Josten, Werner, 151-152
Judd, George E., 164
Judson, Arthur, 237

Kalliwoda, Johann Wenzeslaus, 158
Kansas City Orchestra, 156
Kelly, Cuthbert, 140
Kent, Arthur, 46-47, 197
Kern, Jerome, 7, 15, 149
  Show Boat, 149-150
Keynote, 209
Kiepura, Jan, 45, 111, 232
Kingman, Russell B., 133-135

Kipling, Rudyard, 150
Kipnis, Alexander, 105, 142
Kleiber, Erich, 67-68
Klemperer, Otto, 78, 82, 156
Kohaut, Joseph, 9
Korn, Richard, 197, 199
Kostelanetz, André, 31
Koussevitzky, Serge, 25, 28, 29, 58, 62,
    64, 66-67, 76-77, 83-84, 101, 120,
    128, 150-151, 155, 164, 227, 237, 258
Koussevitzky Music Foundation, 151
Koželuh, Leopold, 9
Krehbiel, Henry E., 158
Kreisler, Fritz, 23, 28, 32, 33, 48, 49, 94,
    99, 101, 170, 204, 228, 234, 242
Kreuger, Karl, 156
Krommer, Franz, 10
Kullman, Charles, 72
Kunkle, William M., 136

Lady Macbeth of Mzensk (Shostako-
    vich), 15
La Farge, Christopher, 151
Landowska, Wanda, 33, 170
Lasso, Orlando di, 11, 230
League of Composers, 150
Lehmann, Lilli, 115
Lehmann, Lotte, 70-71, 105, 109-110,
    142, 145, 234
Leinsdorf, Erich, 81, 155
Lesser, Sol, 19
Levin, Sylvan, 148-149
Levine, Henry, 193
Levitzki, Mischa, 100
Lhevinne, Josef, 49, 93
Lillie, Beatrice, 171
List, Eugene, 197
Los Angeles Philharmonic, 31, 160
Louisville Symphony Orchestra, 196
Luboshutz, Pierre, 176-177
Lust for Life (Stone), 152

Macbeth (Verdi), 153
MacDowell, Edward, 12
Mackay, Clarence H., 164, 166
MacLeish, Archibald, 151
Magic Flute, The (Mozart), 150
Mahler, Gustav, 78, 130
Malcuzynski, Witold, 101

Mann, Erika, 256
Marriage of Figaro, The (Mozart), 149,
    231
Martin, Freddy, 204
Martinelli, Giovanni, 50, 110
Maynor, Dorothy, 35, 108, 180, 184, 185,
    187
McBride, Robert, 193, 232, 233
McCormack, John, 28, 100
Melchior, Lauritz, 34, 45, 82, 112-113,
    115, 143, 145
Mendelssohn, Felix, 10, 72
    Songs Without Words, 72
Mengelberg, Willem, 58
Menotti, Gian-Carlo, 106, 107, 146, 150,
    230
    Island God, The, 106, 146-147
    Old Maid and the Thief, The, 150, 230
Menuhin, Yehudi, 28, 33, 35, 97, 216, 234
Metropolitan Opera Company, 16-17, 30,
    31, 34, 37, 40, 62, 63, 78, 142-147,
    151, 152, 159, 185, 227, 253
Mignon (Thomas), 72
Milanov, Zinka, 112
Milhaud, Darius, 12
Milstein, Nathan, 33, 88
Minneapolis Symphony Orchestra, 31,
    155
Mischakoff, Mischa, 88
Mitropoulos, Dimitri, 21, 31, 48-49, 52,
    65-66, 101, 123, 155
Monteux, Pierre, 155
Monteverdi, Claudio, 11
Moore, Douglas, 24, 151
    Devil and Daniel Webster, The, 151
    Fall of the City, The, 151
    White Wings, 151
Moore, Grace, 28, 34, 45, 111, 112, 113,
    143, 238
Morgenstern, Sam, 23-24
Mosel, Ignaz Franz, Edler von, 10
Mozart, Wolfgang Amadeus, 7, 9, 10, 13,
    81, 88, 149, 150, 153-154, 158, 231
    Don Giovanni, 46-47
    Magic Flute, The, 150, 152
    Marriage of Figaro, The, 149, 231
    Musical Jest, A, 88
Musical Jest, A (Mozart), 88
Mussolini, Benito, 250
Mussorgsky, Modest, 13
Mutual Broadcasting System, 30, 161

Nasolini, Sebastiano, 10
National Broadcasting Company, 30, 150
NBC Symphony, 28, 60, 61, 63-64, 65, 70, 87, 91, 161, 204
National Concert and Artists Corporation, 236
Nemenoff, Genia, 176-177
Netzer, Joseph, 10
New England Conservatory, 192
New Manhattan String Quartet, 197
New Opera Company, 148, 152
New York City WPA Orchestra, 80, 156
New York Philharmonic-Symphony Orchestra, 29, 30, 31, 40, 53, 58, 62, 63, 78, 79, 80, 119-120, 123, 127, 128, 129, 155, 156-159, 163, 164, 166-167, 186, 227, 237
New York Symphony Society, 159
Newman, Ernest, 9, 144
Nine O'Clock Opera Company, 149
Noces, Les (Stravinsky), 22

O'Donnell, Rudolph, 198-199
Of Thee I Sing (Gershwin), 150
Oklahoma! (Rodgers), 150
Old Maid and the Thief, The (Menotti), 150, 230
100 Men and a Girl, 64, 83
Oratorio Society of New York, 135-136
Ordoñez, Carlo d', 9
Organists' Guild, 176
Ormandy, Eugene, 30
Orynwaka, Leo, 196
Otello (Verdi), 153
Our Town, 19

Paderewski, Ignace Jan, 28, 33, 49, 50, 51-52, 56, 91, 92, 96, 97, 98, 103-104, 251, 253
Paisible, James, 9
Paisiello, Giovanni, 9
Palestrina, Giovanni Pierluigi da, 11
Panizza, Ettore, 84-85, 112, 145, 231
Papi, Gennaro, 112
Pelléas et Mélisande (Debussy), 152
Perini, Flora, 205
Petina, Irra, 115
Petri, Egon, 33, 56

Petrillo, James Caesar, 36, 45-46, 164, 201-202
Petrushka (Stravinsky), 16
Philadelphia Opera Company, 148-149, 152
Philadelphia Orchestra, 29, 30, 36-37, 40, 62, 64, 74-75, 94, 155, 163, 165, 204, 207, 227
Piatigorsky, Gregor, 52, 71, 98, 213
Pinza, Ezio, 46, 105, 111, 114, 143, 145
Pique Dame (Tchaikovsky), 152-153
Pittsburgh Symphony Orchestra, 155
Pleyel, Ignaz Joseph, 9, 10
Pompeo, Robert, 197
Pons, Lily, 28, 34, 112, 177, 233
Ponselle, Rosa, 50, 113-114, 177
Porgy and Bess (Gershwin), 150, 188
Porter, Cole, 7, 15, 245
Powell, Eleanor, 88
Praag, Maurice van, 129
Preindl, Joseph, 10
Preyer, Gottfried, 158
Primrose, William, 88, 207
Prokofieff, Sergei, 12, 191
Puccini, Giacomo, 6, 110, 150
Pulitzer, Joseph, 164

Quisling, Vidkun, 116

Rachmaninoff, Sergei, 18, 28, 32-33, 43, 49, 53, 55, 94, 96, 101, 204, 253
    C-Sharp minor Prelude, 18
Ravel, Maurice, 12
Reiner, Fritz, 155
Renardy, Ossy, 197
Rethberg, Elisabeth, 112, 177
Robeson, Paul, 28, 180, 181, 182, 184, 185
Robin Hood Dell Symphony Orchestra, 173
Rodgers, Richard, 15
Rodzinski, Artur, 31, 129
Rolland, Romain, 259
Rome, Harold J., 15
Roosevelt, Eleanor, 181, 187
Rosenbaum, Samuel, 36
Rosenkavalier, Der (Strauss), 17
Rossini, Gioacchino, 158
Rubinstein, Artur, 33, 100, 103

Sacchini, Antonio, 9
Sacre du Printemps, Le (Stravinsky), 22
St. Leger, Frank, 177
St. Louis Symphony Orchestra, 155
Salieri, Antonio, 10
Salmaggi, Alfredo, 147-148, 185
San Carlo Opera Company, 147
San Francisco Symphony Orchestra, 155, 162-163
Sandor, Arpad, 97
Sandor, Gyorgy, 197
Satterfield, Jack, 193
Savitt, Jan, 193
Scala, La, 65
Schang, Frederick C., 238
Schlesinger, Martin, 9
Schnabel, Artur, 33, 50-51, 101, 169, 230
Schönberg, Arnold, 12
Schorr, Friedrich, 82, 105
Schubert, Franz, 7, 13, 73, 89
Schultz, Leo, 134
Schuman, William, 13, 25, 151, 192-193
Schumann, Robert, 13, 25
Schuster, Joseph, 52
Schwanda, the Bagpipe Player (Weinberger), 17
Scott, Hazel, 180
Scott, Léon, 203
Sechter, Simon, 10
Second Hurricane, The (Copland), 150
Seidl, Anton, 113, 158
Seidl, Toscha, 197
Serkin, Rudolf, 33, 169-170, 232
Shakespeare, William, 153
Shaw, Artie, 206
Sheehy, Emma D., 212, 213
Shostakovich, Dmitri, 12, 14, 15, 19, 25, 125, 129, 256
    Fifth Symphony, 15
    Lady Macbeth of Mzensk, 15
    Seventh Symphony, 19, 125-126, 209, 256
Show Boat (Kern), 149-150
Sibelius, Jean, 12, 15
Singer, Jacques, 197
Six Songs of Democracy, 257
Slenczynski, Ruth, 212
Slezak, Leo, 71
Smetana, Bedřich, 154
    Bartered Bride, The, 154
Smith, Alfred E., 141

Smith, Kate, 163
Snow White and the Seven Dwarfs, 88
Society of Timid Souls, 178
Songs Without Words (Mendelssohn), 72
Spalding, Albert, 33, 198
Spirituel-Concerte, 10
Spohr, Ludwig, 10, 129, 158
Stadler, Maximilian, 10
Star-Spangled Banner, The, 43, 250-251
Starzer, Josef, 9
State of Music, The (Thomson), 20
Stellman, Maxine, 114-115
Stewart, Reginald, 162
Stock, Frederick, 31, 155
Stokowski, Leopold, 28, 29-30, 40, 50, 58, 59-61, 62, 64-65, 67, 73-76, 83, 85, 101, 119-120, 128, 155, 204, 207, 227, 232, 237
Stone, Irving, 151-152
Strasfogel, Ignace, 78
Strauss, Johann, 90
Strauss, Richard, 12, 16-17, 72-73, 77, 78, 255, 256
    Don Juan, 77
    Rosenkavalier, Der, 17
Stravinsky, Igor, 12, 16, 22
    Fire Bird, The, 16
    Noces, Les, 22
    Petrushka, 16
    Sacre du Printemps, Le, 22
Struther, Jan, 192
Süssmayer, Franz Xaver, 81
Swarthout, Gladys, 34, 48
Symphony Orchestra of Mexico, 160
Szigeti, Joseph, 33, 35, 47, 93, 96-97, 98, 101, 104, 169, 193, 216, 228-229, 234, 256

Talley, Marion, 108
Tchaikovsky, Piotr Ilyich, 13, 67, 93, 102, 228
    "Pathétique" Symphony, 67
    Piano Concerto in B-flat minor, 204
    Pique Dame, 152-153
Thomas, Ambroise, 72
    Mignon, 72
Thomas, John Charles, 34, 45, 106-107, 111, 112, 143, 187

Thompson, Randall, 13, 150
  Butterfly That Stamped, The, 150
Thomson, Virgil, 13, 20, 150
  Four Saints in Three Acts, 150
Thorborg, Kerstin, 105, 114, 143
Tibbett, Lawrence, 28, 34, 36, 48, 51, 88,
  115, 142-143, 241
Toscanini, Arturo, 21-22, 28-29, 40, 42-
  43, 53, 55, 57, 58, 59, 62-64, 65, 67-
  68, 69-73, 85-91, 101, 103, 110, 120,
  122, 123, 155, 161, 204, 208, 209, 217,
  227, 228, 231, 232, 237, 249-251, 255
Toscanini, Carla, 86
Toscanini, Walfredo, 86, 89
Toscanini, Walter, 86
Traetta, Tommaso, 9
Trapp Family, 140
Traubel, Helen, 107, 143
Tree on the Plains, A (Bacon), 150

Van Rensselaer, Alexander, 165
Varnay, Astrid, 45, 106, 107, 114-115,
  143, 234-235
Vaughan Williams, Ralph, 12-13, 249
Verdi, Giuseppi, 6, 10, 25-26, 57, 150
  Aïda, 25
  Falstaff, 107, **153**
  Macbeth, 153
  Otello, 153
Verdi, The Man and His Life in Letters,
  25
Vermont State Symphony Orchestra, 135
Victor Records, 209
Vienna Philharmonic, 155

Villa-Lobos, Heitor, 13

Wagenseil, Georg Christoph, 9
Wagner, Friedelind, 254-255
Wagner, Richard, 5, 6-7, 113, 150, 153,
  250, 254-255
Wagner, Siegfried, 254
Wagner, Winifred, 254
Wallenstein, Alfred, 30-31, 88, 122, 190
Waller, "Fats," 193-194
Walter, Bruno, 30, 46, 77, 101, 122, 179,
  206
Walton, William, 13
Warner, John A., 141
Warren, Leonard, 143
Waters, Ethel, 180
Weber, Karl Maria von, 158
Weill, Kurt, 12
Weinberger, Jaromir, 17-18
  Schwanda, the Bagpipe Player, 17
Welles, Orson, 19
Westminster Choir, 29
White Wings (Moore), 151
Wichita Symphony Orchestra, 156
Wille, Stewart, 241
Williamson, John Finley, 29
Wilson, Teddy, 180
Winneberger, Paul Anton, 10
Wood, Sir Henry, 68
Wozzeck (Berg), 61
WQXR, 201

Zimbalist, Efrem, 33
Zimbalist, Mrs. Efrem, 165

ABOUT THE AUTHOR

HOWARD TAUBMAN, as a reporter and reviewer of music for the past thirteen years, has heard and met most of the prominent musicians in this country and abroad. He is music editor of *The New York Times*, the author of *Opera Front and Back* and *Music as a Profession*, and the editor of Giulio Gatti-Casazza's memoirs.

As an observer of the musical scene, Taubman is also interested in the human and business side of art, since no art can live by itself. He knows not only the concert and opera stars, but also the people behind the scenes—managers, administrative staff, salesmen, ticket takers, ushers, and fellow critics. Music critics, he assures us, are human beings.